Adam

Best Wishes

Barry

DON'T FLINCH

Barry Alvarez
The Autobiography

DON'T FLINCH

Barry Alvarez: The Autobiography

*The story of Wisconsin's all-time
winningest coach*

**Barry Alvarez
with
Mike Lucas**

**KCI SPORTS
CHAMPAIGN, IL**

CREDITS

ISBN: 0-9758769-7-X

Published By:

KCI Sports, LLC
2005 Emerald Drive
Champaign, IL 61822

Publisher: Peter J. Clark
Managing Editor: Molly Voorheis
Photo Editor: Kristofor Hanson
Cover Design: Terry Neutz Hayden
Book Layout and Design: Nicky Mansur
Sales & Marketing: Bret D. Kroencke, Pat Leahy
Media & Promotions: Scott Bucholtz, Doug Milkowski

Front cover photos courtesy of Michelle Stocker, *Madison Capital Times*

Photos courtesy of the Barry Alvarez family, John Maniaci and the *Wisconsin State Journal*, Jeff Miller and the UW Communications Office, UW Sports Information Office and the Associated Press.

Printed and bound by Worzalla Publishing, Stevens Point, WI

I dedicate this book to my wife Cindy; my daughters Dawn (Mrs. Brad Ferguson) and Stacy (Mrs. Mike Delzer); my son Chad (wife Stephanie); and my grandsons Joe and Jake Ferguson and Jackson Delzer and my granddaughters Grace Delzer and Scarlett Alvarez.

They've been my best fans and they never kept score.

-B.A.

ACKNOWLEDGEMENTS

I'd like to thank all the players I've coached; all the assistants who were committed to the program; my brother Woody and all my great friends in Langeloth and Burgettstown who have supported me through my years as a high school and college player and my whole coaching career; my closest friends, John Flesch, Ted Kellner, Tony Canonie, Larry Jacobson, and Rick "Gordo" Coleman. (In the first printing of this book, John Flesch's name was inadvertently omitted.) And lastly, I'd like to thank all the good fans we've had here at Wisconsin.

FOREWORD

January 1, 1990. At 3:30 p.m., as I was preparing to go to our pre-game meal prior to our contest with the University of Colorado, the #1-ranked team in the country, Barry Alvarez asked if he could visit with me. It was then that Barry told me he had just accepted the head coaching position at the University of Wisconsin and that they would announce his appointment as the new leader of Wisconsin football at the halftime of our Orange Bowl game. I asked Barry if he thought it was a smart move, as Badger football had not enjoyed much success in recent years. Barry said he had no qualms and felt he could build a winning program there for many reasons: Wisconsin was a great school, and had excellent leadership in Donna Shalala as chancellor and Pat Richter as athletic director. In addition, they had great fan support, excellent financial resources, it was the main university in the state, a great place to live and raise a family, decent facilities with a commitment to improve them, and he could recruit excellent student athletes to attend the University of Wisconsin.

He convinced me, just as he had two years ago to elevate him to Notre Dame's defensive coordinator. In the two years he had been the leader of our Notre Dame defense, Notre Dame had won a national championship and won twenty-four games and lost just one. This night we would be facing maybe the best offensive team I had seen on film. They were undefeated and appeared unbeatable, but Barry had put together a great game plan and we won 20-6.

Barry then moved on to Wisconsin, where he has established one of the top programs in the country, a program many have tried to emulate. I had not only lost a great coach, but a very close friend. He is a natural leader. He had a vision for Wisconsin, a plan for success. I knew he would lead by example and be positive in the face of adversity. I had no doubt that he would be successful.

In his first year at Wisconsin he won one game and lost ten, but his faith in Wisconsin and himself never wavered. He built a sound program that ultimately led to three Rose Bowl wins and several Top 10 final rankings and a Heisman award winner. He brought in one of the best staffs in the country and he retained them.

Barry is a smart person who has the unique ability to inspire people to strive for greatness. He has his priorities in the proper order as he is dedicated to his wife Cindy, son Chad, and daughters Dawn and Stacy.

I talk to Barry quite often and I remember one specific conversation when he was being recruited to become the head football coach at the University of Miami, a very lucrative offer. Barry said he was flattered, but he felt loyalty to Wisconsin. Before he could decide to accept the Miami offer he had to first decide if he could leave the University of Wisconsin. In the final analysis, he felt he couldn't. This was the same logic he used when numerous pro teams attempted to hire him.

Barry's morals and values are exceptional. I would trust him with my life; he is committed to excellence and he cares about people. My respect for Barry could best be summarized thusly: When people ask me about Barry I say, "He could write his own letter of recommendation and I would be proud to sign it."

Yes, Barry and the University of Wisconsin have been successful, but more importantly he has been significant. The difference? When you die, your success ends. When you are significant — when you help other people achieve success — that lasts many lifetimes. No doubt Barry has been significant. No doubt Barry will end up in the Hall of Fame in the future, but more importantly he will remain in the hearts of the players, administration, coaches, students, and fans of Wisconsin.

–Lou Holtz

FOREWORD

The first time I met Barry Alvarez was at the Orpheum Theater in Madison. There was a nice crowd in the place and I noticed that the noise level, the buzz, the excitement was really starting to build. Then I heard a single sentence bounce through the ranks of my wife's relatives, who were sitting in the front row. One line kept repeating over and over—"Barry's here. Barry's here."

Suddenly the evening was no longer about my latest bestseller, it was about the fact that Barry Alvarez had actually shown up for the reading.

I married into the Wisconsin family. My wife Sue was a four-time All-American swimmer, then went on to earn an MFA at Wisconsin. Her parents were Badgers as well.

Barry Alvarez was hired at Wisconsin, and he soon became family, not just because he turned around the football program, but because of the way he did it.

Like anybody who roots for the Badgers, I'm tremendously impressed with Barry's stats. He's the winningest coach in Wisconsin history. He led the Badgers to three Big Ten championships. And of course, there are those Rose Bowl wins.

He even has an ice cream flavor named after him at Babcock Hall, a mix of raspberry, strawberry and blueberry. I've had Berry Alvarez — and it's delicious. Another Alvarez winner.

But I'm most knocked out by the fact that every one of Barry's football victories came with class and dignity. He's always preached "talking with your pads" and has made a habit of not rubbing it in once a victory was assured.

Anybody who reads my thrillers knows that I write short chapters, but there's another reason to keep this preface brief. It's because this book has a lot to say about how sports ought to be conducted in our country, and Barry has a unique voice.

So without further ado, the one and only Barry Alvarez, and one of the best sports stories you'll ever read.

-James Patterson

Gilda's Club

Cindy Alvarez has always felt that humor can be a vehicle to help families through adversity. As such, she laughed and cried with Gilda Radner, the former Saturday Night Live diva. Today, she loves how Radner's memory has been preserved through the nationwide efforts of Gilda's Club, a cancer support organization named in honor of the late comedian. Both of Cindy's parents died from cancer, as did Barry's mother. Reason enough for them both to get actively involved in bringing a Gilda's Club to Madison, especially since the club will be a source of support for all ages of men, women, and children.

Barry and Cindy Alvarez have been generous in their time and financial contributions, but they need help. A percentage of the proceeds from this book will benefit Gilda's Club of Madison.

For more information, please visit www.gildasclubmadison.org.

CONTENTS

Dedication . . . .*v*

Acknowledgements . . . .*vi*

Foreword   Lou Holtz . . . .*vii*

Foreword   James Patterson . . . .*ix*

Contents . . . .*xi*

Introduction 13

Chapter One   Barry from Burgettstown 32

Chapter Two   Devaney and the Husker Blueprint 46

Chapter Three   Making a Name in Mason City 60

Chapter Four   Hayden and the Hawkeyes 74

Chapter Five   We're No. 1 and Irish Eyes Are Smilin' . . .88

Chapter Six   All the Agony Without the Ecstasy 104

Chapter Seven   Beginning to Believe in the Plan 120

Chapter Eight   Living the Dream 136

Chapter Nine   Then Along Came Ron 154

Chapter Ten   History in the Making 172

Chapter Eleven   Coping and Moving On 193

Chapter Twelve   A Last Hurrah 211

Epilogue 234

The All-Alvarez Team 246

Barry Alvarez Bio and Year-by-Year Review 251

"Barry Alvarez brought energy, integrity, strategic brilliance and a great heart to Wisconsin football. In the process, he changed the state and the university forever."

    -Donna Shalala, former UW chancellor and current President of the University of Miami

"Barry Alvarez is a great leader and coach who demands toughness and discipline while pushing his players to be great. And because of his relationship with them, they want to perform for him and the team. He has developed Wisconsin football into a perennial Top 25 program and Big Ten contender."

    -Bob Stoops, former Iowa player and assistant and the current University of Oklahoma head coach

"He was an honest and first-class guy who gave us responsibilities and treated us like men. As a player, he was someone you could believe in—you'd run through a brick wall for him—and he made us feel like we had an edge on every opponent and that we could win every single game."

    -Chris Chambers, former UW receiver and current NFL player with the Miami Dolphins

"His personal motivation each day in practice was inspiration to every player. When Coach Alvarez called me for my evaluation of the Wisconsin football program, I told him it was a sleeping giant. Man, did he ever awaken that giant in what ranks as one of the all-time best turnarounds in the history of college football."

    -Hayden Fry, former University of Iowa head coach

"It's not just the X's and O's with Coach Alvarez. He also teaches you how to be a better man. It's always great to return to Madison because he always makes you feel like you're still important to him. There is still so much loyalty and support for his players. You won't find that in many other college programs."

    -Lee Evans, the UW's all-time leading receiver and current NFL player with the Buffalo Bills

"Barry Alvarez brought a unique passion to everything he did. I often hear of players who elevate the play of their teammates. Barry was like that. He made you a better coach, a better teacher. And his players responded to his leadership by doing things they previously only dreamed of doing. Barry made them believe."

    -Dan McCarney, the former UW defensive coordinator and the current Iowa State University head coach

"The thing I remember the most is the confidence that he instilled not only in me as a player, but the confidence he instilled in the team, the athletic department, and the whole university that this could be a top tier, elite program. Barry came in with a whole new set of expectations and demands for everybody."

    -Don Davey, the former UW defensive tackle and NFL player with the Green Bay Packers and Jacksonville Jaguars

INTRODUCTION
Nobody Believed In Us, But Us

My confidence stems from my football background. I've been fortunate to have had very good coaches who have doubled as teachers. In retrospect, they were among the best in the country. People will ask, "Why you? Why have you been successful? Are you surprised at your success? Especially since you're a small-town boy?"

I'm not surprised because I've been around good people who have been successful at high levels. And that type of mentoring provides a foundation for what you do, regardless of the size of the school or where you're from. Maybe I had an advantage over most people who got into coaching because of my association with some of the best coaches in the business.

Through my experiences, I've established a philosophy that fits my personality and developed my plan to win. I've respected everyone I've competed against. But I've never been in awe of anyone in football. I've never let somebody else set my standards. Don't tell me I'm not good enough. Don't tell me I can't do something.

That's why I felt such a tremendous sense of pride with the way we played against Auburn in the 2006 Capital One Bowl, because it was about playing the game and beating a very good football team that nobody thought we could beat.

Even though it was my last game on the sidelines as a college football coach, I didn't get real sentimental, and I wasn't thinking, "Well, this is it. It's almost over. Let the countdown begin. This is my last nine minutes, this is my last six minutes...."

That was the farthest thing from my mind when we got the ball at our own 1-yard line in the fourth quarter. I'm still trying to get first downs and run out the clock. I just wanted to go home with the win. That's the way I've always coached.

It's not about beating somebody by a lopsided margin, running up the score. It's about playing the game the right way, and it's about the bottom line: winning. Wherever I've coached, I've always told my quarter-backs, "My favorite play in football is victory — taking a knee at the end of the game."

And do you know what was the most satisfying thing about being able to finish the Auburn game that way in Orlando? Nobody thought we could do it — nobody thought we could win the bowl game. Nobody thought Wisconsin was good enough to beat Auburn. Nobody gave us a chance. Absolutely nobody.

After the draw was announced for the Capital One Bowl, somebody sent me a newspaper clipping from a newspaper in Alabama. And you didn't have to read between the lines to figure out their media people who cover the team were upset.

Basically, they were disappointed that Auburn wasn't playing a higher-ranked opponent that could enhance the Tigers' profile and standing in the polls. From their perspective, the Tigers weren't playing a "good team" in Orlando. Instead, they were playing us.

Even some of our best Badger fans didn't think we could win the game. In December, Cindy and I went to a birthday party in Milwaukee, where there must have been 300 people, people of all ages, young and old alike. What I heard all night was, "Man, Barry, you're playing Auburn? That's the best team in the SEC? What a bad draw."

Everybody was paying their condolences.

I felt like I was attending my own wake.

Now, I'm not going to argue with people. Especially if their minds are set. So I just listened to their opinions about what a mismatch it was going to be with Auburn, and I nodded my head and said, "Yeah, they're a very good team."

And I left it at that. When we walked out of there, I turned to Cindy and said, "Do you realize there's not one person here who thinks we can win this game?"

She didn't say anything.

I think she agreed with them.

***

Cindy is a classic.

We both went to Orlando to hype the bowl at a press conference with the local media, and afterward she said, "You were a big hit with the media in Florida. They really like you. You may get your ass beat, but they really like you."

She wasn't the only person who felt that way.

Bob Davie, the former Notre Dame head coach and a current color analyst for ESPN, had worked a lot of games in the SEC. And the first time we talked, he's raving about how Auburn is playing the best football in the league at the end of the season. And how they don't beat themselves and how they do this and that. And he's going on and on and on.

Again, I'm not going to sit there and argue with the guy. I knew they were a good team. But in the same respect, I felt we had some things going for us. In fact, that night in Milwaukee, I pulled aside a friend, Ted Kellner, and told him, "I really think it's a good matchup. We'll play with these guys."

I never came out and said that publicly.

But that was my whole approach with the team, and that was the point that I made to our assistant coaches and players. I wanted them to understand that we could win. Leading up to the game, I didn't want them hearing and reading about how we didn't stand a chance and how Auburn was far superior and how we were going to get beat. I didn't want those negative thoughts in the back of their minds for a month.

So I addressed that point right away with the players when we gave our scouting report and began our bowl preparations. I told them, "We can win this game. We've got to play well. But we match up well with Auburn."

Personally, I thought Alabama would have been a better matchup.

Midway through the season, Tom Mickle, the Cap One Bowl chairman, called and said, "Our dream pick is Alabama and Wisconsin."

Mickle had his reasons. Alabama hadn't been in Orlando for awhile, and we had never been there. And I'm thinking, "Alabama sounds good to me."

They were struggling on offense and we were struggling on defense. That's what I liked best about the matchup. But there was another personal motivation.

As a college player at Nebraska, my first bowl game was against Alabama. I thought it would have been kind of special to end my career that way — coming full circle and playing against Alabama in my final bowl game as a coach.

I was a sophomore linebacker with the Cornhuskers, and we were unbeaten going into the 1966 Orange Bowl. I still remember that game well because we were in contention for the national championship, and we had a better team than Alabama.

But we didn't win.

We drove the field on our first offensive possession, and they couldn't stop us because we were too big and physical for them. But we fumbled inside the 10-yard line and they came out throwing — Steve Sloan to Ray Perkins — and we couldn't stop them.

They scored and kept scoring. They recovered an on-side kick late in the second quarter and went into halftime with a 24-7 lead. Overall, they recovered three on-side kicks. My coach, Bob Devaney, took the blame afterward for not correcting a flaw in our return unit.

The second half was a track meet, and our quarterback, Bob Churchich, put up some big numbers, throwing for three touchdowns.

But we were just too far behind and couldn't overcome four fumbles. We ended up losing 39-28. Following the game, they moved up to No. 1 because Michigan State and Arkansas had lost in their bowls. And we dropped from No. 3 to No. 5.

Jackie Sherrill played for Alabama's Bear Bryant. Years later, he told me that Bear had played the race card as motivation to get his team up for the game. They had no black players, and we did. That Orange Bowl was played on January 1, 1966.

Three months later, Texas Western beat Kentucky in the NCAA basketball finals, the game that served as the basis for the film *Glory Road*.

I was oblivious to the tactics Bear might have been using to motivate his players. I'm sure our whole football team was the same way. At the time I was a back-up linebacker, but I wound up playing quite a bit against Alabama. I'll tell you one thing, Bear Bryant really ticked me off after the game.

That night, they held an awards dinner for both teams at a Miami country club. Each coach introduced his players individually and handed out the bowl watches. Devaney just called out our names, and each player got up, walked to the front, got his watch, walked back to his table, and sat down.

Bear Bryant did the opposite. He stood up there forever. For each player, he gave a little speech in that thick, Southern drawl of his.

"Louis Thompson, 6-foot, 195-pounds," he called out. "Little Louie played across from some big 250-pounders from Nebraska today, and I just don't know how Louis survived. But he did wind up with about 15 tackles...."

The Bear rubbed our noses in it.

And our guys were ticked. We lost the game, they beat us. And, quite frankly, Bear Bryant outcoached Devaney that day. But these were two good teams who each had great seasons, and I just didn't think that was the time or place to rub it in.

I log everything. And as a head coach I never forgot what it felt like to be sitting there while the Bear was showing us up. I don't believe in that.

Who knows? Maybe subconsciously that's why I wanted to play Alabama in my final game. When Mickle called and told me that we were playing Auburn, I said, "What about 'Bama, Tom? Can't we still work that out?"

I was kidding.

But I'm not sure Mickle thought I was funny.

***

Bobby Stoops, the Oklahoma coach, called me a few days after the bowl pairings were released. Bobby has been a close friend for a long, long time, and he's one of the people in college football that I bounce things off of from time to time. As we're talking, Bobby says, "You know what? We've got the two worst draws in the whole bowl deal."

Sure enough. Oklahoma is playing Oregon and we're playing Auburn, and outside of USC and Texas, the Ducks and Tigers were maybe the two hottest teams in the country.

Still, I liked our matchup.

And that's what I wanted to get across to my coaches first because I wanted to make sure they sent that message to the players. More than ever, it was important that everybody was focusing on the same things and everybody was on the same page.

To be honest, I was concerned about the potential for distraction with the way some of my assistants were handling the coaching transition late in the season.

In late July, I had named my defensive coordinator, Bret Bielema, to be my successor. There's some risk to the timing of such a decision because you certainly don't want to disrupt the season. That's why I did it when I did — so it wouldn't become a distraction.

From the start, Bret made a point of saying that he wasn't going to make any decisions on his staff until later in the season. We both talked about the situation and the possible ramifications, and I told him, "That's the only way you can do it."

It didn't make sense to do it any other way.

When you think about it, Bret really hadn't had enough time to visualize how his staff was going to look. He had some thoughts. And he had some people that he wanted to get. But he just needed more time for things to play out — to think about the chemistry and the mix that he wanted on his coaching staff, and that was his call.

I knew there would be some challenges because not everybody was going to be retained. From that viewpoint, some of my assistants felt like they should know whether or not they were going to have a job. Well, that wasn't their call.

Bret made a good point. "If I name somebody — let's say one person — to my staff in August," he said, "I'd be in the awkward position of going up and down the football offices and auditioning guys the entire year. You just don't do it that way."

I agreed.

Look, no one wants to be in the position of not knowing where your next job is going to be. But it comes with the territory. That's part of coaching. We've been fortunate at Wisconsin to have had consistency over a long period of time. The staff basically stayed intact, and a comfort level developed.

Change can be difficult.

I never felt the tension until the end of the season when we played our 12th game at Hawaii. Then, it kind of jumped out at me. It was obvious.

Leading up to the team banquet, some wives — of the coaches who were not coming back — made a fuss about sitting at the same table with the coaches and their spouses who were being retained. They wanted their own table separate from the others.

When I conducted my post-season evaluations with the players, a few of them mentioned that we had a couple of assistants who were way too vocal about their situation. That should never happen. The players should have never been involved.

Initially some coaches felt like they were auditioning for their jobs — that was their perception — because Bret refused to make immediate decisions about his staff.

After it all played out, though, some of these same assistants saw the benefits to the way Bret handled everything and acknowledged that there was no way this season would have been as successful if he had done it any other way.

Not everyone saw it the same way. And, ironically, there were some assistants who would have been retained on Bret's staff had they handled the situation better.

For the most part, I didn't feel like much was carried over to the field. I thought my assistants were professional in their coaching and stayed focused.

As a group, they practiced well, they met well, and they did what they were supposed to do in the football setting. In other words, they did their jobs, and they did them very well — which I complimented them for — because they had the kids ready for Auburn.

***

As we were getting ready to leave for Florida, we had a player, Booker Stanley, get into trouble again. I was disappointed with Book because he put himself in that type of predicament. He already had strikes against him for getting into a fight at the Mifflin Street block party in Madison.

From my understanding, the other guy started the fight, and there was a strong likelihood the whole case would have been thrown out. That said, Booker should have never finished the fight. He shouldn't have been there in the first place.

Still, I thought the whole thing was sensationalized — especially the Internet pictures — and Stanley was judged guilty in the media. That's the type of thing that will give your program a black eye, whether there's any substance behind it or not.

The current trend is to pile on.

Fair or not, Booker Stanley knew he didn't have another chance. And he knew the consequences. You only have so many strikes. Everybody makes a mistake. I'm not saying everybody gets into trouble, but young people make mistakes.

If a guy gets into a fight, you don't necessarily boot him from the team. Yet, when there is a second or third time — continued issues — that's grounds for dismissal.

Just the fact that Booker was arrested again eliminated him from the bowl team as far as I was concerned. I didn't even talk to our kids about it. Didn't even bring it up with our players. Didn't need to. The guys who were ready to play were going to play against Auburn, and it wasn't going to be a distraction. I made sure of that.

We were planning on playing with Booker Stanley and Brian Calhoun in the same backfield, a new wrinkle we hadn't shown during the regular season. During our practices in Madison, we had put in a special package for the bowl game.

We were going to send Calhoun in motion in hopes of getting him outside and isolated in favorable matchups. Plus, Booker was a better ball carrier than our fullbacks. But since we didn't have him, we went with something else offensively and didn't look back.

Once we got to Orlando, we didn't have one incident of any kind. All you need is one guy coming in late, one guy getting in a fight, one guy having a problem with the law and that's all you will read about. It can be disruptive and create a distraction for the team.

I didn't have a player curfew the first three nights. That's how I always do it. Let them run, let them get things out of their system.

At the bowl site, we encouraged the kids to take in everything. Every day we had something different planned for them. Many of the things were optional, but I recommended that they do as much as possible.

I told them, "You don't have to spend five hours at Universal Studios, go for an hour. And we'll have shuttles to bring you back to the team hotel. But take it in."

I wanted them to take advantage of the entire bowl experience. I wanted them to experience everything. In short, I wanted them to do all of the things that I didn't do when I was a player at Nebraska.

When the Cornhuskers played at the Orange Bowl in Miami, I was in awe of the beach, the ocean, and the surroundings. For a kid with nothing, it was the prettiest place I had ever seen.

I remember I had a chance to take in Sea World and some other sights, and what did I do? Me and some guys from Pittsburgh went to the dog track.

Next day it was the same thing. We had a chance to do some sightseeing in south Florida, and what did we do? Dog track. I didn't see anything.

It was more of the same the following year at the Sugar Bowl in New Orleans. They had a list of places to attend, but since the activities were optional, I was a knucklehead and slept in, thinking it wasn't a big deal.

A few years later, I'm a high school coach with two kids, making $7,000 a year, and I'm watching the bowl games on TV and thinking, "Look at what you missed out on. You're the dumbest guy who has ever come down the pike. Now you can't afford to do the things you took for granted and didn't think were important."

That's why I've always looked at bowls as being a reward.

I want my players to enjoy the experience and I allow them the freedom to do so. But I demand they know the schedule and I want their full attention when we have meetings and practices.

We had scrimmaged in Madison, and I was going to conduct a 20-minute scrimmage when we got down to Orlando. But after four live plays with the ones against the ones — the number one offense against the number one defense — I just stopped it.

We were clicking so well, I said, "You guys are right where you need to be. We don't need to scrimmage any more."

Our kids were sharp every day. They were focused, they were ready to play, and we didn't have one bad day.

We had two work days prior to the bowl — what I would consider a Tuesday-Wednesday practice on a normal game week. Normal would also entail: you taper on Thursday, and you have a walk-through on Friday and you play on Saturday.

I had never before in any situation given my players a day off during a bowl preparation. Never. But I sat down with my staff and I told my coaches I had made up my mind — before we got to Orlando — to break up the routine and give them some time off. I canceled what would have been the equivalent of our Tuesday practice.

The players were scheduled to get up at 7:15 a.m. I called them together the day before and told them to sleep in and plan to meet at 11 a.m. We had a good talk, too. I kind of gave them an idea of where I thought they were, and I felt they were right on track. They had given us tremendous concentration and effort at practice. I thought they were practicing with confidence, and I didn't want them to lose their legs.

So I gave them the day off.

"Do whatever you want to do," I told them. "If you want to golf, then golf. If you want to lay around the pool, then lay around the pool. If you want to go to one of the theme parks, then go. But I expect a helluva practice tomorrow."

The kids went flying out of that meeting room.

You have to have a feel for your players. I think that's one of my strengths as a coach, and always has been. You have to know what buttons to push; when to push them, and when to back off.

To practice just for the sake of practicing — after the way they'd been practicing — would have been counter-productive. It may have taken a little bit out of them.

More than anything else, I wanted them mentally ready, and fresh. I knew they were in good condition, and I felt like they knew the game plan because we had been practicing it for about two weeks.

That's a must in my book: we always want to put the game plan in, and practice it, before we get to the bowl site.

The next day, the players came back and practiced well again.

***

In talking with Auburn coach Tommy Tuberville, I sensed that he was very confident, and so were his players. And why not? They were the favorites.

Tuberville told me they hadn't practiced much at home before getting down to Orlando. They got to Florida a day after we did, so they had one less practice. I really listen to what other coaches have to say. And I thought that maybe Tommy was telling me something I could use to our advantage.

Tuberville said, "I'm not going to hit them much."

It was exactly what I wanted to hear. Tommy wasn't going to hit his guys, and I really didn't think he was going to push them very hard. To me, that sent a message to those Auburn players that they were going to beat us. That they were better than us and all they had to do was show up.

I'm thinking, "If we start fast, we can really jump on these guys."

I look for any edge I can get.

The week of the game, they had a function for both teams at a local alligator theme park. I was matched against Tuberville in a competition to see who could pull an alligator out of the water the fastest. I got mine, Tuberville didn't get his.

At first, though, I couldn't get the damn thing out because he kept hooking his back feet on something. So I whispered to the alligator's trainer, "Hey, listen, when I tug, give the gator a little flip so he can't latch his feet."

It worked, and I was able to pull the gator out.

The Auburn players were mad because they thought I cheated.

I did.

I cheated.

But it was all in fun. My theory is when you go to a bowl game, you want to win everything.

At the 2002 Alamo Bowl, we had two freshmen get up and win the singing competition, and Brandon Williams won the dance competition. Even though Colorado was favored in the game, our kids walked out of there that night feeling good about themselves.

At the 1995 Hall of Fame Bowl, in Tampa, they held a pie eating contest, and I said, "Get me the guy who's going to eat more Key Lime pies than Duke."

That guy was Mike Galletti, a reserve offensive lineman, who won.

At our first Rose Bowl, we went to Lowry's restaurant in Los Angeles for prime rib, and I made sure that all of our players were wearing sport coats. They didn't have to wear ties, but I wanted them to dress nicer than the other team's players.

I don't care what the competition is. We're sending a message — we came here to win everything we do. To me, the little things can become big things. Some people may think that some of these things have nothing to do with winning a game. But it's all about the attitude, it's all about the mindset. That's just our philosophy.

The night before the Auburn game, the bowl committee had a dinner for the school chancellors, athletic directors, and other dignitaries. Wisconsin's Governor Jim Doyle and his son, Gus, were there. The governor is a good fan. He noticed I was very relaxed.

Normally, I'm a mess, I'm a wreck, the night before a game. In most cases, I wouldn't even consider going out with a group of people. This was different.

I was much more mellow.

Maybe it's like going to a movie and seeing "The End" come up on the screen when it's finished, though I don't know if I had internalized my retirement to that extent.

But maybe my peace of mind was the result of knowing this was "The End" of my career. When this bowl game was over, I wouldn't have to worry about recruiting, I wouldn't have to worry about getting ready for spring practice, I wouldn't have to worry about what's next.

It's over. My legacy had already been established. The End.

That was evident, according to Cindy, in my behavior before the bowl in Orlando.

(Cindy has since noticed the reaction I've gotten from people. Now that I'm retired, it has changed because I don't have anything else to prove. I've already done it. It's usually, "How's the team going to be? Who's your quarterback? Are you going to have a good running back? What about the defense and the kicking game?" Now, when someone comes up to me, more often than not, it's to say thanks.)

There was something else at play before the Auburn game.

It was a no-lose deal.

When nobody thinks you're going to win, or even have a chance to win, there's no pressure. And everyone thought we were going to lose. I thought we could win, and so did our players. That's all that counted. Our staff had developed a good game plan, the team had spent a solid month in preparation to win this game, and everybody had prepared well. I knew my players felt good about themselves.

One of our senior wide receivers, Brandon Williams, was hot all week. He was having fun. He loves big games and being on the big stage. I love teasing Brandon, too.

"Brandon, you're going to light it up tomorrow," I told him. And he looks at me and smiles, and says, "I know it, coach. Just give me the rock."

That same day, I was visiting with a pro scout who was asking me a bunch of questions about our senior offensive center, Donovan Raiola. I know pro football is important to Donovan, and I challenged him.

"This is a money game, Donovan," I said. "That Auburn nose guard is a heckuva player, and he gets a push on everybody. He's disruptive. He's short, he's squat, and he's hard to block. But if you can handle this guy, you can make yourself some money from the pro's because they'll all be watching."

And that's why I told the scout, "Evaluate Raiola tomorrow. Don't look at any other game he's played this season. Just look at how he plays against Auburn because he has been flat-out challenged, and I bet he plays his fanny off."

On the morning of the game, Father Mike Burke always says something to me about what he has observed from our players. "All their eyes are on you, Barry," he said. "They're listening, they're tuned in, they're really focused."

I could feel that.

Before our season opener against Bowling Green, I had talked to the players about going on the field and turning it loose. I wanted them to play fast. And that's how I wanted them to play against Auburn.

"We know the game plan and there's no reason to be hesitant," I said to them in the locker room before the kickoff. "If you make a mistake, you make a mistake. But play fast. Let's go turn it loose, men. Let's have some fun and let's go out there and kick ass. We're going to take a full swing today. We're not taking a check swing. Let's get after their ass."

Going into the game, I was a little worried about their speed at linebacker. They weren't big, but they could run. We hadn't run the toss sweep well all year, and I'm thinking, "What the hell do we have this play in our game plan for?"

Their linebackers run like deer, and I didn't think our guards could block them. They struggled with good mobile linebackers most of the season. The kid at Northwestern, Tim McGarigle, must have had 25 tackles against us. Our guards couldn't get to him, and he doesn't run as well as the Auburn guys.

I did think that we could throw the ball against them.

We had a lot of play-action in the game plan, and a lot of good, solid protections. We weren't going to allow them to come whistling off the edge on John Stocco, especially Stanley McClover. I felt we could create some problems for Auburn with our shifts. We wanted to make them communicate things in the secondary.

Defensively, we had Justin Ostrowski starting again at defensive tackle, back to 100 percent after missing most of the year with a knee injury. With Ostrowski and Nick Hayden, you've got a couple of 300-pounders, and you can jam up things in the middle. We can protect our linebackers more with those two big guys inside.

It's different if you're playing a Kurt Ware at tackle. He's still very green. Or if you've got a Mike Newkirk in there. He's barely 250 pounds. We tried playing Jason Chapman inside, but he was also getting moved and thrown around.

If you can't slow down those guards and center, they can get a lot of people up on your linebackers and our linebackers aren't strong enough to take on a block and get to the ball carrier. But lining up with Ostrowski and Hayden allowed Dontez Sanders and Mark Zalewski some space to run.

With the exception of their season opener against Georgia Tech, Auburn's quarterback Brandon Cox had really played well. I think he finished second in the SEC in passing yards and passing efficiency, and he had thrown for over 200 yards a bunch of times.

But he didn't play well against us.

He didn't play his normal game.

On the second play, he under threw his receiver, and our senior cornerback, Levonne Rowan, intercepted the pass. There's a guy who played his fanny off in the bowl. And the fact is, Levonne strugged his whole career at Wisconsin. I don't know why, either. He's a smart kid with a great attitude.

Rowan has never been a problem for us in school or anywhere else, and I know how badly he wants to play pro football. I can recommend him to the scouts. But they're not just going to take my word alone. They're going to watch every film.

That's why I told him, "Levonne, you can make some hay against Auburn. Play well in this game, and the right people will take notice."

That was a helluva interception by Rowan. It was absolutely a big play, maybe one of the biggest of the game, because their quarterback never responded afterward, never recovered from that. You'd like not to have one play have such an impact on your team. But it can.

You look at our Iowa game. On our first series of the second half, Stocco threw a beautiful pass to Brandon Williams who got behind the defense. That would have been a 79-yard touchdown. And that would have given us a 17-3 lead.

But he dropped the pass. We wound up punting, Iowa scored, and the game is tied. We never recovered from that drop. We didn't have any offense the rest of the game.

I always talk to the players about momentum and how the pendulum can swing. When you lose the momentum, you can't flinch. You can't let losing come into your mind. You have to trust each other and have the confidence that somebody on the team is going to make a play to swing the pendulum back.

Auburn was never able to swing it back. We got the jump on them, and I thought we dominated the first half, even though we left some points on the field. We did some things to hurt ourselves and stop drives — a dropped pass, penalties, a missed field goal. But we still led, 17-0, and controlled the game.

My guys were cranked.

There were some fisticuffs just before the half ended, and one of their players, an offensive tackle, was ejected. I thought some of my players got carried away, too. There was some taunting and a lot of trash talking that I didn't appreciate.

Normally, we go into the locker room and split up to talk about adjustments — offensive coaches and defensive coaches. And I spend time with both. But I felt like I had to say something right away. So I ran into the room with the players, got them all together, and I quieted them down.

"Listen, you're kicking their ass, you're beating the hell out of them," I said. "We don't have to taunt these guys. We don't need this nonsense. Talk with your pads."

I had to get that point across.

There's the temptation in a game like this to sugarcoat what was happening. You know how coaches who have the lead are always saying, "It's still nothing-to-nothing. Let's go out there in the second half and play that way. Zero-to-zero."

That wasn't my message when we were ready to go back on the field.

"It ain't nothing-to-nothing," I said. "We're beating their ass, so let's keep beating their ass. You've dominated the game, and I expect the same thing in the second half."

Talk about dominating.

Brian Calhoun was spectacular. He made one short run in front of our bench where their cornerback is unblocked and right in his face, and he leaps off one foot and hurdles the kid to get a first down. It was one of the greatest three-yard runs I've ever seen.

Calhoun didn't exceed my expectations. I knew he was very talented. You could see that last season, when he played on the scout team after transferring from Colorado. It was the same way last spring. I just didn't know how tough or how durable he was going to be during a long, grinding Big Ten season. Well, he's plenty tough and plenty durable.

Nobody ever gets a solid hit on him.

Calhoun is a different type of tailback than Ron Dayne. We used him differently. When he goes to the NFL level, he'll be able to shift to the slot and be effective as a receiver. You just need to get the ball in his hands. He'll be great in the West Coast offense. He's a guy who can lug it and catch it.

Throughout the bowl game, we felt we could get something with Calhoun running to the weak side of the Auburn defense. If you break us down, we're a tight end or strong side offense — we run a majority of our plays to the tight end's side. Even some of the plays we start on the weak side, like an isolation, will end up bending back strong.

I'm sure Auburn overcompensated because of our tendencies. The first time we called the toss sweep, our guard didn't block anybody, but we still got a long run because Calhoun was able to make the linebacker miss.

Their free safety, Will Herring, is a good player. But he didn't play well against us. Our tackles, Joe Thomas and Kraig Urbik, stretched or hooked their 5-technique, and we were getting things sealed off. Our linemen were knocking their guys off the line and creating big seams and putting the onus on the safety to make plays, and their secondary was missing a lot of tackles.

It's nice to get into that kind of rhythm on offense, where you can run it and throw it, and you can change up on them to keep the defense off balance.

***

In the second half, you could see their quarterback was still off his game. "Heat him up, press him," I kept telling Bret. "Let's get a push inside instead of running a twist because he's stepping up so much. Let's keep somebody in his face."

When you have a quarterback rattled, you have to take advantage of it. Our quarterback was just the opposite. Stocco showed a lot of poise.

From the beginning of the year to the bowl, I thought he progressed light years. John always wanted to be good. And he's a good athlete; a better athlete than most people think. Just watch him play basketball and the way he runs and jumps and competes.

Paul Chryst, who was in his first year back with the program as the offensive coordinator, did a great job with Stocco as far as changing our practice schedule and routine during the season. That gave John a lot more opportunities — repetitions — and looks at what he was going to see in the games.

Stocco developed a feel for his receivers, knowing where they were going to be coming out of their cuts. That familiarity was instrumental in his improvement.

John has always had toughness.

I'll give you an example. There's less than nine minutes left in the fourth quarter — we're leading Auburn, 24-14 — and we take over the football on our own 1-yard line. I still don't understand the spot that we got. They punt, and it should have been a touchback. Ball on the 20.

"Do you guys have different rules in the ACC than we have in the Big Ten?" I asked one of the officials. "Are we playing by different rules today?"

I've been in the game for a long time, and I pride myself in knowing the rules. Not that this call was going to make a difference. If nothing else, we're going to punt the ball to the other end and get it off our goal line.

But I thought the third-down play that Stocco made in the end zone on that series was as good of a play as he has made all season. It kind of exemplified how he played that day, how well he was prepared and how confident he was throwing the ball.

He's standing in the end zone, and he knows that he's going to get whacked as soon as he delivers the ball. But he stands in there and takes the hit and throws a strike to Brandon Williams, who takes the ball out to our 40. That was huge, that was big time.

The rest of that series I'm just thinking about moving the chains. I'm on the headsets with Paul Chryst, and he's calling the plays and I'm directing and watching the clock. I would have liked to get another touchdown on a big play. But they were battling pretty hard to keep us out of there, and then they conceded.

I could tell Paul wanted us to get another score. All my coaches wanted to score again. Hell, all the players wanted to score again.

Raiola comes off the field and says to me, "Coach, you talked about calling an aggressive game, you talked about going after their ass, and you want to take a knee?"

He was teasing me, and I laughed. But we didn't have to rub it in. That was enough.

My first year as a head high school coach, it got kind of ugly because I ran up the score on an arch-rival from a neighboring community. I had a running back who needed 250 yards rushing to break the conference record. I put him out there, and we put it on the other team pretty good. I didn't feel good about it.

Actually...

At the time, I felt good about it, good about how our kids played. But I've been on both sides and I don't feel like there is a place for that. Auburn wasn't using their timeouts, they were white-flagging it, and I just wanted the game to end.

I just wanted the win.

When John took the knee and then sprinted over and presented me with the game ball, I thought that was a pretty nice touch. That was pretty moving and pretty meaningful to me. It was kind of like an exclamation point on the day.

For the first time during a game, I had one of my grandsons, Joe, on the sidelines with me. My daughter Dawn wanted him there because it was my last game. And I agreed that he should be there. He's 11, a good athlete, and I thought he'd appreciate it.

I wanted him to be a part of it. I wanted him to get a feel for everything. He was in the locker room before the game and at halftime, and he probably heard some language he hasn't heard before. But that's part of the deal.

I gave Joe the game ball to carry around.

As I was leaving the field, I wanted to make sure our fans knew how much we really appreciated their support. I wanted to acknowledge them and thank them. They were really into the game and very vocal, even though they were outnumbered by Auburn fans. You will never hear me say anything bad about our fans. They're the best.

I was so happy with our win.

I was ecstatic.

Then I saw Joe Thomas' dad, and I cried with him.

Joe Thomas played both ways against Auburn, offense and defense, and he got hurt just running to the ball while playing on defense in the third quarter. It just kills you when a kid is doing extra to help his team and he blows out an ACL without getting hit.

I had almost the same feeling when Lee Evans, our all-time leading receiver, got hurt in a spring game. I felt so bad for Lee and the two surgeries that he had to go through. But it made it a lot easier on everybody with the way he came back so strong his senior year.

Football is a violent sport, and injuries are part of it. That's the hard part for me. I'll always walk out on the field any time a kid is down. And it's such a sick feeling knowing that he may have to go through surgery and rehab.

After I told Joe's dad how bad I felt, I made sure he knew that we would support Joe, and I assured him everything was going to work out.

***

In the locker room after the game, I thanked the seniors. You always want to thank them for their commitment to the program and the legacy that they leave behind.

I told the younger guys that they have a very bright future — the sky is the limit — and I wanted this bowl victory to be a springboard for them. I emphasized to them that they need to buy into Bret's program, and I wished them the best.

I told the group that they could learn a lesson from this — something they could use the rest of their lives. Some will continue to play football. Most won't.

"Regardless of what you're doing," I said, "don't let someone else build a barrier or establish what you can or can't do. Most people didn't think you had a chance against Auburn. Most people didn't think you could win this game. Nobody believed in us, but us.

"And, against all odds, or so it seemed, you went out there today and proved them all wrong. You did something they said you couldn't do. You didn't flinch."

I thanked them again and reminded them what can happen when everybody in the room is pulling together and believes that the team is going to win.

I expect to win.

That's just the way I was brought up.

CHAPTER ONE

Barry from Burgettstown

I loved coaching in Old Coal Miners games: two teams standing toe-to-toe and slugging it out. Very little passing. Both defenses are pounding each other pretty good. Nobody is moving the ball very much. And everything is played between the tackles.

It's a conservative, hard-nosed, physical brand of football. It's about solid fundamentals and toughness. And it goes back to how I first learned to play the game in Pennsylvania, where the lifestyle, work ethic, and tradition dictated how you played in the '50s and '60s.

An Old Coal Miners game is not about finesse or spreading the field and dinking and dunking the ball. It's not the West Coast offense. When you change possession, you want to gain yardage. But not every possession is going to be a scoring possession. And you're always working toward shortening the field.

That's what it's all about; field position and being smart with the ball — avoiding turnovers, foolish penalties, and mental errors, especially in the red zone. It's about working hard to move the chains and getting first downs with your tailback.

Every once in a while you throw a pass. But it's not about taking chances that might put you in a hole. On the contrary. It's about staying away from all negative yardage plays. It's about the kicking game, and punting the ball to the other end of the field, and playing good defense.

Our 2004 Big Ten Conference opener against Penn State was an Old Coal Miners game. We knocked out two of their quarterbacks, including Michael Robinson, and we wound up playing a 270-pound fullback — Matt Bernstein — at tailback because of injuries to Anthony Davis, Booker Stanley and Jamil Walker. We won 16-3.

Bernstein ended up bringing a lot of personality and punch to the offense. And we rode him. Did we ever. On one of our scoring drives, we gave him the ball on 11 of the 17 plays. That was just the type of game it was. Tough, physical, defensive football.

Ron Dayne came of age in an Old Coal Miners game; our 1996 game against Stanford. There was nothing pretty about it, except the final score, 14-0.

Stanford had a highly-touted quarterback in Chad Hutchinson, who signed a major league baseball contract before moving on to the NFL. I knew their coach, Tyrone Willingham, was high on Hutchinson. But we shut down their offense.

Middle linebacker Pete Monty was all over the field and had something like 13 unassisted tackles, while Tarek Saleh and Bryan Jurewicz wouldn't let Hutchinson get comfortable in the pocket. The pressure resulted in five sacks and four turnovers.

Offensively, we also had turnover issues: three interceptions and a fumble. And when Stanford loaded up the box with eight and nine defenders, we couldn't run the ball with Carl McCullough and Aaron Stecker. We had two net yards at halftime.

Stanford was a good defensive team, particularly with Kailee Wong rushing off the edge and Chris Draft at linebacker. They were determined to take away the run and force our quarterback, Mike Samuel, to make plays through the air. It was a solid game plan. And it worked until we took the wraps off Dayne.

Our assistant coaches were reluctant to move a true freshman ahead of our two returning tailbacks, McCullough and Stecker. I remember Chilly — Brad Childress, our offensive coordinator — flipping out when Dayne got into the UNLV game the week before.

"What the hell is he doing in the game?" Chilly demanded from the press box.

"I put him in," I said on my headset.

"Well, maybe then I should throw Scott Kavanagh in there," he said.

Kavanagh was a freshman quarterback.

I nixed that idea.

Chilly wasn't sold on Dayne being ready to play so early in his career. I was. I always thought Dayne was special, and I felt he was ready. He had 90 yards in the second half of our win against UNLV, and he made the difference against Stanford. Ronnie took control of the game, rushing for 75 yards.

We rode him, too. Dayne had eight straight carries and all but one of the yards on our fourth-quarter touchdown drive that sealed the win. Samuel scored on a quarterback sneak on the ninth and final play of the drive. My kind of drive.

***

Hayden Fry and Lou Holtz were opposites when it came to protecting a lead. Hayden wouldn't hesitate to punt on third down and put the defense back on the field. I remember winning some close games that way when we had our good defenses at Iowa. Lou, on the other hand, wanted to control the ball and wear down the opponent's defense.

The first game I coached under Lou Holtz at Notre Dame — we won 26-7 at Michigan — I learned some things about time management. After the Wolverines had cut into our lead, our defense didn't get off the sidelines again for a while because we're rushing the ball with our running backs, getting first downs and eating up the clock.

That's the way I tried to coach at Wisconsin — managing the game by controlling the ball and dictating field position. That was especially true when we had Dayne.

People laughed at Don Morton and his veer offense. I laughed, too.

But in my final game at Notre Dame — the 1990 Orange Bowl — we beat Colorado 21-6, in what was an Old Coal Miners game. And basically all we ran was the veer. It wasn't Morton's split-back veer, but we were running inside and outside veers and giving the ball to our fullbacks when our quarterback, Tony Rice, wasn't running.

So it's not so much the style of offense you're running, but the execution that makes the difference in how you are running those plays and moving the chains. I've always felt comfortable in a field position game. I know how to play that game; the Old Coal Miners game.

I've been in a lot of them, too. You could say I was a product of my western Pennsylvania environment. That part of the state was once a melting pot for Europeans and a spawning ground for a generation of football coaches. And there was a correlation.

Many immigrants came to the United States to work in the coal and zinc mines and steel mills. Although they lived and worked in different towns up and down the rivers in western Pennsylvania, they all had the same interest in sports and the same focal point.

Their kids.

That's why Friday night football was so big. The games were played for entertainment and bragging rights among all those miners and mill workers in those little communities. My fondest recollection of the rivalry we had with another high school in the area?

Bonfires and fights.

That was the culture. So there was a major emphasis placed on athletics, whether it be high school, junior high, midget football, or Little League baseball. Consequently, the coaches were advanced, the playing facilities were dynamite, and the kids learned how to play the game playing whatever sport was in season. That was the commitment. And, ultimately, it became a means to an end for many who used athletics to get out of working in the mills.

My parents always talked about respecting people, and I learned about hard work from them because that's all I saw around me — blue-collar people, hard-working people. Most of all, I saw people who loved athletics. That shaped who I am.

But I never wanted to set foot in the mills. Nobody working there seemed happy. I just didn't want any part of that life. So I ended up being a student of the game. I tried to learn as much as I could, and I absorbed everything that I was taught. I never lost that foundation, either. That's one of the common threads between all of us who grew up that way in western Pennsylvania and went on to coach football.

Bill Cowher is from Crafton, west of Pittsburgh, and went to Carlynton High School. Kirk Ferentz went to Upper St. Clair, and Dave Wannstedt went to Baldwin High in Pittsburgh. (Wan's dad, Frank, worked in the mills.) Marty Schottenheimer is from Canonsburg and went to Fort Cherry. So did Marvin Lewis, who's from McDonald.

Mike Ditka is from Aliquippa. Joe Walton is from Beaver Falls. Bob Davie is from Sewickley, as is Chuck Knox, who went to Ellwood City High School. Knox is the son of a steel worker who emigrated from Ireland. What was Knox best known for as a football coach? Ground Chuck. Run the ball and play field position.

We all coached the game the same way.

Football is a tough, physical, hard-nosed sport, and there are no short-cuts. That was ingrained at an early age.

***

I grew up in Langeloth, a small community of about 1,500 just outside of Burgettstown. I was raised with Spanish kids, Polish kids,

Slovenians, Irish, Serbians. And I never felt like I was a minority. Everybody took pride in their nationality.

My dad, Anthony Alvarez, was born in Springfield, Illinois. His father and mother came to the United States hoping to make enough money to go back and buy property in Spain. (I found out recently that the only thing my grandfather could say in English was "son of a bitch." That was his response to everything.)

When my dad was 10, the family moved back to Spain and bought a beautiful piece of property that butts right up to the cliffs overlooking the Bay of Biscay. We still have about 35 first and second cousins in that region.

With the outbreak of the country's second civil war in the late '30s, my dad declared as a loyalist and refused to fight for dictator Francisco Franco. As a result, he was imprisoned in a POW camp for his political beliefs.

His older brother negotiated with the American consulate, and they exchanged my dad for a French prisoner. He was released on French soil. Being an American citizen, he had no interest whatsoever in going back to Spain.

I didn't know any of the specifics about what my dad lived through — because he never talked about it — until I was in grad school at Nebraska and I was assigned to do an autobiography. Cindy found out most of the details.

Anthony — Tony — worked his way back to the United States. He stayed with an uncle in New York for a while and eventually settled in Pennsylvania.

A number of Spanish people had relocated to Langeloth. They found the same type of work there that they had in Spain — zinc mining.

My mother, Alvera, was born in Langeloth, a true company town. Sebastian Langeloth built a zinc plant there and lived in the biggest house I'd ever seen at the very top of the hill. That was for the owner as per the old caste system.

After the war, Gus Barbush, a Greek, literally bought the town. He owned every house and everyone paid rent to him, including my dad.

We lived at 414 Fourth Ave., one of the cement houses. My dad lived there until he was 85 and we had to put him in an assisted living facility.

While I was growing up, Tony worked seven days a week as a groundskeeper at Williams Country Club in Weirton, West Virginia.

Alvera worked as a waitress.

My mom and dad were blue-collar people. They taught me about respect and working hard and treating people right. They taught old-fashioned values.

Have pride in yourself. Have pride in your family. Be proud of your nationality. And, whatever you do, make sure you do it the right way.

My dad was very sensitive and very observant. He was a good judge of people. And I probably inherited that trait from him. My mom was very outgoing, a people person. She enjoyed being around people all the time. And that's the way I've always been.

I'll never forget my mom's reaction to what Lou Holtz had to say on national television after we beat No. 1-ranked Miami during the '88 season. Lou was being interviewed on the field, and he said, "It's the spirit of Notre Dame that won the game for us today."

Almost immediately after he said that, my mom was on the phone with Cindy saying, "Spirit of Notre Dame? My ass. It was Barry's defense that won the game."

She hated John Cooper. She used to watch Cooper's TV show all the time. And after we beat Ohio State in 1992, she called and said, "Cooper chaps my ass. Here he is talking about how Ohio State beat itself, and he's not giving you any credit."

That was Alvera.

My parents always showed support. They were always there for me, regardless of what sport I was playing. And they showed their appreciation when I did well. One thing about Spanish people, they dote on their children. They make a fuss over them. They make them feel special. That's the way my younger brother and I always felt.

My brother's given name is Tony Mark. But I gave nicknames to everybody, so Tony Mark became Woody — Woody Alvarez. There was five years difference in our age, so we each had our own circle of friends. Woody was more like my dad — very laidback and kind. He could have been a good athlete, but he got hurt playing sports. He was only 120 pounds when he graduated from high school.

Cindy always felt that it would have been easy for Woody to be jealous because of my accomplishments as an athlete and all the attention that I got in our home and around town. But he shared in my success. He and my dad would drive to our games at Ohio State and Indiana. Woody has always been 100 percent supportive of me, and still is. I'm indebted to

Woody for taking care of our parents the last six or seven years of their lives, when they weren't able to take care of themselves. Out of necessity, they became his life.

***

When we were growing up, my maternal grandmother, Elvira, lived with us in Langeloth. I called her "Wella," short for Abuela — the Spanish word for grandmother. My Greek friends tell me Yia-Yia was their equivalent word.

In any language, Wella was a great influence.

I spent more time with her than anybody. She basically raised me because my dad worked all day and my mother worked from 4 to midnight. Wella was tough as hell. She didn't speak much English, and she'd raise Cain with me when I didn't speak Spanish. I actually learned Spanish before I learned English.

I wish I would have stayed with the language. But when you're young and impressionable, you don't want to be Spanish, you want to be American. Whenever I talked to my grandmother in English or broken Spanish, she'd get very upset with me. Like I said, she was tough and demanding.

Even later on, when I was 16 or 17, if I tried to sneak back into the house late at night — my parents would be sleeping — she'd hear me coming in and would come out of her bedroom and whack me. She made sure I didn't get away with much.

For some strange reason, she loved watching the old *Perry Mason* show on television. I don't know how much she understood, but that was her favorite.

American Bandstand was on at the same time, and that's what my brother and I wanted to watch. Since we had just one TV, we had a conflict.

That prompted me to change all the clocks in the house. I moved them back an hour. So, we're giggling and dancing to Dick Clark, and my grandmother is thinking that she still had time before *Perry Mason* was scheduled to come on.

We thought it was the slickest thing.

"No Perry Mason?" she'd say in broken English.

"Not this week," we'd tell her.

It didn't take long for her to catch on to our shenanigans, and we paid for it. Still, I remained her favorite. And we were always very close.

My uncle John — John Vallina — probably had the most influence on my life. He was like a big brother and a dad. He picked me up whenever I was down.

Uncle John owned a convenience store which also had a butcher shop. I worked for him on weekends and after practice. I learned how to cut meat, and I delivered groceries when I was 12 or 13. I was too young to have a license, but I'd load up the car and deliver anyway.

I'd also go out with my Uncle John when he collected bills. He was a tough sucker. And he'd fight at the drop of a hat. I remember one time seeing him go right through a screen door because some guy — who owed him money — was getting smart.

I liked being with him, but I didn't want to pay his bail.

Uncle John was always supportive of me. But he would kick me in the butt when I needed it. He was a character, always teasing and antagonizing people. I liked hanging out with him at the store.

Most of the mines in the area had shut down by then. But the steel mills would send buses to pick up guys and some of them would park their cars across the street from the store. I'd see them going to work every morning and coming back the same way — tired and filthy — from a hard day of labor.

Except for one guy. He had a college degree, and he wore a shirt and tie and worked as an accountant for one of the steel companies.

He always sat in the front of the bus. When the bus stopped, he'd jump out and sprint home. He always had a bounce in his step. He was happy as hell, while the other guys getting off the bus were dirty and dragging, carrying lunch pails.

That left an impression. It seemed like they had nothing to look forward to except maybe the Friday night football games. And that sent a strong message: you didn't want to be sitting in the back of that bus.

That was not the life for me.

One summer I almost got trapped into working at Weirton Steel. When I came home from college I learned my dad had lined up the job. I even went through a physical.

That's when I made a phone call to Nebraska and begged the coaches to get me into summer school. They said yes, and I got on a plane and went back to Lincoln.

I knew they were getting paid well in those mills. But I had made a vow to myself that I would never set foot in one. And I kept that promise.

***

As a family, I knew we had some limitations financially. But I never felt like I was poor. I never wanted for anything.

Woody likes to tell the story about how I wanted a new baseball glove, a Wilson A-2000. My parents didn't have the money to buy it. But my dad did some things on the side, some odd jobs, trimmed some trees, and bought it for me. I was maybe 13 or 14, and I wore that glove out.

My dad was a big baseball fan. He loved baseball more than any other sport. There's a softball complex in Langeloth and there wasn't a game played there without my dad's car parked beyond the outfield fences, a good vantage point to watch the kids.

I loved baseball, too.

I remember falling asleep — with a transistor radio to my ear — listening to the Pittsburgh Pirates. Their play-by-play announcer, Bob Prince, was awesome. He was informative and entertaining, and his style went over big in western Pennsylvania.

If you listened closely to Prince, you could learn about baseball. He would talk about strategies, about moving runners, and what the Pirates were attempting to do. I was always trying to learn more about the game, and Prince was a good teacher.

A lot of things he talked about stayed with me. When I became a head football coach, I always used to tell my players, "You need to think like a shortstop."

That meant, to me, that you needed to think one play ahead. You had to be conscious of the game situation. In baseball, you had to be aware of base runners and the count on the batter. You had to have a feel for what he was trying to do at the plate. You had to anticipate the ball being hit to you — and you had to position yourself accordingly, so that you knew where to go with the throw.

I was using that example all the time. But it dawned on me one day to ask, "How many of you know what I mean when I say, 'Think like a shortstop?'"

Maybe one-third of the players in the room had played some baseball and knew what it meant. The rest of them didn't have any idea what I was talking about, and here I was using the phrase and assuming everybody knew.

I was a catcher, not a shortstop.

I also played a little first base and outfield. I could never run very fast and, for a catcher, my arm probably wasn't strong enough. But I could hit, I mean, I could really hit. As a ninth grader, I lettered on our high school's varsity baseball team.

I loved following the major leaguers. Every Sunday morning I would devour the baseball statistics in the newspaper. I remember studying every average. And I could tell you what everybody in the National League was doing.

My dad would take us to a few games every year in Pittsburgh, but he really hated to go because he didn't like to deal with traffic. We had a good parks system in our town, and they'd load up the buses for special promotions like Kids Day or Little League Day.

I even won some free tickets from the local Ford dealership when I correctly identified some Pirates players who were pictured with their backs to the camera. I could tell who they were just by their body size. Roberto Clemente was one of my favorites.

I liked Dick Stuart, too. Dr. Strangeglove. The hardcore fans had a saying, "Don't boo Stu, he's overdue." I never saw anybody hit a ball so high and far as him.

I would have loved to have gotten some autographs. I would have loved having Elroy Face's autograph or Bob Skinner's or Rocky Nelson's. But I could never get close enough to them. We were always sitting out in right field in the peanut gallery.

Forbes Field seemed so big, and we were so damn far away.

***

My best friend was Jim Nicksick. We were like brothers.

His uncle was Mike Nixon, who was an assistant for the Washington Redskins under Joe Kuharich and Buddy Parker, and later the head coach of the Redskins for two seasons. In 1965, he was the head coach of the Pittsburgh Steelers before being replaced by Bill Austin, a former assistant under Vince Lombardi in Green Bay.

Jim Nicksick's parents used to take us to Steelers games. I loved watching John Henry Johnson and Bobby Layne. But my favorite player was Ernie Stautner. He was only 6-1 and 230 pounds, which was small for a defensive tackle. But he was a Pro Bowl player, and he was always the toughest guy on the field.

I had an appreciation for how he played, and how the Steelers played. I was still learning about the game. But I had come a long way from the first time I went out for midget football when I was a sixth grader and the coach said, "Line up at fullback."

To be honest, I didn't know what a fullback was. I didn't know any position. I was starting from zero. I was a 9-year-old playing with 12-year-olds. That's a helluva difference. But I was always able to compete.

You have to be very careful in youth football because sometimes you can get coaches who are trying to live vicariously through the kids, and they'll take out their frustrations on them instead of really teaching them the game. Some think coaching is just screaming at a kid, and you can really disillusion youngsters.

I had a great youth coach, Johnny Marcucci. He was really a teacher. I remember him teaching us how to take tackling angles and what to look for in blocking schemes. He taught us how to block, how to tackle, how to be tough, how to play with your face up. That's where I learned to be physical.

We had a very advanced team for midget football. We were drawing more people than the high school. It was big time. And it was really a good foundation. I was like a sponge and listened to everything Marcucci had to say about gaining an edge on your opponent by studying and knowing tendencies.

As a ninth grader, I couldn't make weight for the midget team, so I played on the high school's junior varsity. I was the quarterback. Why? Because they didn't have many guys out and nobody else wanted to play the position. We had a four-game schedule, and we won all four. Could I throw the ball? Hell yes.

As a sophomore, I played linebacker and some offensive guard on the varsity. Pat McGraw was the coach of the Burgettstown Blue Devils. He was a tough old Irishman who always had a tobacco chew in his mouth. He was all about toughness. And he coached that way.

McGraw always took pride in his teams being more physical than other teams. Before the start of every season, he'd line up scrimmages against bigger schools. We had about 30 guys out for football, and we'd show up in our black high tops and grubby practice gear that we had been wearing twice daily. We were a motley crew.

The other team would come racing out of their locker room in their big stadium, about 100 guys all dressed in game uniforms. We didn't even have numbers on those grungy ribbed jerseys. We would all be thinking, "Holy Mackerel, this was only supposed to be a scrimmage."

That turned out to be a good lesson for me. I remember McGraw telling us, "I don't give a crap what they're wearing or how many they have. All I know is they can put 11 on the field, and that's all you have to know. Our 11 will kick their ass."

And we did. We beat the hell out of them. Beat them good. That was McGraw's attitude: "You're going to be tougher than they are, and you're going to hit, and if you don't hit, you're not going to be playing for me."

I liked to hit.

I was always a physical player, and I never backed off.

I liked contact.

I was starting to get a lot of attention from college recruiters near the end of my junior year. We had a good team, and I had a good year. I did whatever was asked of me, including place-kicking. We didn't have anybody else, so I just did it.

I remember missing four extra points in one game. I don't remember how I missed them, but I missed them. We still won, 24-0.

You'd think I'd have great compassion for kickers as a head coach.

I don't.

By the time I was a senior, I weighed between 215 and 220 pounds. That's pretty big for a linebacker. Back then, the offensive guards were 225 and 230. I wasn't very fast, but I was athletic enough and big enough to play. And I was really playing well, too, when I dislocated my elbow the third game of my senior year.

And that scared me. I didn't know if I would get a scholarship or not.

I missed about four games, and I was pretty worried about my future. But I had good enough film and schools like Miami (Fla.), Virginia, Wake Forest, Duke, Arizona State and Nebraska were still interested.

I'll never forget my last high school game. We played Hopewell, the same school that produced Tony Dorsett and current Penn State linebacker Paul Posluszny.

We lost, and I cried like a baby.

I was crushed, and I couldn't stop crying. We had a dance that night at the school, and I cried through the whole dance. I was emotional not because it was my last game as a senior but because we had lost.

That's how I learned to play. Football became my life, my livelihood.

It became me.

***

I really entertained the idea of playing football at Miami. I wanted to go there out of high school, but my mom wouldn't let me. The Miami coaches would call the house, and my mom would tell them, "He's not interested." She was afraid I'd party too much. For some reason, she had a picture of Miami being a big party school.

Frank Kush tried to recruit me to Arizona State, and I'll never forget the night that Kush showed up at our house in Langeloth. My dad was working, so my Uncle John sat in with my mother. It didn't take long for Uncle John to offend Kush.

"Are you an N-C-Double-A school?" he asked.

That really ticked off Kush, who made a point of telling my uncle that the Sun Devils were ranked No. 10 in the country and had a helluva team.

When I took my visit to Arizona State, I couldn't believe their practices. Frank killed those guys. He beat them up. He had them running laps and sprinting every time he blew that damn whistle. I wasn't crazy about all that running.

You talk about a tough old coal miner from Pennsylvania. That was Frank Kush.

Years later, when I was coaching at Notre Dame, we were getting ready for the national championship game at the Fiesta Bowl, and Kush was part of a Tempe group that was playing host. I'm walking through a buffet line, and Frank comes up from behind — I didn't see him coming — and gives me a kidney punch.

He says, "This is the SOB who didn't come to Arizona State when I recruited him." Every time I see Frank, he'll whack me for not going to school there.

Now, you can imagine the reaction to a guy showing up in Burgettstown wearing a red felt hat with a feather on it. That was Nebraska's Bob Devaney. And my high school coach, McGraw, still talks about Devaney wearing that damn hat. There was a magnetism about Devaney. That was undeniable.

Any time he was passing through the area, he would call my father, and they'd get together at the Slovenia Club, a private club where they'd have drinks and laughs and shoot the breeze and tell stories.

Everybody at the club was really into athletics, and Devaney felt comfortable there. The next day he might be in Pittsburgh at a black tie event. He was the type of person who could feel comfortable with anybody.

A *Newsweek* article once suggested that Devaney's appearance — he was called paunchy and pudgy — didn't match the new breed of college football coaches.

The writer said Devaney wasn't as suave as Ara Paraseghian, John McKay, or Darrell Royal. He wrote that Devaney was more like Wallace Beery than Kirk Douglas.

Another writer called Devaney "the poor man's version of Willy Loman" because of his colorful wardrobe. Devaney took everything in stride. And he was able to laugh at himself. He always viewed the press as an ally, not an enemy.

In his autobiography, Devaney related a recruiting story about a player, Tony Jeter, who was from my neck of the woods. When Devaney walked into the home, Jeter's mom was playing the organ, so Devaney sat down and began singing hymns.

"Tony told the local newspaper that once his mamma heard my Irish tenor," Devaney said, "there was never a doubt where he was going to college. He was coming to Nebraska to play for that nice Mr. Devaney."

One of Devaney's assistants was John Melton, who was from Slovan, a neighboring community to Langeloth and Burgettstown. He went to high school with my mom and knew my Uncle John. He recruited four or five players from western Pennsylvania every year.

My mom trusted him. So did I.

Nebraska was my choice. I wanted to leave the area because I thought that was part of growing up. That's just what you do — you get away from home.

A week or so before I was scheduled to leave for Lincoln, I was jogging around our high school practice field when some guy challenged me to my face. I think he was someone who had worked in a steel mill all his life.

I remember him saying, "Now we'll find out how tough you are, Alvarez. Wait 'til you get there with all those big guys. We'll find out."

I didn't say anything to him. Instead, I just kept running and thinking to myself, "I'll show him. I'll show him."

CHAPTER TWO

Devaney and the Husker Blueprint

During my recruiting visit to Nebraska, I got the sense that I was entering the world of big-time college athletics. People in Lincoln made a fuss over the players wherever they went. There was a commotion when you walked into a restaurant.

Football was important.

The Cornhuskers were coming off a 1963 season in which they went 10-1 and beat Auburn in the Orange Bowl. They were already in the midst of what would become an NCAA record streak of 262 straight sellouts at Memorial Stadium.

They had a couple of NFL first-round draft choices in Bob Brown, who went to the Philadelphia Eagles, and Lloyd Voss, who was the No. 1 pick of the Packers.

Bob Devaney's first starting quarterback, Dennis Claridge, was also headed to Green Bay after leading Nebraska to its first two bowl wins in school history.

Prior to Devaney, who replaced Bill Jennings, the Cornhuskers were one of the worst teams in the nation, with just three winning seasons since 1940.

How bad was it in Lincoln?

Devaney inherited a program that had gone 15-34 over the previous five years. But he didn't waste any time in changing the culture of Nebraska football.

He was such a likable guy, too. When you were being recruited, Devaney made you feel wanted. And it follows that if the head coach feels like you can play for him, then you feel like you can play to his level of expectation.

Since I had already gone up against some of the Pennsylvania guys on the Nebraska roster — and had done well against them in high school — I thought I could come in and play. I thought I'd fit in. That's why I couldn't wait to fly to Lincoln and get started on my college football career. I was ready to take on the world. Or so I thought.

Once I got on campus as a freshman and saw what I was getting myself into — it was like a scene out of *Animal House* — it didn't take long for me to start thinking, "What the hell am I doing all the way out here?"

That was my first day.

I flew out to Nebraska with Dennis Richnafsky, a wide receiver from Clairton, Pennsylvania. He was kind of like me. Slow. He couldn't out-run anybody. But he knew how to get open, and he didn't drop any passes. He knew how to play the game.

We got picked up at the airport by Cletus Fischer, one of the assistants on Devaney's staff, and dropped off at the dorm. All the frosh stayed on the same floor. My first-semester roommate was Al Fierro, a quarterback out of Texas. (Freshmen, by the way, had no status back then, 1964, since they were still ineligible to compete.)

After putting our stuff in the rooms — I had all my belongings in a foot locker that I had bought from an Army surplus store back home — we went to the cafeteria, where the team was eating lunch. The varsity guys had already begun practicing; they were in the middle of two-a-days.

Nebraska had big numbers in those days. So there were well over 100 varsity players chowing down. And they all looked the part of veterans, upperclassmen who had been around the block more than once and had experienced a lot of different things during their lifetimes.

It was pretty intimidating. The varsity players were all dressed in tank tops, shorts, and flip flops. Richnafsky and I walked into the room together in suits; shirts and ties.

The inmates noticed right away. They all started hooting and hollering and cat-calling us. It felt like we were walking into a prison cell block and trespassing on their turf.

That was scary. I was 17 years old, young for my class. (Heck, I barely shaved once a week when I was a senior.) And all of a sudden, I'm looking around at these guys, and they're men. A couple of them had even been married and divorced.

The transfers showed up with the freshmen. Some of them had been to Big Ten schools, like Wisconsin, and flunked out. Some had been to junior colleges. Most of them were 21. It was a whole different world.

Richnafsky and me? We couldn't have looked more out of place in that cafeteria. I know I felt like a little kid going through a fraternity hazing.

But the one thing I discovered is that it all balanced out once you put on the pads. It didn't matter how old or mature you were, or even how big you were.

It always came down to the same thing in football: whether you were willing to hit. That's the case at any level of competition. There are only so many guys who will stick their face in somebody's sternum and really cause a collision.

As a high school coach, I used to sit down individually with my players who were going on to college and visit with them about what I felt it took to succeed.

"Don't worry about anything else," I told them. "If you're physical — if you're willing to hit — they'll find a place for you."

***

They issued me jersey No. 33, but I wasn't happy with the number. In high school I was No. 38, and I just felt like No. 33 was a running back's number, not a linebacker's number. In my mind, I was suited to play one position, linebacker. That was my mentality.

But you didn't complain about such things in those days. As a first-year player, you weren't in a position to demand anything, particularly at a school like Nebraska.

Our freshman team was made up of 75 players who came from all over the country. I went back and counted, and I think 12 may have completed their career in Lincoln. That's 12 out of 75, and I'm not talking about starting or anything else. That was the number that made it to the finish line.

We were all on one-year scholarships unless we got something else in writing from Devaney. That was the leverage he held over his players. And it was like a death march; only the strong survived because Devaney would weed them out.

Whenever you stepped on the field in the spring, the stakes were really high because you were fighting for survival — fighting to be in the two-deep or close to it.

There were so many guys practicing that Devaney used to scrimmage in shifts. The first three teams would practice in the morning, and the fourth and fifth teams in the afternoon. The competition was a great motivator.

At the end of the spring, Devaney would meet with each player, and he'd tell the ones who weren't coming back, "We really enjoyed you here. We appreciated your effort. Now, where would you like to go next year?"

Guys would transfer to Drake or North Dakota State or North Dakota or Northern Michigan. They'd go anywhere for a chance to prove themselves.

Wayne Meylan was in my freshman class, and he became one of my best friends. Meylan was a nose guard, but he could run faster than most of the tailbacks and he was over 240 pounds. He was stronger than anyone I had ever seen. Farmer strong. Didn't lift a weight.

Physically, we had some really good players in our class, players who had raw strength and speed, like Meylan, Jerry Patton, and Ben Gregory. I didn't measure up to a lot of them, but when we got on the field, I felt like I belonged.

Like many of the power schools in that era, Nebraska had unlimited scholarships and a surplus of athletes. These were largely five-year programs; very seldom did you see a true sophomore playing. I was one of the few who didn't redshirt, along with Richnafsky and Gregory. And we all just happened to be from Pennsylvania.

I completed my senior year, played in two all-star games, and I was still 20. I grew up in a hurry. That was the byproduct of playing in a system like Devaney's and at a school like Nebraska. It made you think about a lot of things, too.

***

I took an inventory during the first semester of my freshman year. I did a little soul-searching and self-reflection, and asked myself, "What do you want to do with your life?"

Coming out of high school, I had heard all the stereotyping of dumb jocks. That was the perception most people had of athletes, but I thought, "I'm not going to be that way."

So I signed up for a bunch of business courses. There was only one problem. I had no background in business. None. I hadn't taken anything like that in high school, and I was really struggling — spinning my wheels — and thinking, "This is not what I want to do."

What I wanted to do was coach.

That's all I thought about.

Some people are good at working with numbers and equations. Some love writing and philosophizing. Some love politics and debating. It comes easy for them.

Me? I loved football, and I wanted to coach. Off the top of my head, I could make up a practice schedule or a game plan. Those types of things came easy.

That's when it first dawned on me that I really wanted to be doing what the guys around me were doing for a living. That included Devaney and some of his assistants, like George Kelly and Monte Kiffin. Football was important to them, and me.

I listened and absorbed. I watched how each coach dealt with his players. And I patterned myself after the ones I responded to the best.

Kelly coached at Marquette before coming to Nebraska, and he was a holdover from Jennings' staff. Devaney didn't have a defensive coordinator, per se. But Kelly handled the front and the linebackers.

In '63, the Huskers led the nation in total defense. Kelly went on to coach at his alma mater, Notre Dame, for Ara Parseghian, Dan Devine, and Gerry Faust.

I just liked the way Monte Kiffin coached. Still do. He has been the defensive coordinator of the Tampa Bay Bucaneers since the mid-'90s. Monte was gung-ho. He was a great motivator who was consumed by football. The minute you set foot on campus, he sold you on the pride of being a Cornhusker. He was from the state and a Nebraska alum.

Nebraska was the perfect place for me. By the end of my first year, I realized I was much better off at Nebraska than any of my other options, including Miami. The football program was like a melting pot, and you learned how to get along with different people, much like where I grew up in western Pennsylvania.

Football was your family unit in Lincoln. And I developed some close friendships right away, like with "Gordo" — Rick Coleman, a linebacker from Pittsburgh, who was two classes ahead of me. He was my recruiting host, and he's still one of my best friends.

When I was a sophomore, Gordo cut me a deal on a car, a 1952 Buick. I paid 50 bucks.

The same weekend I bought the car, I made a road trip to Scottsbluff, which is on the other side of the state from Lincoln. I was traveling with a teammate, Mick Ziegler, Ziggy. We stopped for gas along the way and after the service station attendant checked for oil, he forgot to put the pressure cap back on. Halfway to Scottsbluff, the engine basically melted down, and we coasted off the interstate.

That was my first introduction to Lexington, Nebraska (which just happened to be Kiffin's hometown). Someone finally came along, saw us in distress, and stopped. His name was Norman Reynolds. He was about 6-foot-4 with silvery, white hair, a Lexington rancher who loved athletics.

Making conversation, he asked if Ziggy and I were students and if we were going to the Orange Bowl to watch the Cornhuskers play Alabama. When we told him we were players — Devaney's players — he was impressed enough to loan us his car for the weekend. He turned over the keys to us. Just like that.

That's how revered Nebraska football players were in the state. And that tied in with the hero-worship we received on campus.

I know that's how Cindy got a good grade in an anatomy class. She wasn't crazy about the subject, but the teacher was a big Cornhusker football fan, and since she was dating a player, she got an A in the course.

To be honest, I was never a serious student. Cindy likes to tease that I had a 3.5 grade-point average my freshman year — but it was on a 9-point scale. Early on, my goal was to stay eligible for football. That changed when I got older and closer to graduation, and I got more serious about what I was doing in the classroom.

From the very beginning, though, I studied Devaney, and I really listened to what he had to say. I respected and admired him. And I think I did pay more attention to him than some of my teammates, who may not have realized at the time how advanced Devaney was in his thinking about football.

In the mid-60s, Devaney and Alabama's Bear Bryant ran the bowl system. You can talk all you want about the Bowl Championship Series and what we have now, but in that era, it was Devaney and Bear who set all the key matchups. They were the power brokers in college football.

In a lot of respects, Devaney was ahead of his time. What stands out probably more than anything else was his practice organization and the way he dealt with people, particularly his players. He was also very consistent with his staff. He tried to take care of his assistants, and some of them were making $12,000, which was a lot of money back then — more than some head coaches were making.

At the time, for a young person like me, someone who wanted to be a head coach, Devaney was the guy I tried to emulate starting with the way he practiced.

He was unique.

If you go back and study coaches from that generation — Frank Kush or the Bear and his protégé, Kentucky's Charlie Bradshaw — you recognize the common denominator was their aggressiveness. That was especially true in the South.

It was not uncommon for coaches to obsess over breakdowns that may have cost their teams a chance at victory. Like missing an extra-point. They might spend an hour and a half during their Monday practice beating up their players on that one facet of the game. It was more about the punishment and coaches taking out their frustrations. And there was never any rhyme or reason for what they were doing.

Devaney, by contrast, was a revelation. He never scrimmaged during the season. Never. *Sports Illustrated* did a big story on him because he was such an exception. Everybody else was beating the heck out of their players, and Devaney never hit them. He always said, "We're not playing against each other. We're going to get ready for the next team we play. I don't have to play against the guys on my own team."

Everybody stole from Devaney, including me.

Devaney believed in the Gestalt theory, the whole being greater than the sum of its parts. That was the basis for Devaney's practice structure and the learning process at Nebraska: whole, part, whole. You'd progress incrementally from individual periods to group work to team work. Devaney taught the big picture, piece by piece.

Good team morale was an important piece. "You have to be serious and work hard," he used to say. "But you have to enjoy what you're doing and also have some fun. You can have the best players in the world — and lose — if they won't play for you."

***

In 1993, when I was coaching at Wisconsin, I arranged for Devaney to be the featured speaker at the Wisconsin High School Coaches Association Hall of Fame dinner. While he was in Madison, he came out and watched practice at Camp Randall Stadium.

Or, at least, he made a brief appearance.

I remember him coming up to me shortly after we had started practice and saying, "Barry, you don't mind if I leave before it's over and go back to my hotel room?"

I didn't mind because I knew what was coming next.

"I didn't like practice when I coached," Devaney reminded me that day, "and I like it a lot less now as a spectator."

Devaney was single-minded and very quick-witted. They still tell the story around Lincoln about how Devaney was so upset by the way his team had played during the first half of a game that he purposely stayed out of the locker room until just before the players were getting ready to return to the field. And then he popped his head in the door and said, "Sorry, ladies, I was just looking for my team."

The Huskers dominated the second half.

Devaney did what all good head coaches did: he sold his program and what he believed in. I can't say that he was a great motivator. At times, he would get you cranked up. But he had built such a pride in Nebraska football, and what it stood for, that each player felt like he had a responsibility to play well.

In that system, there were so many good players. If you weren't competing, if you weren't producing, you weren't going to be playing. That was motivation in itself.

It wasn't unusual for Nebraska to have preseason All-Americans or all-conference players listed on the second team of the depth chart. If you wanted to play, you stayed motivated because if you slacked off, somebody would pass you up.

Devaney was kind of a walk-around coach at practice, leaning more toward offense than defense. And he was not necessarily known for his X's and O's.

But he showed his flexibility and willingness to change after back-to-back 6-4 seasons in '67 and '68. What he was doing offensively was somewhat antiquated, and he had to change because people were catching up to him.

Devaney even brought in Hayden Fry, who was then at SMU, because he wanted to learn more about spreading the field and throwing the football.

One of Devaney's assistants, Tom Osborne, had the most influence on the offensive changes and transition, from the unbalanced, full-house T-formation to the I-formation. Tom was the wide receivers coach when I was there. He was very bright and innovative, and with the installation of the one-back sets and pro sets, he pushed Devaney into the future.

Osborne was well-respected for being a straight-shooter. He also was very religious and very quiet. He became Devaney's hand-picked successor at Nebraska, even though they had completely opposite personalities.

If I'm not mistaken, there were three other assistants on the staff who thought they were going to be the hand-picked successor. They had each been with Devaney at Wyoming, and they were initially very upset. One of them, Carl Selmer, got the Miami job.

***

Devaney was one of a kind.

People like to make fun of Lou Holtz and his reputation for being the consummate sandbagger, someone who builds up the opponent with the idea of making them overconfident, while talking down his team in hopes of gaining a psychological edge. Lou always took on the role of the huge underdog, regardless of the competition.

Holtz was good, but Devaney was the master of that strategy. He used to warn us, "Don't ever believe anything I say in the newspapers."

Sure enough, if you read what Devaney was saying on game week, you would have sworn that we were playing the greatest team in the history of the world and we had little chance of winning. That's what he told the press. That's not what he told us.

Devaney did a good job of explaining how he wanted his players to deal with the media. Never criticize your opponent, never give them any bulletin board material. Always praise your teammates and team. Those were some of the things that he stressed out of habit.

And nobody really crossed the line. We had some great athletes, but they weren't brash, not T.O. brash. We didn't have any T.O.'s — Terrell Owens. The players knew the Devaney plan, and they didn't bring undue attention to themselves or the team.

I thought Devaney did it the right way, and I modeled my approach after his. He absolutely impacted the way I dealt with the media when I became a head coach.

As a player, I got interviewed — not a lot, but enough. I can't say I was a good quote, but I never got burned. I was going to stay within the prescribed boundaries and not say anything outlandish. I always used the company line. That's what I demanded of my teams, too.

There's the misconception in sports that you're supposed to treat everybody the same, equal. Sometimes people don't want to admit it, but that's not the real world.

Jimmy Johnson made that point in his autobiography. He used to tell his players that everyone is going to be treated differently, and how you're treated will be determined in large part by how good of a player you are and your value to the team.

Devaney believed in the same things. For example, Devaney could be a disciplinarian, but that usually depended on the player he was disciplining.

The fact is he treated his better players differently than the others. And you learned that in a hurry. If you were borderline or a bad player, you had better not mess up.

People have asked me, "Who did you like the best? Who were some of your favorite players?"

My response is always the same: "I liked the best players the best."

With Devaney, it was clear-cut. Then again, he could basically do what he wanted to do. Nebraska football was that big and important, not only on campus — and in Lincoln — but also in the entire state. Football was never out of season.

People fussed over players and made us feel special. And the media was writing something about the team 365 days out of the year. There weren't many other places like Lincoln, Nebraska. A few, but not many. We were sold out every week. And we learned to appreciate that loyalty and support when we played on the road.

***

I still remember my first trip to Madison as a player. It was during my junior year, 1966. I didn't know much about the program. The Badgers were just another team to us, a Big Ten team. We were the defending Big Eight champions, and I don't think anybody thought Wisconsin was special — at least not compared to the opponents that we were accustomed to playing on our schedule. (Devaney never lost to a Big Ten team while he was at Nebraska.)

That Friday afternoon, we had a team walk-through at Camp Randall Stadium, and I remember looking out of the old dressing room windows at all the grass practice fields surrounding the stadium — areas which are now the site of the McClain Indoor Facility and the parking ramp behind the north end zone.

My Uncle John and one of his friends came to visit me that weekend. As a team, we were staying at The Edgewater Hotel, and Uncle John had never seen anything as beautiful as the view from my room overlooking Lake Mendota.

He was right. The view was absolutely gorgeous.

I roomed with Meylan, who was out of Bay City, Michigan, and he got paranoid over all the Langdon Street partying that Friday night. He thought they were making noise to keep him awake. To his way of thinking, rowdy behavior had nothing to do with a typical party night along Madison's frat row, but instead was all about keeping Cornhusker Wayne Meylan from getting his sleep.

That's how he motivated himself, and he got all stirred up for the Badgers and went out the next day and blocked a punt that we recovered in the end zone for a touchdown. It wasn't much of game at that point. We ended up winning 31-3. Offensively, we pounded them with our running backs, Harry Wilson and Ben Gregory, who just wore them down.

Our defense didn't give up a rushing first down. We stuffed the run with Meylan, Patton, Jim McCord, Carel Stith, Lynn Senkbeil, and Langston Coleman.

The Badgers lost the ball three times on fumbles, and their quarterbacks — John Ryan and John Boyajian — threw four interceptions.

I had one of the picks, which I returned 25 yards. I got caught from behind and brought down along the sidelines by an offensive lineman. Over the years, my runback has become a punch line at banquets. I wasn't tackled — rigor mortis set in.

And they ribbed me about the way the radio announcer handled the play-by-play of the interception: "Alvarez is at the 41, the 42, the 43...."

I ran about a 5.2 in the 40-yard dash — 5.2 seconds, not minutes.

As I mentioned earlier, Devaney really didn't treat Wisconsin any differently than other teams we faced. On Friday night, he went through the whole kicking game. It was the same talk he gave every Friday night.

Before we took the field on Saturday, he would read off the starting lineup. He might say a little something else but not much. It wasn't rah-rah. He prepared us all week to go out and win. That was his approach, and it worked.

Devaney never came out and said that he wanted me to be a leader. But I do remember coaches telling me that they expected me to lead the team or the defense.

What does leadership involve? I always believed it to mean there was more expected of you than just playing on the field. As a more mature player, you have to lead by example — making sure that things are done the right way. You have that responsibility to the team.

Leadership is a very difficult thing to define. A leader can be someone who gets others to do things that they normally don't want to do. And he can get them to do those things for a specific cause — like winning a game.

That's not always easy to do — to get everybody on the same page — because some people are very self-centered. I don't know that you learn how to become a leader as much as you either know how to lead or you don't. I think leaders are born.

When you go to a playground and watch youngsters playing, there always seems to be one kid who everybody else is following.

I know that I wouldn't have been as good of a coach if I hadn't played college football at Nebraska and learned from a leader like Devaney, who taught a winning system.

I played with some very good captains, like Mike Kennedy and Frank Solich. But I didn't dwell on what made them good leaders because I was just trying to survive. I was trying to figure out a way to get on the field and play. Every year was like that.

***

Before the start of my senior year, I got engaged to Cindy.

We had met a couple of summers earlier. Cindy grew up in Omaha, but when she was 10, the family moved to Lincoln. Her dad was an adjutant general in the Nebraska National Guard and trained officers.

After Cindy got out of high school, he went to work at the Pentagon in Washington, D.C. (And that's where we got married, in a chapel overlooking John F. Kennedy's gravesite at Arlington National Cemetery. Cindy hasn't let me forget that we spent our honeymoon at a Pirates game. She says she should have known what she was getting herself into and bolted right then.)

Cindy started her schooling at Mundelein College in Chicago. But since they didn't offer a journalism major, she transferred after her freshman year to Nebraska.

The summer after my sophomore year, she and a friend showed up unannounced at a house I was renting with some teammates. They had heard there was a football party.

There wasn't.

I had just gotten home but invited them in anyway and made them something to eat. I got Cindy's number and called her for a date. She accepted, but when I showed up at her apartment — she was living with some other girls — she got cold feet and hid in the closet.

She felt bad about how that turned out, so she called to apologize and we started dating. Cindy was always a very serious student, and she helped settle me down.

Cindy still talks about the pressure that came with dating a Nebraska football player and all the time she spent thinking about what she was going to wear to the games. Most of the players' girlfriends wore red Cowboy hats. Hers had a No. 33 on the back.

***

I had a very good senior year, despite tearing my Achilles tendon. I never got back to playing at full speed, and I wasn't very fast to start with. But I compensated in other ways.

I felt that as a unit we had one of the better defenses in the country, and I had a record number of assisted tackles, a record I held for years.

I had a couple of good performances in postseason all-star games and thought I would be drafted into the NFL. But when I wasn't, I made up my mind to get started on a career as a coach. A lot of NFL teams wanted to sign me as a free agent, but I really wasn't that interested. Devaney changed my thinking.

The Minnesota Vikings had contacted him.

"They would like you to go up there," Devaney said.

"I don't want to do it," I insisted.

"Go ahead, give it a shot," he encouraged me. "If it doesn't work out, I'll hold open a spot on my staff and you can come back and be a grad assistant."

I agreed to give it a chance, and I might have had a fair shot of making the Vikings, but I had the wrong attitude. I was miserable.

I admitted to Minnesota coach Bud Grant, "I'm here for all the wrong reasons. I know what I want to do. I want to go out and coach."

Grant said simply, "That's what you need to do."

I called Cindy with the news, and she hung up on me.

She was heartbroken.

She thought we were going to have money and glamour and all of those things that go along with being the wife of an NFL player.

Instead, she was marrying a coach.

CHAPTER THREE
Making a Name in Mason City

At the end of my senior year, I got the news from Pennsylvania. It came out of the blue, and I was crushed. I was really devastated.

My parents were getting divorced.

When my dad called and told me, I was floored because I wasn't expecting it. And it was even tougher to deal with because I was in Lincoln and so far away from home. I felt so helpless to do anything about it.

I really struggled. It took a long time for me to reconcile with their divorce. I was disappointed. Maybe even more than feeling disappointed, I felt a little betrayed.

I didn't talk to my mother for three years.

And I didn't know whose fault it was.

Cindy asked me, "Why did you choose your dad over your mom?"

She knew how close I was to my mother. I called her every Sunday when I was in college. Subconsciously, I may have looked at which one was the weakest — my mom or dad — and tried to determine which one needed me the most. That was my dad.

When I thought about it, they were total opposites.

My mother loved to be active and do things. The grass never grew under her feet, while my dad just wanted to come home from work and sit. They didn't have much in common.

I found out later that it was my mother's initiative to get the divorce. She wasn't happy, and they had just grown apart. What did I know? I was always living in the present, and, selfishly, I was not thinking about who was happy or unhappy.

As hard as it was on me, it was even harder on my brother. Woody was still in Langeloth, in junior high, and he had to live with it on a daily basis. I didn't.

It was Cindy who got me and my mother back on speaking terms. Cindy wanted to make sure our children knew their grandmother, so she stayed in contact with her until we gradually worked things out.

I owe Cindy for that one.

***

When I got back from the Viking training camp, I began coaching as Kiffin's graduate assistant on the Nebraska freshman team. Jim Walden, who had been a high school coach, was also a grad assistant. He went on to be a head coach at Washington State and Iowa State.

I was in charge of the linebackers, and it was great training.

Cindy still had a year of undergrad left, and I needed six hours that first semester to get my degree. To make ends meet, I took a job with the Lincoln police department.

They had a deal where if you were going to college, they would pay for your tuition, and that's how I wound up getting my master's and paying for Cindy to finish school.

I worked as a beat cop, a cruiser officer, and a detective.

When I was walking the downtown beat, I worked from 10 at night until 7 in the morning. I had Mondays and Tuesdays off but worked weekends.

On a typical school day, I would attend class in the morning and coach football in the afternoon. Right after practice, I would go home, grab something to eat, and head out to walk the beat. When you're young, you have a lot of energy.

I liked police work. But I didn't like guns.

I never pulled my gun. I hated guns. I didn't want them around the house. After my shift, I always used to wrap my gun and holster and leave them in my police locker.

But the department adopted a rule that made it mandatory to carry your gun — to and from work. I started taking my gun home, but I would unload it first.

One night before sending us out on the street, they had an inspection and checked our guns. I held mine up, the captain opened the cylinder, and saw there were no bullets. They were still in my locker. I had forgotten to load the gun.

Even Barney Fife carried a bullet in his front pocket. Me? I'm going to walk the street with an unloaded gun. That cost me. I had to work two days without pay.

While I was on the force, I was involved in the longest high-speed car chase in Lincoln. I was riding shotgun in a cruiser car when we jumped in behind a guy who was going as fast as 110 miles per hour. For a while we were one car length away from him at that speed.

Along with the county police, we chased him for about 45 minutes. He ran through two road blocks before they finally shot out his tires to stop him. That's about as close as I got to the "real action."

Just before I got my first full-time coaching job — as an assistant at Lincoln Northeast High School — I was pulling a double-shift as a detective when there was a situation.

We received a report of some rioting and gun shots in one section of town. When I saw the bullets flying — ricocheting off the pavement — that was enough for me.

Not that I didn't enjoy what I was doing. I had even applied for the FBI. I went through the physical, sat through an interview, and took the written test.

At the time, I was still teaching and coaching at Northeast. I taught driver's education, and I was an assistant wrestling coach in addition to football. I was lucky to get work in Lincoln.

Life was good.

If you're in a teacher's college at the University of Nebraska — the Harvard of the Midwest — you want to stay in Lincoln and teach. And about five graduates every year would be hired for that opportunity.

I was making $7,500 a year. Cindy had a part-time job and taught half-days; we had a brand new house and a new baby daughter and we thought we had it made. It doesn't get much better than this in Nebraska. Except for one thing.

We didn't have any money.

Every Tuesday, we ate liver and onions because liver was 29 cents. It took us a full year to save $600 bucks for the closing on our house, and then we still came up short and had to dip into the $1,000 my dad gave us for a refrigerator.

Everything we bought was used. I remember Cindy wanted a new dishwasher, and I told her she could have it if she could catch three passes in the backyard.

I lobbed the first two and really drilled the third one. But she caught all three, and she got her dishwasher.

I found ways to make extra cash, including officiating basketball games. One summer, Cindy even worked at the Daily Double window at the local horse track.

When you don't have any money, you have to make your own entertainment. And that's what we did in our neighborhood, going from house to house. We were involved with a gourmet cooking group and a couple's bridge club. We stayed active.

But nothing sidetracked me from my passion: coaching.

I was fortunate to be working for someone like Bob Els, a former assistant who had been elevated to the head coaching job at Northeast. He gave me a lot of leeway and let me coach. I was the only assistant working directly with Els and the varsity.

Frank Solich was the head coach at our rival, Lincoln Southeast. Solich was a close friend and former teammate. He was a member of Devaney's first recruiting class, an All-Big Eight fullback, and a co-captain of our 1965 team.

As I look back, critiquing myself as a high school assistant, I drilled way too much and I didn't teach near enough. I always got along with the kids, and I had a good feel for the game. But I don't think I was as good of a teacher as I needed to be.

I got better as an assistant coach. And I think Els got better as a head coach. By figuring out what we had to do to win, we got better as a team. (Bob Els has since been inducted into the Northeast High School Hall of Fame.)

We ended up winning the state championship my third year at Northeast, and we had a pretty nice team my fourth year there, too, when I got another job offer.

Make that offers, plural.

I had to make a choice. Between coaching and the FBI.

I had been on a waiting list with the FBI when I got a call telling me that I had been accepted. I really thought that I would like that type of work. But I had one concern. With my Spanish background, I figured I would end up in New York City or Miami or Los Angeles. And I didn't want to live in any of those places.

One of my Nebraska teammates, Ron Kirkland, had gone that route and made a career of the FBI. We had worked on the Lincoln police force together. And maybe I would have followed that path, too, if I didn't feel like I would have a chance to be a head coach someday.

I knew I didn't want to be an assistant high school coach forever. After four years, in my mind, there was no question I was ready to be a head coach. I even had some options. I interviewed for two jobs on the same weekend.

One was in Kearney, a college town of about 30,000. There's a University of Nebraska campus in Kearney. I thought they would probably offer me the high school job.

I also interviewed in Lexington, a much smaller town of about 6,000 on the Platte River in southern Nebraska.

Lexington?

The coincidence didn't escape me. That's where my '52 Buick had broken down on the way to Scottsbluff, and I first met Norm Reynolds.

Lexington smells like burning grass all the time because of the hay mills. Cindy and both of our girls, Dawn and Stacy, had allergies. And since Cindy had lived in bigger cities, I knew what her choice would be.

As we were driving back to Lincoln, I turned to Cindy and said, "If they offer, I'm going to take the Lexington job."

She cried all the way home.

She didn't know if she could live in such a small town.

"It's temporary, this is going to be a stepping stone," I tried to assure her. "It's a good football program, and we're going there to win some games, and then we're going to move onward and upward."

I don't know if she bought it.

But she never questioned it after that.

And it turned out to be one of the best moves we ever made. In Lincoln we still had all our college friends, so we were always socializing with the same group of people, the same clique, and we were in our own little comfort zone. We really didn't grow.

That's why Lexington was such a refreshing and much-needed change of pace for our lifestyle and an important step in my professional career.

Monte Kiffin helped get me the head job. His brother-in-law, Jim Murphy, was a successful businessman in the town, and he and his wife, Ann, were like surrogate parents to Cindy and me. They took us under their wing, introduced us to people we needed to know, and got us involved in the community.

In the process, we developed our own identity — an identity separate from that of being college students in Lincoln. We really did grow as a couple.

We developed a lot of confidence in what we were doing and broadened our horizons. We're pretty fast learners and adjusted to the situation, and we made our own social life. Cindy started a gymnastics school, and we were both happy in Lexington.

Especially me.

I liked being the boss.

I liked making decisions.

I liked running my own football program.

Lexington had a heckuva sports reputation. Kiffin was one of their more famous alums, along with Mick Tinglehoff, a pro bowl offensive center for many years with the Minnesota Vikings.

Lexington was a small town, but the school competed at a high level, the second-largest class in the state. They had a 25-game winning streak in football. They hadn't lost in two years and had been awarded the mythical state title in 1972 before the advent of play-offs.

They were also the state champs in wrestling and the runners-up in basketball and track. Athletics were very important.

That spring, I drove up to Grand Island, where the Lexington track team was participating in a district meet. I was looking around the stands and spotted Norm Reynolds. We kind of rekindled our friendship and reminisced about our first roadside meeting.

One of the reasons I took the Lexington job was because I knew we could win right away. With all the success they already had, there was a strong commitment to football and that appealed to me. They had a system in place. I just had to teach them a new system, my system, and get them to buy into what I was selling.

***

I thought I had all the answers.

Until I lost my first game at Lexington. That snapped the long winning streak. And I thought my head coaching career might end in a hurry. I got humbled.

We made a good recovery that season — behind a sophomore quarterback, Doug Holtmeier — and finished with an 8-2 record. That included beating the No. 1 team in the state. The following year, we had another good team in Lexington, and we were 8-2 again.

During those two seasons, I stayed in close touch with Solich, who was still at Lincoln Southeast. We talked football non-stop.

Since Frank had been a fullback, he liked talking to me about defense, and since I had been a linebacker, I liked talking to Frank about offense. We covered other things during our conversations, like how to practice and how to deal with parents.

We'd regularly go to football clinics together all the time.

I'd go at the drop of a hat. I wasn't making a whole lot of money, but I never hesitated when I was presented with an opportunity to learn more about football from somebody else. Cindy was supportive, and she'd just tell me, "Go."

If I heard that a George Kelly or a Monte Kiffin was speaking at a clinic in Minneapolis, I'd jump in the car and go.

I tell young coaches all the time, "If you want to move up the ladder, you need to expose yourself to other people's thinking and learn as much as you can. Listen and be inquisitive. Be a sponge for knowledge."

I firmly believe in seeking out the best coaches and asking questions. If you can learn one thing, one teaching tool, one drill, one different way of doing things, you're ahead of the game. You just need to take that information and fit it to your own philosophy and what you believe in.

One spring, Solich and I got money from our administrations and went on a tour of college campuses. We stopped at North Texas State, Oklahoma, and Kansas. We left on a Wednesday and went the whole weekend. I took one of my assistants with us, and all we did was talk X's and O's.

Hayden Fry was the coach at North Texas.

He didn't have much for facilities and he didn't have the best players, but he was beating good teams. Solich and I both had good quarterbacks returning, and we wanted to spend some time with Hayden because his teams threw the ball so well.

Hayden was very creative in what he did, and he would take advantage of what people were doing defensively against him. That's the one thing I studied.

North Texas had nothing going for it — compared to a Nebraska. And that's why I was so impressed with Hayden and the way he ran things. He had everybody convinced that North Texas was a big-time program. That's just Hayden.

***

While I was in Lexington, if Devaney was in the area, I'd go see him and he was always cordial. But we didn't stay close, and we didn't talk that much.

That's because I was so involved with my job. I was obsessed with what I was doing and that carried over to the off-season when I coached wrestling. I was always looking for different ways to motivate and condition my guys.

As a football coach, I wasn't worried about taking the next step. I was just trying to win as many games as I could. My goals hadn't changed.

I wanted to be a college head coach. My goal was to take a down program like Devaney had when he took over at Nebraska, and I wanted to build it up and sustain it.

Cindy knew what I wanted to do, and we worked as a team.

No matter where we were, she would jump in with both feet. Bob Els' wife, Jeri, at Northeast was that way. She was good at involving the staff, fostering a close-knit group, and doing things socially.

Cindy was like another assistant on my staff. When she wasn't working with the cheerleaders, she was having the players over to the house for meals or she was having bake sales to earn enough money to send coaches to clinics.

She always got involved, and she was always in the middle of things — knowing how committed I was to the profession and moving ahead.

I thought I'd win the state championship my third year at Lexington. I had all of my key players coming back, like Holtmeier, wide receiver Ed Stuckey and fullback Ron Newton. I knew that nobody was going to be better, nobody was going to beat us.

That April, I got a telephone call out of the clear blue from Roger Clough, the superintendent of schools in Mason City, Iowa.

"Barry, I'm originally from Nebraska, and I've been following your career," he said. "I've been the super here for a year, and we've changed football coaches. Since the season was over, we've been conducting a search and we can't find anybody we really like. Would you be interested in coming here for an interview?"

My response was, "No, not really."

I figured I'd have another winning season in Lexington, and I'd be able to take one of the bigger high school jobs in Nebraska, preferably in Lincoln.

Clough didn't take no for an answer.

"Talk to your wife," he said, "and we'll fly both of you up here for a weekend so you can take a look at the place."

If we had anything going, anything on our schedule that weekend, we wouldn't have gone, we wouldn't have taken him up on the invitation.

But since we had nothing planned, Cindy said, "Let's go."

We got a baby-sitter and took off for Mason City.

It's a nice town of about 35,000 with one public high school. During our tour, they told us Mason City was the hub for northern Iowa and the birthplace of Meredith Willson.

That night, Cindy said, "I'm glad you didn't say anything when they brought up the name of Meredith Willson because I know that you have no idea who Meredith Willson is."

"Sure I do," I said.

"Well, who is he?"

"Meredith Willson," I said, "is on Monday Night Football with Howard Cosell and Frank Gifford."

Cindy still doesn't know I was pulling her leg.

After our visit to "River City" — we saw the bridge in Mason City that was the backdrop for Willson's Broadway play *The Music Man* — Clough called again and wanted me to come back for a second interview.

I was set to go when I got another call from somebody in personnel at the high school. "Do you know who your competition is for the job?" he asked.

"No, I don't," I said. "And, quite honestly, it doesn't make any difference. Why are you asking?"

"Well, we've got some of the top coaches in the Chicago area who have applied, including one candidate from New Trier High School."

"Did you already hire somebody, is that why you're calling me?" I asked him. "Because if you've hired somebody else, that's fine with me."

"No," he replied, "but I just want you to know your competition."

Without hesitating, I said, "Listen, the best guy for that job will show up tomorrow. I'll see you at 2 p.m."

That's how confident I was.

John Melton, my old freshman linebacker coach at Nebraska, was the difference-maker and really swung my thinking on the job.

I called John for advice on what I should do. I knew he recruited the Mason City area, and I wondered if he had any suggestions for me.

"Everybody in the state of Nebraska knows who Barry Alvarez is," Melton said. "You've already made a name for yourself. So why don't you go out and make a name for yourself in the state of Iowa?"

He kind of challenged me.

And when they offered me the job, I accepted.

***

To make the move from Lexington, I rented a U-Haul and borrowed a hay truck. We got everybody's attention when we drove into our new neighborhood in Mason City since the hay truck had a wooden balance beam hanging out of the end with an American flag attached. We made quite an entrance, and those neighbors laughed for years.

The facilities were good in Mason City, but the program was no laughing matter. It was in bad, bad shape. They hadn't won in a long time, and nobody was interested in football.

When Cindy was asked after I took the University of Wisconsin job if it was hard coming to Madison in 1990, she pointed out that we had already been through something like this before — in Mason City.

When we got there, we didn't know a soul so we just started grinding. Basketball was the No. 1 sport in a high school of over 1,800 students.

When I took over the football program, we had 30 kids on the varsity level. I was planning on calling our team "The Dirty Thirty."

Then I was down to 27 after losing three guys in a bar fight.

That first year was really a struggle. We just didn't have any players, but we managed to compete and play everybody tough. We finished 3-6.

Near the end of year, we were playing Cedar Falls at the University of Northern Iowa's domed stadium — the UNI-Dome. That was also the site for the annual state championship game.

We were down to 25 guys on the varsity, and I didn't want my kids to be embarrassed because we were outnumbered — with only a handful of players on the sidelines. So I promoted seven or eight sophomores to the varsity. Some of them had already shown the potential to develop into good players, like Scott Raridon and Mark McManigal.

We didn't win the game, but we played pretty well for being so out-manned. By the time we got back to Mason City — it was a two-hour bus ride — it was nearly midnight. I drove each of the sophomores home. McManigal was always inquisitive and asked, "Coach, why did you dress us tonight? Why did you take us to Cedar Falls?"

I was prepared for his questions and emphasized, "I wanted to get all the sophomores accustomed to playing in that dome because when you're seniors, we're going back there and winning the state championship. That's what we're building for."

I had worked out in my mind how I wanted to develop the program, and the following year, I got the numbers up to where they needed to be: 25 seniors, 50 juniors, and 75 sophomores. And I had all three junior highs running my system.

We built a program in a year.

By the second year, we were pretty good. At the time, only four teams made the state playoffs, otherwise we would have been in. We were 7-2, and I'm not so sure that we weren't the best team in the state that year.

For some reason, there were a lot of big kids in Mason City while all the schools in Waterloo had a lot of speed. I was looking for an edge, so I sold our kids on being bigger and stronger than everybody else in the league. "We're going to out-lift them," I said.

In order to do that, we needed a new weight room. And that meant raising money and literally taking a sledgehammer to the old room. I got together with Ed Lenius, my offensive line coach, and that's what we did on weekends. We didn't ask for permission. We just started knocking down walls and shoveling everything out of a window on to a truck.

We hustled all the products, too. A guy in the metal shop built the benches, and we got a place in town to donate the mirrors for the wall. By the time the fundraising project was over, we had $10,000 for the equipment, and our weight room was a show piece.

It was better than what they had at Iowa State in Ames and the University of Iowa in Iowa City. Nobody could match our out-of-season program, and we were the strongest team in the state within three years. We were also the best team.

Mason City hadn't won anything in two decades, and then in 1978, we won the Class 4-A state championship. We beat Dubuque Hempstead 15-13 in the title game. We won on fundamentals and toughness.

Nothing else mattered. It didn't make a difference what plays you were running as long as you were executing them well. But you had to have good fundamentals, and you had to be tough. That's how it had to be.

***

I was very demanding.

And I refused to compromise.

There were some parents who were upset with me because I didn't play their kids — older kids who looked the part. I didn't play them because they weren't tough enough. They weren't physical. It's pretty simple.

The parents didn't understand. They wanted their kids playing. But I had to be true to the program and true to myself and what I believed in. I just knew if we stuck to the plan, we'd be pretty good, and we were.

When you're a high school teacher, you learn how to carry over the teaching to the football field. There's a direct knowledge of dealing with the people in the community and the school and tying them together, getting them involved.

That's the way I was. I just didn't coach those kids. I tried to get everyone involved at every level because I needed to sell myself and my program.

I started my own weekly radio show in Mason City. I had a kid on the team whose dad had a car dealership — Don Lafrenz Ford — and he sponsored it. He was later my car dealer at the University of Iowa.

When I arrived for my first show, I just assumed somebody would be there to serve as the studio host and interview me.

Not the case.

They just gave me the headsets and sat me down in front of the microphone. I had a half-hour to kill and absolutely no training in radio.

But I started talking about our players and the program, and I got a feel for what I was doing right away. I didn't get paid for doing the show — I wasn't smart enough back then to put a price on my air time — but it was a good training ground.

By that third year, I had plenty to talk about, too.

Seven players off that 11-1 state championship team earned college scholarships in Division I-A, I-AA and Division II programs.

McManigal went to Nebraska-Omaha. Dave Kilpack and Greg Lewis went to Drake. Mark Salz went to Northern Iowa. Raridon went to Nebraska (and later became my first strength and conditioning coach at Wisconsin) and John Judge went to Iowa.

Dan McCarney was one of Hayden's top recruiters in the state. He really worked hard and cultivated the high school coaches. I liked Dan.

Who didn't?

He'd come to Mason City and I'd invite him over for dinner. He wanted to get close to our program because we had a lot of good players.

That's how we got to know each other.

I didn't know if Mason City was going to be my springboard to a college job. I had seen where some other guys had made that jump from high school to college.

Had Earle Bruce stayed at Iowa State, I think he would have hired me. But following the '78 season, Earle left for Ohio State and Donnie Duncan took over in Ames. Duncan talked to me about possibly joining his staff when I got the Iowa offer.

Hayden had asked Dan, "Who's the best high school coach in the state of Iowa? Who should I talk to?" Dan recommended me.

When I interviewed with Hayden, he asked me about my background, what I believed in as a football coach, and what I could bring to the Hawkeyes' program.

For starters, I knew that I could coach and recruit. I told him I could help recruit in Pennsylvania, Ohio, Nebraska, and Iowa.

I wanted to get to a Division I school so bad, and to be lucky enough to start off in the Big Ten, well, I could care less that it was Iowa and not Nebraska.

I had no anxiety whatsoever about whether I could get the job done. I just felt it was time. I was ready to learn more about football in a situation where I didn't have to worry about teaching or coaching another sport, like wrestling. It was pure football.

Mason City had prepared me for the jump.

I knew if I had stayed, we would have kept winning championships.

You always remember your first and that first state title is still as big a win as I've ever had as a head coach, including the Rose Bowl wins at Wisconsin.

That '78 team was so special that I wanted to buy the players jerseys so they could keep them as keepsakes, memories of what they accomplished.

Somebody has to pay for it, though. And that's how I came up with the crazy idea of shaving my head. That was my threat — if we got to the state finals, I'd shave my head.

As it turned out, we won the game we needed to win, and Mason City got to the finals. And all the local TV stations sent crews to cover the big event.

They sat me down in a chair and shaved my head. And the cheerleaders collected the hair and auctioned it off during a fundraiser to get those jerseys.

I'm not sure Hayden Fry knew what he was getting with his new assistant coach. But he probably wasn't expecting the Spanish Telly Savalas.

CHAPTER FOUR

Hayden and the Hawkeyes

I always thought Bob Devaney was a much better coach than Woody Hayes. Obviously, I was biased on the subject, having played and coached for Devaney.

But I always asked myself, "How good of a coach would Hayes have been if he had coached at Nebraska? Would Devaney have ever lost if he had coached at Ohio State?"

The guys who worked for Woody respected Woody. I just didn't always agree with the way he went about his business or some of the things that he believed in.

I spoke with Woody once at a coaching clinic when I was still at Mason City. It was about a year or so before Woody was forced into retirement following the 1978 Gator Bowl incident where he took a swing at the Clemson nose guard.

Woody spoke for 45 minutes on the fullback power play. That's the only thing he talked about — how the Buckeyes executed that play. When he was done, he took questions.

Someone raised his hand and observed, "Coach, you've won a lot of games during your career at Ohio State. There has to be more behind it than just the fullback power."

You could tell Woody didn't like the tone. He was visibly upset.

"Bob Commings isn't winning at Iowa," the questioner continued. "We want to know why you're winning all those games at Ohio State. What's the secret?"

Woody paused before speaking and said calmly, "Well, I've got better players."

Nothing like cutting to the chase.

"But," Woody went on, "as a young coach you better understand that when we run this play — the fullback power — we're going to run it right. Over the last 45 minutes, I've tried to show you all the intricacies of running the play.

"And that's the point I'm trying to make. You don't just draw plays on a board. You have to be thorough and understand why they will work and why they won't."

***

Woody Hayes could be very persuasive, among other things, and one of his most famous lines was, "You win with people."

That entailed recruiting. And, from my standpoint, if you're going to be a good college football recruiter, you have to be able to communicate. People have to like you, too.

I liked recruiting. After being a high school coach in Nebraska and Iowa for nine years, I enjoyed getting on the road and trying to build relationships with different people.

One of the keys is to develop your instincts. As a young recruiter at Iowa, I went through a trial and error adjustment period. I found out what works and what doesn't.

I learned through the process. I made some good decisions and some bad ones. There were some kids I probably should have taken, but turned down. And vice versa.

If you're new to a recruiting area, where do you start? Who do you recruit? Who are the good players? Who do you have a chance of getting?

Well, the first thing you have to do is talk with the high school coaches and establish who you are going to try to sign. When I recruited in the state of Ohio for the Hawkeyes, I went to see Ron Stoops, Sr., the defensive coordinator at Cardinal Mooney High School in Youngstown, which is only about 20 miles west of the Pennsylvania border.

I'd have dinner at his house, shoot the breeze, and find out who could play and who I should be looking at. His brother, Bobby, was the head coach at Youngstown South, and he was also able to put me on the right guys. Sadly, though, Ron died from a heart attack in 1988 while coaching on the sidelines during a game. He was only 54.

Ron Stoops' sons — Bob, Mike, Mark, and Ron, Jr. — have all wound up in the coaching profession. Bob, Mike, and Mark played at Iowa. Bob is the head coach at Oklahoma, and Mike is the head coach at Arizona. Mark is Mike's defensive coordinator.

As I recall, during one of my early visits with Ronnie Stoops, he tipped me off to a quarterback prospect at Boardman, a suburban Youngstown school. He kept saying that even though the kid was skinny and he threw the ball kind of funny, he could play, and I needed to take a look at him.

I took his word and took a look. But after evaluating the quarterback, I didn't even take the film back to Iowa City. I just didn't think he was that good.

The quarterback?

Bernie Kosar.

You know the rest of the story. Kosar winds up at Miami, wins a national championship, and plays 12 seasons in the NFL.

Things like that happen. That's why recruiting is such an inexact science.

One year, I remember working hard on a high school quarterback — Ken Karcher — in Pittsburgh. I developed a good relationship with the family. I liked the kid, and I think the kid liked me. That was the signal that he was sending out.

Hayden Fry, Bill Snyder and I flew into Pittsburgh for our home visit with Karcher, but he was still undecided. He had set a visit and then canceled.

In the meantime, Bernie Wyatt, one of Iowa's top recruiters, was on a quarterback named Doug Strang in New Jersey. We all flew to Atlantic City, but there was no way this kid was going to come to our place. He was headed to Penn State.

So I picked up the phone and called Karcher, and he says, "Coach, I'm going to Notre Dame." Now we're out of that deal, too.

Hayden and Snyder still had one quarterback on the line, a kid out of Wheaton, Illinois, whose only offer was from Northern Illinois.

The quarterback?

Chuck Long.

Not a bad Plan B or Plan C, either.

Long threw for over 10,000 yards and led Iowa to a couple of Big Ten championships and Rose Bowls. As for the other prospects, Karcher transferred from Notre Dame and finished up at Tulane. Strang started at Penn State. But he was no Chuck Long.

***

The best advice I could give to a young college recruiter is that you have to build solid relationships with the high school coaches who can help you close deals. They have to trust you, and you have to trust them. And it goes without saying that you also have to get close to the recruits for the same reason, trust.

One of the keys in recruiting is finding the hot button. What is the most important thing to the kid? And who's the most influential person in his life?

Bill Snyder was the chief recruiter on Larry Station, who turned out to be a great linebacker at Iowa, and it was one of the great jobs in recruiting. All the other schools and recruiters were working the coaches and the high school principal and mom and dad in Omaha.

But the most influential people to Station were his girlfriend and a female high school counselor tucked away on the second floor of the building.

Snyder landed Station, who went on to start 42 straight games for the Hawkeyes. He led the defense in tackles in each of his four seasons and was a three-time All-American.

John Alt is another good example.

Alt was from Fridley, Minnesota — he played at Columbia Heights High School — and nobody thought he had any interest in leaving the state. His mother had passed away, and his dad was in a wheelchair. So it only made sense for him to stay close to home.

But Dan McCarney did a super job getting close to John, his sisters, and the grandparents. They loved Mac, who convinced John to sign with Iowa. And he turned out to be one of the best offensive tackles in school history.

Everybody is different. And your sales pitch has to change accordingly. You can scare off recruits by being too aggressive. Yet there are times when you need to be aggressive if you're not getting much feedback.

How do you learn to be a recruiter if you never recruited? I was lucky enough to have quality recruiters come to my door in high school. And I saw how different coaches, like Frank Kush and Bob Devaney, presented their arguments and sold themselves.

When I first got to Iowa, I spent some time with Bernie Wyatt, who had been retained on the coaching staff when Hayden Fry replaced Bob Commings. Bernie had already established himself in the Big Ten as a top-notch recruiter, and I wanted to learn from him.

Bernie was a New Yorker — a prep All-American out of Amityville — and a former high school head coach in Lindenhurst, New York. That background helped him get around New York and New Jersey. He knew the territory and didn't waste any motion or time getting between high schools. And he did a good job networking the coaches.

Bernie got close to them, and they trusted Bernie. They knew if they sent a kid to Iowa that Bernie would look out for that kid the whole time that he was in school. Even if that kid wasn't necessarily a good football player, Bernie would take care of him.

Frank Verducci was a Hall of Fame coach in Newark, and Iowa had four captains from that high school, including Andre Tippett and Norm Granger. Whenever Verducci had a good player, he'd send him to Bernie because of the trust factor. And because he liked Bernie.

In this sense, people really like Bret Bielema. He's a lot like Bernie in that he puts a strong emphasis on developing relationships with high school coaches. Bret's strength as a recruiter was one of the reasons why I felt he was the right choice to replace me.

Bret has gotten so close to some high school coaches in Florida — which was his recruiting area when he was an assistant at Iowa and Kansas State — that they're not only good buddies but allies who are looking to help Bret find good players. Bret has cultivated his contacts in Florida, like he will in Wisconsin.

He's easy to like.

Sort of like Dan McCarney. He was young, but a good recruiter when I got to Iowa. Mac was initially the tight ends coach for the Hawkeyes. But when the defensive line coaching job opened up, Hayden moved Mac there, and that opened up a spot on the staff. Along with Mac's recommendation, that's how I got hired.

***

In recruiting, the natural progression is to get better with time, and I did. The more I recruited, the better I got to know the areas, the better I got to know the coaches, and the better they got to know me. Those relationships are invaluable.

I developed a rapport, and I put stock in what coaches would tell me, especially when they said, "Look, this kid's film might not be that good, but he can flat-out play. He's the best athlete in the county. He can run and he competes hard."

Those are the things you're looking for — things you don't always see on film.

I really liked watching kids play in other sports, whether it was wrestling, basketball or track. I liked seeing how they competed. As a high school wrestling coach, I realized there was some carryover to football. The power and explosion in football comes from your hips, and you also have to have good leverage and hips in wrestling.

Being a good recruiter involves work and follow-up. Not only do you have to win over the high school coaches, but you have to win over the parents — particularly the mother, who has to feel comfortable with the way you're recruiting her son.

I tried to be consistent as part of gaining their trust. If I said I was going to be at a certain game, then I went to the game. If I said I was going to call at a certain time, that's when I called. The lasting impression that you need to leave with the recruit is that he's going to be treated right once he leaves home and steps on your campus.

When I got to Iowa, I wanted Hayden Fry to know that he could rely on me recruiting good players. I didn't want to be an anchor on the staff and drag everybody else down. That's why you fight like hell to succeed and do your part.

One of the first kids I signed was Mike Stoops. His brother, Bobby, was already a redshirt freshman in Iowa City. I recruited Mike Hooks, who was out of Omaha, in the same class with Stoops. And the next year, I signed Jonathan Hayes and George Little.

One of the best players I recruited to Iowa might have been running back Nick Bell. An old friend of mine — Jim Nicksick from B-Town — was coaching in Las Vegas and he put me on Bell, who went in the first round of the NFL draft. Brad Quast was another very good player for me.

One of the players I should have offered, but didn't, was from Youngstown South — a defensive back, Brian Marrow, who went on to have a nice career at Wisconsin.

I lost some good players to winning programs, like Garcia Lane, who went to Ohio State, and Jerry Diorio, who went to Michigan. Rejection always bothers you, especially when you develop a rapport with the prospect and you feel like you have a good shot, but you lose him to a school with more tradition.

***

What happened early on at Iowa — when we were selling blue sky — reminded me of how it was when I first came to Wisconsin. That's all we had to sell — the promise of things getting better, blue sky. At least Hayden had won at North Texas, and we were selling Hayden, pitching the challenge of building a program and being a part of the turn-around.

Hayden wasn't much at opening the door to a recruit. But he stayed on top of recruiting, and he did a good job of making sure everybody was on top of their recruiting areas. He knew what was going on, and he was a really smooth closer. When he turned on the Hayden Fry charm, people loved him. The kids liked him and responded positively to him.

I always had a lot of confidence in Hayden, and I learned a lot about organization from him. To be truthful, there was nobody as organized as Hayden. There was a plan and unbelievable attention to detail at Iowa. Everything was covered.

I will guarantee you that all the assistants who came off his coaching staff and started their own programs, regardless of who else they worked for, used Hayden's blueprint to set up their own organization. That's what I did at Wisconsin.

Hayden was very structured. He had a reason behind every move. If you were going to meet with your position group for 90 minutes, then everybody started at the same time, and everybody ended at the same time. Even though the quarterbacks might have more to work on than the defensive linemen, they were all on the same clock.

Hayden didn't want any morale problems. He didn't want one position group to meet for 30 minutes and another to meet for the full 90 minutes. And that's how he managed his program. He'd tell us, "I've been shot at and hit so many times, I've tried everything, and these are the things that work and these are the things that matter."

Hayden also believed in having the starters leave the practice field on a positive note. His rationale was that if they had success practicing, they would feel good about themselves and that would carry over to Saturday. He never matched the No. 1 offense against the No. 1 defense. Never. The No. 1 offense always practiced against the scout team. They knew what the defense was going to be, and they were going to be successful.

Lou Holtz was just the opposite. He didn't think you could get better without challenging yourself every day in practice — good against good. He pushed his starters to compete at their highest level. And he kept pushing them. That's what I believe in.

Hayden was not an especially good motivator on game days. He would always give a weather report. Our first year, we're playing on a cold day, and Hayden, who had never experienced cold weather in his life, is telling the players how to keep their feet warm by putting a pair of socks on, then a baggy, then another pair of socks.

I couldn't stop from laughing because Devaney was just the opposite. At Nebraska, he taught us that you never talk about the weather or complain about it because that's something you have no control over, and you just have to deal with it.

What I took from Devaney, Fry, and Holtz is that there are different ways to get the job done, and everything you do has to fit your personality. That's because you've got to be able to sell the plan to your staff, and your assistants have to be able to sell it to the players.

As a young head coach, you can't just steal someone else's way of doing things. I couldn't be Hayden Fry or Lou Holtz. But I could be myself, and I could incorporate some of their beliefs into my coaching. That's what I did.

At Iowa, I really developed as a coach. I kept learning more about the game, and I gained more and more confidence. I coached the tight ends that first year. In high school, I had coached everything and called every play on defense and offense, and since I had worked with the offensive line, I could bring some things to coaching tight ends.

Hayden brought some unconventional thinking to the position. When he was at North Texas, he moved a wide receiver to tight end. Instead of having him take the traditional three-point stance, he had the tight end standing up on the line of scrimmage before the snap. That allowed him to get a better read on the defensive coverage.

***

There's a whole different tempo of doing things at the college level compared to high school. As a first-year coach, I spent time with Bill Snyder learning pass routes and releases and that type of thing.

I had to listen to what was important. That was one of the first things I learned at Iowa. Carl Jackson, one of Hayden's offensive assistants, taught me that principle: teach what is important. In your position group meetings, you needed to make sure your players were all on the same page and knew what was going to be run in practice, otherwise you might screw up the team periods and you would have to deal with an angry head coach.

Hayden Fry always came off as the down-home, Hee-Haw character, this funny, wise-cracking rube — the ultimate schmoozer — what with the sunglasses and white pants.

Let me tell you something. He was very demanding on his staff. He was a disciplinarian, a tough guy, and very explicit in what he wanted, particularly on offense and special teams. That's what he cared about the most.

Meanwhile, he turned the defense over to Bill Brashier, who came to Iowa City with Fry in 1978. Brashier was one of the best football coaches I've ever been around, and it's really a tragedy that he didn't have an opportunity to coach his own team. Brashier was very even-keeled and consistent with what he did on a daily basis.

He really had a good sense of what was going on, and Hayden trusted him. That's why he entrusted Brashier with the defense. The young assistants all looked up to Brashier as a mentor. A lot of the things I believe in defensively, the X's and O's, I learned from him.

Hayden put a great staff together. He had been around a long time, and he knew exactly what pieces fit into the puzzle. I happened to be in the office the week he was bringing in people to interview for the offensive line job in 1981. We had the potential for a good team and a good O-line, and everyone assumed Hayden would hire a veteran coach.

Instead, he brought in somebody with just two years of experience as a graduate assistant coach at Pittsburgh and Connecticut. His only other coaching stint had been at Worcester Academy, a prep school.

Kirk Ferentz turned out to be a great hire, though.

I don't know what separated Kirk from the other candidates in Hayden's mind, but he proved that he had a good feel for people and how they fit in. Kirk was very even-tempered and very smart, a real student of the game, the same way he is today.

***

Somebody asked me if I knew Bill Snyder had the makings of a head coach when he was at Iowa. None of us thought that way because we didn't know if we'd ever get out of Hayden's web. He wouldn't allow other schools on campus in the offseason. He didn't want anybody seeing what we were doing. As a result, none of Hayden's assistants got much exposure. Nobody had the chance to say, "Boy, they've got some good coaches there."

They didn't know that, and Hayden wasn't going to advertise. All of us probably thought the first guy who would have that chance to go would be Brashier. Personally, I never thought about who was going to become a head coach. I was so immersed in my own job. Plus, we were taught, "Take care of your responsibility and don't second-guess anyone."

As assistants, we were all a little different; we had different strengths. But we respected each other and how each coach handled his own business and players.

Because so many of Hayden's assistants went on to run their own programs, people wonder all the time what those staff meetings were like when you had the presence and influence of so many good coaches, like Bill Snyder, Dan McCarney, Kirk Ferentz, Don Patterson and the Stoops brothers, Bobby and Mike, both of whom were graduate assistants.

Truth is, there was never any doubt about who was in charge during those staff meetings. Hayden let everyone speak their mind. But if a vote was taken and it was 9-1 — and Hayden had the one — that's the only vote that counted. That was his democracy.

You can't argue with the results. Hayden Fry took a losing program and turned it into a winner. And the one thing I learned from him about turnarounds is that it comes down to what you demand of your players 12 months of the year, not just those 11 Saturdays in the fall.

Whether it's classroom attendance or taking hats off at training table or holding players accountable for meetings and appointments and out-of-season workouts, it's a process. How you run your program will determine how much you win.

Hayden Fry, the psychologist, got big play in the media. That was his shtick. Like the pink visitors' locker room at Kinnick Stadium. We used to laugh about all the attention that got from the writers. But it seemed to get into the heads of opposing coaches.

Michigan's Bo Schembechler went to the trouble of putting butcher block paper on the walls before the Wolverines played us. And an Ohio State assistant told me that one of his best players on defense kept yawning at halftime and nearly fell asleep.

***

No doubt about it, Hayden Fry created waves in the Big Ten. And while he was different from some of the other coaches in some of the things that he did, it showed that if what you're doing is sound, and everybody believes in the plan, you will be successful.

That came to fruition in 1981. We opened the season with a huge upset win over Nebraska. But we turned around and lost to Iowa State, a team that wasn't very good. And then we beat a ranked UCLA team. It was that kind of a roller coaster ride.

It looked like we would have to fight like hell just to get to a bowl game. In mid-October, Tom Nichol, a freshman place-kicker from Green Bay, kicked three field goals in a 9-7 win at Michigan. That momentum was short-lived.

We lost consecutive games before trouncing Purdue, and that set up a showdown in Madison against Wisconsin. We were 4-2 and the Badgers were 5-2 and still very much in contention for the Big Ten title and a trip to the Rose Bowl.

We weren't very good on offense. We were more efficient than good. Gordie Bohannon was our quarterback — Gordie was tough (his son, Jason, will be playing basketball for Bo Ryan and the Badgers beginning with the 2006-07 season). Phil Blatcher, Eddie Phillips, and Norm Granger were the running backs. And they each had their assets.

Where we excelled was on defense and special teams. Mark Bortz, who was from Pardeeville, and Jim Pekar, who was out of Cudahy, were the defensive tackles. Pat Dean was the nose guard. Andre Tippett and Brad Webb were the defensive ends, and Mel Cole and Todd Simonsen were the linebackers. Simonsen was a tough guy from Racine.

As a senior, Cole played as well as anyone in the country. He was kind of foul-mouthed — like me — and Hayden used to get all over both of us for our language during practices. But on game days, Hayden would turn to Cole and ask in that Southern twang of his, "Melvin, do you have anything to say to the guys?"

And Cole would go off and get everybody cranked up. You see, it was OK to swear when it was appropriate. Hayden was cunning that way.

We inherited many of those kids on defense. The Badgers had the first crack at Bortz, but turned him down. They didn't offer a scholarship. But we didn't use the Wisconsin kids for extra motivation in this particular game. We were playing for so much in Madison, we didn't have to use it.

As a defense, we held Wisconsin to a little over 40 yards rushing. We also had three interceptions, and Bobby Stoops recovered a fumble that set up a touchdown, so we took a 17-0 lead at halftime. The final score was 17-3.

Nobody could move the ball consistently against our defense. We also had a weapon in punter Reggie Roby, who averaged almost 54 yards per attempt against Wisconsin. Hayden had so much confidence in Roby that he had him punting on third down in the fourth quarter, even though we could have run more time off the clock before kicking.

Hayden was smart. He was not about to take a chance on fumbling, and he knew the Badgers couldn't move the ball against us. Roby was a big part of our defense because he forced opposing offenses to drive nearly the length of the field on every possession.

After beating the Badgers at Camp Randall, we got some help from Ohio State, which knocked off Michigan. And then we helped ourselves to a share of the Big Ten title and the Rose Bowl with a 36-7 victory over Michigan State at Kinnick.

That also ended the drought.

***

Iowa had gone 19 years without a winning record.

And after going 5-6 and 4-7 his first two years, Hayden Fry was taking the Hawkeyes to Pasadena. That Rose Bowl was very special to me.

And what I learned from our mistakes in preparation for that game — we got crushed 28-0 by Washington — I later put to good use at Wisconsin.

For one thing, we were at the bowl site too long. We didn't have an indoor practice facility at Iowa, so when finals were over, we took off for California. Once there, we killed the players. We had an early wake-up call. It was hurry up and go to an activity. And it was hurry up and practice. We repeated that every day.

By contrast, Washington's players had no curfew the first week and slept in. Our kids were burned out by the second week.

We really mismanaged our schedule, and by the time the game rolled around, our kids were in a trance. I took mental notes and when we started putting together our Rose Bowl itinerary for our '93 Badger team, I did everything the opposite of that first trip.

I will say this, it was fun to get on a roll at Iowa. Starting with that breakthrough season in '81, the Hawks went to bowls annually, including the '85 Rose Bowl, where we had some personnel issues and got whipped by UCLA, 45-28.

During that stretch, we recruited well and had good players, and you gain confidence when you know you can play with anybody. It's not as much fun when you're not as good and you have to rely on everything falling into place just to have a chance — as opposed to knowing, if your guys play well, you're going to win.

At Iowa, sustaining the success was more about consistency than anything else. It was about not getting too high or too low. Hayden Fry enjoyed every win, which was the opposite of Lou Holtz, who fretted about everything.

Hayden was always consistent in the things that he demanded from the players. He never varied, which allowed them to get into a routine. They knew how to work and prepare for games, and they went out and played with that type of consistency from week to week.

***

As a family, we were very happy and comfortable in Iowa City. Dawn was just graduating from high school, and Stacy was just starting. I really wasn't looking to leave. If anyone called to measure if I was interested in a job, I just said, "No."

The calls weren't like, "We want you. What is it going to take?"

But people did express interest.

Kurt Schottenheimer and I were recruiting in Chicago when he asked me if I would be interested in coaching at Notre Dame. Kurt was the younger brother of Marty Schottenheimer and had played high school football against me.

Kurt was on the Irish staff in 1986. "I've never really thought about coaching at Notre Dame," I told Kurt. "It was never my dream to coach there."

About a week later, I ran into Kurt again, and he said he was moving on to the NFL to take an assistant's job with Marty, who was the head coach of the Cleveland Browns. He also said my name had come up in one of Lou Holtz's staff meetings at Notre Dame.

Soon after, Lou called to see if I would be interested in leaving Iowa.

He said if I wanted the job, the job was mine. I still remember his recruiting pitch.

"What do you want to do?" he asked.

"I want to be a head coach someday," I said.

"If you want to be a head coach," Lou said, "you have to be a defensive coordinator first, and you're not going to be one at Iowa because Bill Brashier is not going anywhere.

"But if you do a good job for me — as our linebacker coach — and if Foge Fazio leaves, you'll get first crack at being the defensive coordinator. I know Foge is looking around for a head job or an assistant's job in the NFL. He's not going to be here much longer."

That got my wheels turning. I didn't know how much he was going to pay. I didn't care. And I didn't know whether I was going to be coaching the inside linebackers or the outside linebackers. Didn't matter. It was too much of an opportunity to turn down.

All I wanted was a shot.

Hayden had talked to me about handling all four linebacker positions, and he said he was going to make a subtle shift in his staff. I told him about the Notre Dame offer, and perhaps if he had handled it a little differently, I might have stayed. Then again, what he did or said probably didn't make a difference.

The timing was a little awkward because all of us — Hayden and the assistants — were getting ready to take our first cruise together. We were going to the British Virgin Islands. I told Hayden that I was going to Notre Dame, but I wasn't prepared for his reaction.

He took my tickets away.

I had spent eight years with him at Iowa, and now, because I was trying to advance myself in the profession, he wasn't going to let me go on the cruise.

I didn't say anything.

Not long after that scene, Hayden came back into my office and put the tickets on my desk. I went on the cruise and had a helluva time.

I had told Lou about the cruise, and I asked him whether he wanted me to skip it altogether and get to work right away at Notre Dame.

"Don't worry about it," he said. "Come whenever you're ready."

I was ready.

CHAPTER FIVE

We're No. 1 and Irish Eyes Are Smilin'

During one of our open dates in the schedule at Iowa, I traveled back to Nebraska and visited with my old head coach, Bob Devaney.

"Set a goal for yourself," Devaney advised. "You should try and get a head coaching job by the time you're 42."

When I got to Notre Dame, we talked again.

"You're at a great place to learn," Devaney said. "And Lou Holtz will give you responsibilities and the space to grow as a coach."

And then he brought it up again: the timetable to be a head coach.

Devaney had arbitrarily set the number for me: 42.

Although he was 41 when he was hired for his first head coaching job at the University of Wyoming, he was 42 when he coached his first game for the Cowboys. He coached there five seasons, and that was his stepping stone to Nebraska in 1962.

Devaney liked telling the story about how he nearly left the coaching profession before he even got to the college level. He always figured that he'd wind up sitting behind a desk with an administrative job before anybody would take a chance on him.

He had been coaching high school football in Michigan — Big Beaver, Keego Harbor, Saginaw, and Alpena — when he supposedly got an offer to be a PR guy for a car company.

As the story goes, he was ready to make the move when he got a phone call from Duffy Daugherty, a Michigan State assistant.

Daugherty, speaking on behalf of Spartans head coach Biggie Munn, offered Devaney a job on Munn's staff in East Lansing.

Devaney accepted and worked under Munn and Daugherty before leaving for Wyoming. He was 46 when he got to Nebraska.

The rest is history — how he inherited a doormat in Lincoln, rebuilt the Cornhusker program, and won back-to-back national championships in the early '70s.

***

I was 40 when I got to Notre Dame, and what Devaney had said about setting a goal to be a head coach — by the time I reached 42 — made sense. It was something to shoot for, something to set my sights on.

In coaching, you have to roll the dice sometimes, you have to take chances. If you want to be a head coach, you can't get too comfortable in a job. You have to make career moves, and that's what Notre Dame was for me.

There was risk involved. In 1986 — Lou's first season in South Bend — the Irish had a losing record, 5-6, the same record Gerry Faust had in his final season with the Irish.

Beyond that, I knew Lou Holtz could be very demanding, very tough on assistants. That was well-documented by those who had worked for him. But I had always respected Lou because wherever he went, he won and he won right away.

When I was coaching at Mason City, I took my whole staff to Arkansas during Lou's first season there, and I watched how he conducted his practices. Monte Kiffin was Lou's defensive coordinator with the Razorbacks, and that was my connection.

The one thing about Lou Holtz you recognized immediately was that he had a distinct way of getting things done. He is one of the unique characters in the sport, and one of the great public speakers and motivators of all time.

As I got to know him better at Notre Dame, I was really impressed with his vision and how he prepared a team — just the things that he said to the players. He sent a message, and he got everybody focused and on the same page. That was his strength.

Lou wrote all of his notes on manila folders. One day, he was jotting down what he was going to say to the team before a game. I picked up the folder, and he had already written on the back what he was going to say AFTER the game.

He was always one or two steps ahead of the curve.

Lou Holtz had a plan for success, along the lines of, "This is how we're going to win." It's about fundamentals, it's about chemistry, it's about teamwork, it's about taking care of the seven areas — or elements — of a football game.

** Turnovers

** Kicking Game

** Big Plays

** Goal Line Fundamentals on Offense and Defense

** Mental Errors

** Minus Yardage Plays

** Foolish Penalties

At Wisconsin, that's what I would check every Sunday morning. Each of my assistants had to file his own report. I wanted to know how many times a defender had been knocked off his feet, how many missed tackles we had. And I'd go over those seven elements with our players every week. "This is why you won or lost," I'd tell them.

If we were in double-figures in mental errors, then maybe the players didn't understand the game plan well enough. That's why it's so critical to make the other team beat you. Before you can start winning, I told them, you have to stop losing.

That was Lou's plan.

I spoke at Urban Meyer's clinic at the University of Florida, and he's got the same plan because he once coached wide receivers for Lou at Notre Dame.

The Holtz emphasis — on doing things the right way — was always the same, too. Lou never cared about what defensive scheme you were using, as long as you were playing with fundamentals. Everything had to be sound. Lou was also going to be the spokesperson. He made that clear to everybody: the head coach speaks for the team.

Whereas Hayden Fry tried to intimidate the press at Iowa — he wanted it one-sided and if anybody second-guessed or crossed him, he wouldn't talk to them — Lou was more forthright and accessible to the media at Notre Dame.

"I'll make all the statements about the team," he always reminded his assistants. "You praise your players and the opponents. And you don't have to worry about different schemes or why we did specific things, I'll handle that."

No detail was too small, and Lou was so well-organized that he wrote down everything. He covered how you treat players, how you treat assistants, along with his philosophy on recruiting and winning and a number of other things. These were the things he felt strongly about and believed in.

When I took the Wisconsin job, I went to Lou's secretary and got his team meeting notes from the three years I was on his staff. He put everything down on those manila folders; preseason, mid-season, spring-ball.

One of the many things I took from him was how he handled recruiting weekends. Lou always finished up by having the players over to his house on Sunday morning for brunch. After the prospects ate, everybody went into his office, one by one, and talked. I thought it was a nice personal touch, and I did the same thing for my 16 seasons with the Badgers.

***

When it comes to recruiting, Notre Dame has always had unbelievable name recognition, which allowed you to get into any living room in the country.

As an Irish assistant, I had to make changes in the way I recruited. At Iowa, you went into every area to establish a rapport with the high school coach. At Notre Dame, your recruiting area is much larger, and you don't have time to work all the schools.

Vinny Cerrato was Lou's recruiting coordinator, and he was on the road all the time. He decided who we were going after, and he'd give each assistant a list, identifying the players we needed to see. We'd go in and make the appointments.

Vinny was a great evaluator and did a tremendous job.

What I tried to do was lock up commitments before Christmas. I'd bring them in on a visit and pressure them to commit early. And you can do that — put leverage on somebody — if you know they really want to come to your place.

Notre Dame might have gone through a slump on the playing field during the Faust Era, but it was still Notre Dame. I really didn't know much about the history or the tradition of the school until I got there. And it was almost an endless list to digest.

The pep rallies.

Rudy.

The Friday noon luncheons.

George Gipp.

Touchdown Jesus (Our Lady on the Dome).

The Four Horsemen.

We're No. 1 Moses (The statue of Moses — right arm and index finger extended to the heavens — that sits outside of the library).

Leahy and Rockne.

Fair Catch Corby (Another campus statue that doubles as a football landmark).

Walking as a team to the stadium on Saturdays you could feel the electricity in the air. It gives me goose bumps just thinking about it. That's why Notre Dame is a totally different animal than any other place. And boy, you learn that in a hurry.

One of my former Nebraska coaches, George Kelly, was an administrative assistant at Notre Dame when I joined Lou's staff, and he kind of took me under his wing. I'd stop by his house frequently, and he would kind of clue me in on how things worked.

Father Joyce talked to me about doing things by the rules, what it meant to be an assistant coach at Notre Dame, and what was expected of me. Father Joyce — Edmond Joyce — was an executive vice-president and second-in-command to Father Theodore Hesburgh.

I always liked visiting with Ara Parseghian, who coached there from the mid-'60s to the mid-'70s. What a classy guy. At first, he was reluctant to come around Lou's program because he wasn't sure anybody wanted him there. Can you imagine that?

Lou made sure that Ara knew he was always welcome.

I also liked talking with Johnny Ray, who coached the defensive line and linebackers for Ara. I tried to draw from their experiences. Here were reasons why they won. And Parseghian, like Devaney, took over a struggling program, won immediately, and sustained that success. To me, Ara Parseghian always epitomized Notre Dame.

I'm the type of person who loves gravitating to old veterans who have been successful. Edward "Moose" Krause was still alive when I got to South Bend, and he was one of the all-time great characters in school history. I'd go into his office and find him surrounded by his entourage, telling stories about his days as the Irish basketball coach and athletic director.

Moose was an All-American basketball player at Notre Dame and a starting tackle on Knute Rockne's football team. Along with Frank Leahy — Leahy's Lads won three national championships during a four-year period in the '40s — Moose can educate you on the history of Rockne and his "Win one for the Gipper" speech.

***

We didn't win 'em all my first season at Notre Dame. But we went 8-4 and won more games than anyone anticipated. There were no expectations, no pressure. I really enjoyed coaching the linebackers and working for Foge Fazio.

I was starting to see the big picture more than just coaching a position group. And when Foge took an NFL job after the '87 season, Lou named me defensive coordinator.

For a time — after Foge left, defensive line coach Joe Yonto retired, and secondary coach Terry Forbes went into private business — I was the only one on the defensive staff.

In assembling my assistants, Lou said, "Recommend somebody to me and if I feel comfortable with him, we'll hire him."

It worked the other way, too. Lou recommended a secondary coach whom he had worked with before, and I said, "Coach, I don't feel comfortable with him."

And we went in another direction.

There are many things that factor into putting together a staff. The worst thing you can do is get a bunch of people like yourself. You want a variety of personalities. But while you want different opinions, you don't want to battle everyday over them.

You have to hire people who are team players, who can get along with other people and buy into your system, and who understand their roles.

Hayden Fry did a great job in this area. Everybody knew exactly what their responsibility was. Nobody tried to step on anybody else's toes. Nobody second-guessed what somebody else was doing. And everybody took pride in their job.

I went to school on that Iowa model.

Lou tried to help me out by bringing in Joe Moore, an old Pittsburgh guy. Joe was Kirk Ferentz's high school coach and mentor. And he was one of the all-time great offensive line coaches at Pitt. He had great wisdom. But he had never coached on defense.

I met with Joe for about an hour, breaking down film. And I spent the whole time arguing with him. I finally got up and interrupted one of Lou's offensive meetings.

"Joe needs to be on offense," I said, weary from battling with Joe on everything. "Why don't you give him the tight ends? I'll take Beef Stew."

That was George Stewart, who coached the tight ends and ran the special teams, and had a tremendous rapport with the players. He was a really emotional coach — the kids loved him — and I thought he would be perfect for defense, even though he had never coached it.

I said to Lou, "I'll teach him."

I wanted his temperament.

My next hire was John Palermo, who had coached with Holtz at Minnesota. When I was at Iowa and we played the Gophers, I liked the way John's kids played. I knew that he didn't have the greatest players, but they always played well against us.

John was a good technician and teacher, and that's what we needed with the defensive line. We had some young guys who hadn't played that much, like Jeff Alm and Boo Williams. I needed someone who could school them on the fundamentals, and I felt like John Palermo could get them where they needed to be.

Next, I really wanted to get a strong secondary coach, someone who had coached in big arenas, big games, pressure games. I didn't feel comfortable teaching the techniques. I knew the responsibilities, but I needed somebody back there who I could really trust.

Chuck Heater was my guy. He had worked at Wisconsin for Dave McClain, and he had been at Ohio State. Heater completed my staff, and the four of us got started on building the defense. We had a group of no-names — like Chris Zorich, a converted linebacker at nose guard — who hadn't accomplished a whole lot but developed into great players.

The key was controlling and coaching the three linebackers, the Three Amigos: Frank Stams, Wes Pritchett and Michael Stonebreaker.

Everybody on the team, everybody on campus, loved them. But they were pranksters and ornery as hell, and it was probably questionable whether they belonged at Notre Dame. I knew if you could find a way to harness their ability and control their exuberance and playfulness, they would be team leaders.

"I know you like to have fun, and I like to have fun, and together we're going to have fun," I told them from Day One. "But when it's time to work, we're going to work our asses off because the most fun you'll have is in winning."

They bought into it, and I don't know that I've ever had as much fun or enjoyed coaching anybody as much as I did coaching those three.

Digger Phelps' basketball office was right next to mine, and Digger used to come in all the time because he knew the Three Amigos would be hanging out there.

I used to love shooting the breeze with Digger, and we got to be pretty good friends and talked all the time about motivating people and competing at the highest level.

Digger was very confident, maybe even arrogant. He was 29 when he got the Notre Dame job. I've always believed you can draw from coaches — how they prepare for an opponent, how they interact with their players — regardless of the sport they're coaching.

***

As a defense, we didn't put up with nonsense from anybody. And it all started with our linebackers — Stams, Pritchett and Stonebreaker. They were street fighters. I remember a fight broke out with Miami during the pregame warm-up, and I didn't think it would ever end. Miami tried to intimidate them. Damnedest thing I'd ever seen. You didn't try to break it up because you couldn't.

That was the type of leadership that we got from them. If it was a big game, an intense, four-quarter game, those guys weren't going to let you get beat. Lou called them "toe to toe heavyweight fights where you're going to find out who's going to flinch."

Our guys didn't flinch.

At the end of the 1988 regular season, we played in one of those "big on big" games. For the first time in the history of the Notre Dame-USC series, it matched No. 1 (us) against No. 2 (them). And we were a betting underdog because nobody had slowed them down.

On Friday, the day before the game at the Memorial Coliseum in Los Angeles, Lou called a staff meeting and said that he was suspending Tony Brooks, our leading rusher, and Ricky Watters, our leading receiver, for being late to a team meal.

"I've got to kick them off," he said.

Nobody argued with him.

Lou called the seniors together and announced what he was doing. They agreed on his decision to suspend the players. Next, he called a team meeting and asked if anybody had anything to say.

One kid stood up and said, "Brooks and Watters have been important contributors to our team all season, and I don't think it's right to kick them off now."

That didn't go over well with Frank Stams, who jumped up and went nuts.

"They haven't followed the rules," he yelled, "and if anybody in this room doesn't think we can win without them, then get the hell out of here."

We won 27-10. Our defense abused USC quarterback Rodney Peete, and Stams wound up with nine tackles and three sacks. They couldn't block Stams or overcome four turnovers in the first half. And they had no answer for our quarterback, Tony Rice.

I remember Lou saying after the game that he thought we were under-rated despite being the No. 1-ranked team in college football. He was frustrated from reading all the articles about Notre Dame being lucky and Notre Dame not being a pretty team.

We weren't very pretty, but we played the toughest schedule in the country, and we played together as a team. And that's what it takes to win a national championship. You need good players, you need tremendous team chemistry, and you need guys who can handle the pressure of big games.

And when you get into one of those types of games — big on big — you have to realize that you can drain your kids by getting them too cranked up, too emotional. The players are smart enough to know what's on the line. They know it's a big game.

The emotion will take care of itself. Just concentrate on the game plan and don't try to be superhuman. Don't change who you are or what you do. There's nothing magical about the formula. Your great players have to play great.

True, you need some luck, some bounces here and there. Most of all, you need a group of people who can really stay focused. Study any championship team, in any sport, and the one common thread is the ability to eliminate outside distractions.

That's what we did in 1988, and we capped our unbeaten season by beating West Virginia, 34-21, in the Fiesta Bowl. Right after the game, I went up to Lou's room and he asked me, "What do I have to do to keep you here?"

Lou had anticipated somebody coming after me. I had had some feelers from other schools, but nothing serious, and I really wasn't interested in pursuing anything, either. I didn't think there was anything real appealing on the market.

My daughter Stacy was going into her senior year of high school in South Bend, and I told Lou that I wasn't planning on going anywhere. If I had any brains, I would have asked for a raise, but I didn't even think of it. I remember Lou lecturing us, "You don't coach at Notre Dame for money. You coach at Notre Dame because it's Notre Dame."

I did have one request.

"Coach, you can do some things for me," I said. "You can throw me some bones. You've got all of those speaking engagements and some aren't paying quite as much you're used to making. Just give me the opportunity to do some of those."

One other thing...

"Give me more responsibility," I said.

That seemed to surprise Holtz. "How can I give you more responsibility," Lou shot back, "you're running half the team now."

"Teach me how to be a good head coach then," I countered.

He followed through by putting me in charge of team meetings when he was gone. I would stay in touch and report back to him — keeping him updated on what was happening on campus and what we were doing during the winter workouts.

I really wasn't on a timetable — mine or Devaney's — to be a head coach.

I just knew I was going to get a job when the time was right.

***

After the 1989 regular season, I was sitting in a staff meeting just before we began bowl practices. We had gone 11-1 — and had been the No. 1-ranked team until our loss to Miami in late November — and we were now gearing up to play the team that had replaced us at the top of the polls, Colorado, in the Orange Bowl.

Lou Holtz got the meeting started by reading off the list of job openings around the country. And he wanted all those who had interest in a particular school to identify themselves because he was more than willing to get on the phone and help them get the job.

"Rutgers?" Holtz said.

I raised my hand

"Have they contacted you?"

"Yes," I said.

"Pittsburgh?"

I raised my hand.

"Have they contacted you?"

"Yes."

"You interested?"

"No."

"Wisconsin? Anybody interested?"

I raised my hand again.

"Talked to anybody yet?"

"Yes."

"UNLV?"

I raised my hand and finally, someone else did, too, Jim Strong. I had gotten a call from UNLV, and I had always loved Las Vegas. I thought that would be a great job. But now I'm feeling embarrassed because I had been contacted for all of these jobs.

"You've got enough options, Barry," Lou said. "We'll let Jim take this one."

I really didn't want to interview at Pittsburgh, but Lou convinced me that I needed to take a look at the job because it would be good experience. Problem was, I already knew it was a set-up.

They were going to elevate an assistant, Paul Hackett, to replace Mike Gottfried. But they wanted to appease some of the alums by talking to western Pennsylvania guys, so they wanted to talk with me and Dave Wannstedt.

It was a farce. I was so mad about the way they mishandled everything that I left the interview early. "I'm out of here," I said.

***

I had already set up an interview with Wisconsin and Pat Richter in South Bend. We had talked on the phone but hadn't yet met face to face.

I picked up Pat at the airport. He likes to tell the story how he was worried that he was getting ready to hire a short little guy who looked like Danny DeVito.

Pat said he was so relieved when he got off the plane and saw me. "Pat, I was a linebacker at Nebraska," I made a point of saying to him. "How short could I be?"

I drove Pat over to my house, and we must have talked for three hours. From the very beginning, I was very impressed with him, and I thought we had a good rapport, a good dialogue. Pat asked most of the questions, and I had all of the answers. I was confident, and I wanted to send him one message — loud and clear — that I was ready to be a head coach.

When Pat asked about Iowa and the Big Ten, I was talking facts: "I did this, this and this." I had done my homework, and I was really prepared to discuss issues, particularly about the situation at Wisconsin.

Chuck Heater had stayed in contact with people in Madison, and he really schooled me on what the problems were, what was lacking, and what fences had to be mended.

One of Iowa's Rose Bowl teams had 11 kids from Wisconsin on the two-deep roster, so I knew there were players in the state. And I knew what had to be done to get them. I had recruited there and had two Wisconsin kids already verbally committed to Notre Dame: Jim Flanigan, a linebacker from Southern Door, and Greg McThomas, a fullback from Milwaukee Marquette.

The kids I had recruited were looking for reasons to leave Wisconsin. There was no pride in the program. But that didn't deter me. I've always been one who could rally the troops. I learned that if you make something important, people will respond.

"Number one, you have to win over the high school coaches," I told Pat. There was a rift between the coaches and the university.

They didn't want to send their kids there.

And you know what? I didn't blame them.

The Wisconsin program wasn't being run right. As a high school coach, you want to send your players someplace where they'll have a chance to win and where they'll be coached the right way. That wasn't happening in Madison.

Not only did I tell Pat who I was going to be recruiting, I told him who the recruiters were going to be; I outlined my coaching staff and the assistants I wanted. And I also presented him with a pecking order, in case some weren't available.

***

"Lou, if I don't get the Wisconsin job, I'm coming back to Notre Dame," I emphasized to Holtz. "But that's the job I want. That's the one I've had my eye on all along."

Holtz, in turn, told me if I was going to leave, he wanted to lure Dan McCarney away from Iowa to replace me. But he reconsidered and said, "I'd like to hire McCarney, but you need somebody you can trust, somebody you can use as a sounding board at Wisconsin."

It was time for Mac to grow professionally.

"Dan McCarney is coming," I told Pat.

And I was trying to get Mac to recruit Bernie Wyatt. I wasn't sure if we could get him because it was going to be so hard for him to leave Iowa City. But I knew Mac would work him hard, and I thought we might be able to get Bernie caught up in the emotion of things in Madison. We kind of ambushed him that way.

I had two other guys on my list: Kevin Cosgrove and Bill Callahan. I was under the impression they would be available. They had coached for Mike White at Illinois, and I had recruited against them. These guys were pit bulls.

You know what you're going to get out of an assistant if he's worked for a Hayden Fry or a Mike White — you're going to get a guy who knows the Big Ten territory and how to work and how to win. He won't be overwhelmed by anything.

***

When Pat Richter left my house in South Bend after our first visit, I'm sure he left thinking, "This guy has a plan and this guy knows what the hell he's talking about."

What I wanted to know was if there was a commitment at Wisconsin — whether the people there really wanted to win. Pat was convinced that Chancellor Donna Shalala wanted football to be successful. That was important. I needed to hear that from him.

And I got that same feeling from Donna when I met with her in Madison. She mapped out what she wanted to accomplish. She said that she would get actively involved with recruiting and be in the middle of everything, and I really embraced that — knowing how committed she was. I remember telling her, "I'll do a good job for you."

Every year there are "hot" assistants, and I knew Pat had interviewed Michigan defensive coordinator Lloyd Carr and Ohio State offensive coordinator Jim Colletto. Both were coaching in "name" programs that had won. I also knew Pat was high on West Virginia head coach Don

Nehlen, and he was up front with me about his interest in Nehlen.

"I don't know how much interest Nehlen has in us," Richter said, "but I have to follow up on this. He's got a big name and he's a proven winner."

I was aware of Nehlen's credentials, having played against his West Virginia team the year before in the national championship game at the Fiesta Bowl.

But I thought to myself, "Don Nehlen is not going to pack up and leave what he has built at West Virginia and take over a program like Wisconsin that is flat on its back."

It didn't make any sense to me, unless he was going to be a combination head coach and athletic director, and I knew that wasn't on the table. I wasn't worried about Don Nehlen.

That's what I kept telling myself.

Richter later told me that he had talked with Nehlen the morning after West Virginia lost to Clemson in the Gator Bowl, and Nehlen was disconsolate and still noncommittal.

Nehlen's emotional and financial attachment to West Virginia, and his lack of commitment to starting over from scratch at Wisconsin, may have prompted Richter to eliminate him as a candidate. Pat called Nehlen and informed him the school was moving in another direction.

Meanwhile, on December 30, my birthday — I turned 43 — I called Pat and told him what was on my mind.

"If you're going to hire me, you need to hire me tomorrow," I stressed, "because we're playing Colorado on January 1. They're the No. 1 team, and we'll have a great TV audience."

I wasn't just blowing smoke.

I said, "Wisconsin can't afford to miss out on that kind of publicity because it will be second to none. We can make a big splash that will help us in recruiting."

There was silence on the other end of the phone line. "Well, I don't think I can do that," Richter said. "I've got to get permission from the Athletic Board."

"I don't care what you have to do or how you do it," I told him. "Get it done. Otherwise, we're missing a heckuva opportunity."

The night before the game, Lou Holtz was finishing up his final meeting. I was sitting outside one of our conference rooms when I saw my dad walking down the hallway. He was crying. I've never seen him that emotional.

"Pat Richter just called," my dad said excitedly, "and he told me that he was going to offer you the Wisconsin job. He'll call back in 30 minutes."

When Holtz came out of the meeting, I told him that I had gotten the Wisconsin offer, and he confided, "I don't know whether I should tell the team or not."

After a brief pause, he said, "No, I'm going to tell the players."

That was pretty neat because the kids were really happy and excited for me, and they went out and played that way on defense in the Orange Bowl.

Colorado had been averaging 34 points and over 470 yards of total offense, and we held them to six points and a little over 280 yards in a 21-6 win.

The game took forever to play. Or so it felt. There were a lot of postgame ceremonies and media interviews. I didn't get back to the hotel until 1:45 in the morning.

Lou had asked me to come up to his room, and we visited for a while. Mostly I took notes on everything he said — the same notes I would turn over to Bret Bielema, my successor at Wisconsin, when I retired from coaching.

"First thing, when you take the job, don't treat those players you've inherited like red-headed stepchildren," Holtz said. "Make sure they understand that you didn't have anything to do with the other coaches getting fired.

"Also, if you are going to pick a fight or fight a battle, make sure it's worth losing a friend over. And, in general, when you have problems, break them down to their simplest form and then make your decision and solve them."

It was really late when I finally got back to my room. Pat had slipped a note under my door asking me to give him a call. We laughed about it later because he said a lot of things went through his mind while he was waiting for my phone call, including whether someone else had come up with a better offer and I had taken a different job.

When I finally did get a hold of Pat — and with our defensive effort against Colorado still fresh in my mind — the first words out of my mouth were, "How was that?"

From that point on, whenever we had a big win at Wisconsin, we would greet each other with, "How was that?"

At the Orange Bowl postgame party, I presented Pat with a St. Christopher medal that was given to the Notre Dame players and coaches at Mass every Sunday.

It would become a symbol of our friendship.

***

I was going strictly on adrenaline at my introductory press conference in Madison. That morning, before we got over to the McClain Facility, where the media was gathering, Pat asked, "Do you want to jot down some things on paper?"

"No, I'll just go up there and talk from my heart," I said.

I didn't have to write down anything. I had a plan and I knew exactly what I was going to do. And even though I was going on about two hours of sleep, I was excited.

One of the first questions I got was about the dwindling fan support for Badger football and all those empty seats at Camp Randall Stadium at the end of the Morton era.

"What do you tell those people who are maybe skeptical," I was asked, "about what's going to happen here?"

Now, remember, I was pretty damn cocky.

We had won at Iowa. We had gone to six straight bowls and two Rose Bowls.

We had won at Notre Dame. We had been arguably the best team in college football over the last two seasons, winning 24 of our last 25 games.

When the question came up — about building a fan base — I couldn't help but think what Devaney had done at Nebraska, too.

"People want good football in Wisconsin," I assured the audience. "And people have to be patient. They have to understand that things aren't going to change overnight.

"But let me say this — they better get season tickets right now because before long they won't be able to."

That's what I thought. It wasn't a contrived statement or anything like that. I believed what I was saying. And I thought I had all the answers.

But I had no idea how bad it was here.

CHAPTER SIX

All the Agony Without the Ecstasy

The 1990 season was a nightmare. We went 1-10, and I didn't handle the losing very well. But I kept telling myself, "I can't flinch, I can't show any sign of weakness, and I can't let anybody know that I'm in the tank," even though I was.

At staff meetings, I tried to come off really strong and positive with my coaches because I was turning them loose on the players. And there was a domino effect between how I acted in front of the assistants and how they acted in front of the team.

"Guys, we're not going to take any crap from anybody," I'd tell my staff. "We're going to run this program the right way. We're not going to change our values. We're not going to compromise on anything that we're doing.

"And one last thing, we're going to keep recruiting our asses off. We just need to go out and get better players because I know what it takes to win and I know that what we all believe in — all of us in this room — will make us successful."

After the meeting, I'd go back into my office at Camp Randall Stadium, close both doors, and curl up on the couch in the fetal position.

I was miserable.

I had gotten used to winning at Iowa and Notre Dame, and now the losing hurt so much my body ached. I had this terrible empty feeling in the pit of my stomach all the time. It was brutal. But I couldn't let anyone see the emotional toll it was taking on me.

Take it from me, though, there's nothing worse than feeling helpless.

A head coach usually has a sense of what is going to happen the night before a game. You've got butterflies and you're nervous. But the night before our Michigan game that first season, I knew that we could get every break in the book and play well, and we still weren't going to win. That's a sad feeling.

Nobody wants to be embarrassed.

I can remember coming off the road on a Friday night after scouting some high school players. We were getting ready to play Michigan the next day, and I turned on the TV to watch the local news block at 10 o'clock. Van Stoutt was then the sports director at one of the Madison stations, and he was also the host of my television show.

At the end of his sportscast, Van predicted a Michigan win. And he started laughing about how bad the Wolverines are going to beat us. It wasn't so much that he was picking us to get beat. Nobody in their right mind would have picked us to win.

But I felt like he was ridiculing us, and that's something I won't tolerate. I cornered him after the game and said, "Don't you ever do that again. You don't have to pick us to win. But for you to laugh at us and ridicule us on TV is wrong. Especially when you're doing my TV show. That's just not right, and it won't happen again."

Keep in mind, I'm a first-year head coach in the Big Ten, and I'm trying to prove that I can coach at this level. You only get one chance at these jobs, and if I don't win here, I'm not going to get another shot. That's why I stood up to people who were attacking us. I said what was on my mind. And, early on, that probably led to some issues with the media.

I admit that I was very impatient. I wanted it to happen fast at Wisconsin. But I soon realized that that was a pipe dream. It was going to take time. I didn't know how far away we were from turning the program around, and I didn't know how long it would be before we were going to get better. That was depressing, and I was depressed throughout that first season.

"You were shell-shocked, not depressed," Cindy would correct me. "You were shell-shocked because the all-invincible coach was having to fight his way up. You didn't realize how hard it was going to be. You just thought something magical was going to happen at Wisconsin because you're Barry Alvarez, and you thought you had all the answers."

Cindy reminded me that my mother flew to Madison to see one of our games during the 1990 season. We lost, and I was in the tank, and I didn't talk to my mom the rest of the weekend. She never came back to watch another Big Ten game, not one. My mom told me that I wasn't any fun to be around. So, instead of regular-season games, she would come back for spring intrasquad games because she knew we were going to win.

She was right. Cindy was right. I wasn't any fun to be around after those losses. Cindy said that she didn't see any futility on my part. She felt all along that I still had the belief in my mind that I could make it happen at Wisconsin. That's true.

But I was worried.

Can I really get it done here? Will they give me the time? They had just gone through five straight years of losing, and I'm 1-10. And, if I go 1-10 again, what really has changed?

It got so bad that I almost thought I was having a heart attack.

I wasn't.

But I did go to a doctor for a physical because I was dealing with so much tension and stress. I didn't eat the best, and I wasn't in the best of shape. And, obviously, I wasn't sleeping at night because all the losing was so hard to accept.

My cholesterol was 378 or some ridiculous number like that. It was off the charts. I had a hard time getting life insurance until I changed my diet and cut out a lot of the junk food I loved eating. And I tended to eat more when I was depressed.

As a player, I had had stingers resulting from physical contact and upper-body collisions which cause damage to nerve endings.

By the end of the '90 season, I was experiencing some of the same tingling sensations that I'd gotten from a stinger. I had little or no feeling in my left arm.

I've learned over the years that I tend to hold all my stress in my neck and shoulders. I had never had a back massage before. But I started getting them on Friday mornings to relieve some of the tension, though they didn't help me sleep any better.

I wasn't sleeping. But when I got home, it was still good to have someone like Cindy to bounce things off of. She stayed strong. Sometimes she would be sympathetic. Sometimes she'd kick me in the ass. Which I needed.

"You've got to believe in what you tell your players," she would emphasize to me. "You've got to live by what you tell them. You talk all the time about dealing with adversity, well, you need to deal with it first."

She was right, again.

"I know you're worried about how long it's going to take to turn this program around, and maybe you have some doubts," she'd tell me. "And

I also understand that you can't show weakness to anybody — but me."

Although I was hurting, I never second-guessed my decision to take the Wisconsin job. I always felt as an assistant, unless you're elevated to head coach in a successful program, you're not going to start off at the top.

That's why you have to make it a good job. I felt we had good assistants, and I had the support I needed from Donna Shalala and Pat Richter to succeed. I felt confident we would win. I just needed a little time to recruit our guys into the program.

To reassure myself, I must have called everybody I knew in the profession that first season. I specifically remember a conversation I had with Jim Walden, who was at Iowa State. And I remember asking him, "How the hell do you handle losing?"

Iowa State had a history of losing.

"Before you stand up and talk to your team on Sunday," Walden said, "you've got to get the previous loss out of your system. You'd better be able to move on to the next game because your players are going to be reading you."

I took his advice to heart. And as hard as it was sometimes — some losses were tougher to get out of the system than others — I tried to remain upbeat and positive whenever I got in front of our kids the day after a loss.

I wasn't the first coach who went through a 1-10 season. Or the last. Misery loves company, and over the years I've had a number of head coaches call and ask how I dealt with the pain that comes with losing.

"Don't take any short cuts," I told Mike Stoops, who was 3-8 his first season at Arizona. "Don't let somebody get away with something just because you're not winning. If you cut corners, you're in trouble. Build a foundation around what you believe in."

It also helps to have a soft couch.

***

I didn't go into the football offices at Camp Randall for the first two or three days after I was hired. I was too busy recruiting. But when I finally got around to checking out my new home at the stadium, I couldn't believe how dingy the offices were. The ugly carpeting was enough to give you a headache, and the secretaries were all smoking, so there was a cloud of cigarette smoke hanging over the front desk.

Why are these things important? When you take a job like this one — when you take over a losing culture — you have to develop a mindset with everyone who touches the program and everything that touches you. You have to teach winning 365 days a year. And you have to educate people on how they need to go about their business.

First impressions are critical, and that's why appearance is so important when you walk into the football offices for the first time. That goes for visitors and the players, too.

When I walked in that first day, I said, "Okay, I'm going back on the road to recruit this afternoon, and by the time I get back on Friday, I want this carpet torn up and new carpet in. I want this antiquated phone system corrected. And I want the ceilings dropped."

Then I lowered the boom on the secretaries. No more smoking. They needed to upgrade how they dressed and their general appearance before our first recruiting weekend. My famous last words were, "Get it done." That's how I left things.

While I was on the road, I got a call from Pat Richter who notified me that I was already in hot water with the administration.

"I understand you've got your bleep in the ringer," he said.

"For what?"

"You can't just go around ordering all of these things to get done," he reminded me. "You've got to get permission."

"Well, what is done is done."

I came back Friday, and people were working on getting things done; they were working towards achieving an objective. That was a start.

A rebuilding project, from my perspective, is about creating an attitude and image — my assistants are going to wear a tie to work every day — and it's about making a statement: "This is the way we're going to run our program."

That was the message I sent to the returning players the first time I met with them. When I walked into the room, it was pretty much what I expected — most of the guys were slumped in their seats with their baseball caps turned around on their heads.

"All right everybody, sit up straight, take your hats off, put your feet flat on the floor, get your eyes on me and pay attention," I demanded. "When we meet, it's going to be important. We're not holding meetings just to meet or to kill time. When we meet as a team, we're going to give you some information that is going to be important."

There was a rustling in the seating area.

Guys were sitting up straight.

To this day, if you talk to players who were at that first meeting, they will tell you that they realized immediately it was going to be different around here. They were now entering a no-nonsense zone. No hats, no facial hair, no earrings, no excuses.

"This is going to be a disciplined program," I told them. "A lot of you won't buy into it. But those of you who do are going to win championships. We'll do it my way. I've been successful, and I know how to win and the assistants I've hired know how to win."

I tried to make sure they knew I was sensitive to change.

"I know you all were recruited by other coaches," I said. "I didn't have anything to do with their firing. That was somebody else's decision."

I wanted them to know that they were going to be treated fairly, but there were going to be expectations. And there were some guys who tested me right away.

One kid had just tested positive for marijuana, and I called him into my office. He gave me a typical song-and-dance about his circumstances or whatever, and I said, "Fine, but we're going to test you randomly until the end of the school year."

That next week, he doesn't show up for an appointment.

I call him back into the office, and he gives me another story and excuse.

"If you have appointments, you keep appointments," I explained. "And if there's an emergency, you pick up the phone and let people know. I already told you how things were going to be handled. You're done, you're off the team."

I never gave any thought to how many players left the program that first year. I wasn't keeping track. But I hadn't seen anything like that before.

At Iowa, we worked them hard, and we had a few guys leave. But not a mass exodus. Not like we had at Wisconsin. And you know what? There wasn't one guy, not one single guy that made me think, "Boy, I wish he wouldn't have left."

I was just trying to instill in them a work ethic. Many of them were coasting and doing their own thing. Many of them didn't know how to work. I don't think there had been many demands placed on them in the weight room before we arrived.

The previous strength coach was also the director of football operations and the recruiting coordinator. I had never seen anything like that. I think they had an equipment guy also handling their video. There were some really crazy combinations, and it was like they were running a one-double A or Division II program.

That carried over to the players. I'll never forget one kid who came into my office and started whining about how he didn't think his heart was into playing football anymore.

I had heard this story a thousand times already, and I stopped him in mid-sentence and said, "I'll make it real easy for you — get your ass out of my office right now. I don't want to hear the rest of your story and I don't want you on this team."

Didn't bother me one bit. We had guys who weren't going to school and weren't doing what they were supposed to be doing. And we weren't going to waste time with them.

Some players thought we were trying to punish them with our out-of-season conditioning program, the same things I've done at every place I've coached, the same things we do now. We're actually more intense now than we were back then. We do more in the summer.

But our older kids have been in a successful program and have learned how to work. When the young guys come in, they get big eyes over what we're asking them to do. But the old guys kick them in the ass and teach them, "This is how we work."

Nobody complains about how hard they work or how hard they're pushed. And they learn how to carry that attitude and work ethic over to the football field.

Our 2005 team wasn't one of my better teams, but we still won 10 games. Much of our success had to do with the way we run our day-to-day business. Certain things are ingrained. Our kids expect to win, and they believe in what we're telling them. They also have a physical maturity because of how they've worked.

That's one of the differences between my last team and my first one in 1990. There were about 140 players, including walk-ons, who were sitting in the room during my first team meeting. Many of them didn't know how to work and didn't know how to win. And many of them knew they didn't belong at Wisconsin or in the Big Ten.

We needed to bring in tougher kids who had their own identity — separate from the identity of most of the guys who were already in the program. And that's what we did; we found kids who were as tough as hell and really bought into what we were trying to do.

Those who didn't — left.

I did have a soft spot in my heart for at least one player who tried to quit.

Brian Patterson, a center from D.C. Everest, and Dustin Rusch, a defensive tackle from Milton, were in the 1990 recruiting class. They were roommates, and midway through the 1991 season, they were both talking about transferring.

When Dustin came into my office, I could tell that his mind was already made up. He was struggling academically, and he needed to go someplace else.

Patterson walked into the office right after Rusch, and he tells me that he's going to transfer, too. He says, "Coach, you always challenge us with the same things, 'Can I trust you? Are you committed?' And I don't know if I am committed."

I knew his background, and I knew Brian Patterson belonged at Wisconsin.

"Bull-crap, Patty," I said. "I'm not listening to any more of this bull-crap. I'm not going to let you quit this team. Get out of my office, and I'll see you at practice."

I think he was dumbfounded and shocked over my response.

In the end, Brian Patterson was a reliable backup on our first Rose Bowl team. He even started a game at center during our 1993 championship season. The kids called him "The Microwave" because things heated up on offense when he was on the field. He was good friends with Cory Raymer, our starting center, and close to a lot of the players.

Years later, Patty recounted the "I want to quit" story at one of our golf outings, and I still laugh at the thought of him leaving my office and returning to his apartment where he had to tell Rusch, "He won't let me go. Alvarez won't let me quit."

That was the exception, not the rule.

***

One of the first things I did when I got on the Madison campus was look up a former Wisconsin coach, John Jardine, who had also taken over a losing program and had led a similar transition in the '70s. At that time people had lost most of their interest in the Badgers, but John was able to restore faith in the product and fill Camp Randall on Saturdays.

When I was at Nebraska, I had heard about Jardine. One of our graduate assistants had worked with John at Chicago Fenwick. And George Kelly was a close friend.

When I got here and contacted John, I knew he had separated himself from the program and the program had separated itself from John. From the day I took the job, anytime I was in town, I would have breakfast with John Jardine.

He introduced me to the people I needed to know and identified the people I needed to stay away from. He put me in touch with some bankers who could get some nice interest rates for my assistants, and he basically clued me in on what I needed to know about community and campus politics. I used him as a sounding board to get my program started.

I was looking for a link to what had happened at Wisconsin — someone who had been through it all — because I wanted to learn the history behind everything. I wanted to identify certain hurdles, and I wanted people to identify with me and what I was trying to accomplish. I felt John Jardine was the best person to help me. From talking with others, I knew he was a hard-nosed coach and we were probably alike in how we wanted the game to be played.

John had recruited heavily in Chicago and the Midwest, my areas at Iowa and Notre Dame. So we were in agreement on the type of players that were needed to compete at the Big Ten level. It's funny, or maybe not so funny, but I took one look at Wisconsin's recruiting list — the list of players Morton's assistants were on before the coaching change — and I wrinkled it up and threw the list in a waste basket.

We were starting from scratch.

***

I felt we had to keep the kids in-state. That was a priority. I had to get Brent Moss, a running back from Racine; Jeff Messenger, a defensive back from Marinette; and Mike Thompson, a defensive tackle from Portage.

Mike Verstegen, a potential offensive lineman from Kimberly, was evaluated as somewhat of a "tweener" because he was about 215 pounds as a high school senior and some of my assistants weren't sure we could put enough weight on him. But I liked his attitude.

I knew we could get Mike Roan, a tight end from Iowa City. The Hawkeyes couldn't make a decision on him, so Dan McCarney closed the deal. It didn't hurt our chances, either, that Roan had taken my daughter Stacy to the prom.

Most of my assistants tapped into recruiting areas where they had been successful in the past. McCarney had contacts in the Twin Cities, and he went up there and landed Mark Montgomery, a good-looking running back out of St. Paul.

One of Bill Callahan's friends called and tipped him off to a prospect who wasn't getting any recruiting traffic because his high school was way out in the country. But the kid was big, tough and fast. And after watching some film, we didn't hesitate to snatch up Carlos Fowler, a defensive tackle from Pontiac, Illinois.

That's the way it went. We got such a late start on recruiting that we had to go out and find players. Most of the high-profile ones had already committed to college programs. In the process of finding out who was available, we also had to find out who was a solid commitment and who might be wavering and willing to jump ship.

My cousin, David Vallina — I nicknamed him "Bimbo" — was checking out some different leads in the Burgettstown area when he came across a player from Belle Vernon, Pennsylvania. Bimbo called and said, "Barry, there's a kid on the basketball team who's about 6-2 and 245 pounds, and he can stuff the basketball. He's a great athlete."

Even though most of the college recruiters didn't like Joe Rudolph as a linebacker, we liked Joe's intangibles, and he turned out to be a helluva offensive guard for us. Rudolph fit our mold. He was a tough kid who liked football. That's who we brought in.

Since two Wisconsin kids — Southern Door's Jim Flanigan and Milwaukee's Greg McThomas — had committed to me at Notre Dame, I decided to take a run at them to see if maybe they would be interested in following me to Wisconsin.

McThomas was ready to flip and told me that he was coming. But his mother wouldn't let him make that choice, and he eventually wound up at Michigan.

"Are you sure you want to go to Notre Dame?" I asked Flanigan.

"No question, coach. I want to go there."

"Fine," I told him. "But do me a favor. Take a recruiting visit to

Madison and give me some credibility. Come here, and have a fun weekend. I'll leave you alone. I won't even invite you into my office. I won't try and twist your arm or change your thinking.

"But after your visit, I want you to talk with the newspaper media and say some positive things about me and the Wisconsin program."

And that's what he did.

Fact is, we had gotten positive publicity when I took the job, a lot more than they had had here in years. I had the ball rolling, but I wanted to keep it rolling. And I knew I could because I had guys who could recruit: McCarney, Callahan, Wyatt and Cosgrove. My pit bulls.

In the office, I had Rob Ianello to organize recruiting. He was my "Vinny" — the equivalent of Notre Dame's recruiting coordinator, Vinny Cerrato.

Ianello didn't evaluate prospects, per se. But he determined who was going to be on the road, where they were going to be recruiting, and where I needed to be. He really did a good job on the phone, organizing our recruiting weekends.

In retrospect, it was unbelievable what we were able to do in such a short period of time that first year. With about three weeks left before the signing date, we went out and recruited a class that formed the foundation of our first Rose Bowl team.

What's even more remarkable is that we didn't have anything to hang our hats on. Kids wanted to go to bowl games — and, hell, the Badgers hadn't been to a bowl since 1984. So we were selling blue sky, or the promise of things to come.

"When I went to Nebraska," I told recruits, "they were losing until Bob Devaney came in and turned the program around. And today, those players who were part of the turnaround are still considered special in the state of Nebraska.

"When I went to Iowa," I went on, "they were losing until Hayden Fry came in and turned the program around. And today, those players are still revered in the state because nobody believed you could win there — except them — and they made Iowa a winner.

"You can do that here, you can be part of the process at Wisconsin," I said. "Be special. Don't be afraid to separate yourself from others. It's easy to go to a program that has been winning. But if you go to a Michigan, you're just another guy there.

"If you come to our place, though, if you come to Wisconsin, you can be really special. You can be part of the turnaround. You can play sooner than you can play anywhere else. And you won't find a school where the coaches will care more about you."

***

Recently, I had a former NCAA compliance employee relate an interesting story. He was working compliance when I took the Wisconsin job, and he said I wouldn't believe the number of recruiting violations that other schools had filed against us the first few years.

He said it was a ridiculous number of accusations, and that the predominant complaint the NCAA kept hearing from our competition was, "Wisconsin can't be getting so many good players, especially on the East Coast, without cheating."

One of the NCAA's top people, David Berst, called a meeting specifically to discuss Wisconsin and all the accusations that had been submitted.

After checking out everything, Berst said, "There are some coaches out there who just work harder than other coaches. Some just get it done. Some know how to win and recruit, and I think that's what we have here with Wisconsin. These other coaches have expressed their concerns about the Badgers, but they really haven't done anything wrong."

Case closed.

When you take a new job, you're naturally aggressive. We knew the rules, and we followed the rules. But other coaches were intimidated by our presence because they wanted to maintain the status quo. Wisconsin had been losing and anchored at the bottom of the Big Ten, and a lot of people didn't want to see us climbing the ladder.

They didn't want the Badgers to be good.

One of those schools, Illinois, was more worried about what we were doing than what they were doing. And they were one of the schools that kept turning us in. They've had something like five different head coaches over my 16 seasons at Wisconsin.

Case closed.

Back in the early '90s, I had some real grinders on my staff. I had guys who would go out on the road and hustle and rattle cages. They weren't going to take no for an answer. And we didn't back off anybody. We didn't care who else was recruiting them. We felt if we could get a player on campus, we could sell him. We just had to survive that first season.

***

One of my first reality checks in 1990 came while I was watching our returning players during an out-of-season workout. We had some big linemen, but they couldn't move very well. We had a couple of quarterbacks who were out of their league. And we had no running backs. None. So I'm thinking, "How the hell are we going to move the ball?"

Defensively, I felt we could do some things.

Don Davey is what you look for in a defensive tackle. He could have started at Notre Dame. He could have played anywhere. He was intense, he was competitive, and he was very smart. He bought into our program and realized we knew what we were doing.

I can remember making our whole team watch defensive game film. "Now, watch No. 91, watch Don Davey, watch his speed," I said, using Davey as my teaching tool. "He's playing faster than anybody else on the field because he's turning it loose and playing hard. We need more guys to play like Don."

When we got here, Troy Vincent didn't have much confidence in himself as a defensive back. But he was just loaded with talent. I can remember telling Troy that he was a better player than Todd Lyght, who was a starting corner on our national championship team at Notre Dame. Troy was a little bigger, faster, and more physical than Todd.

As Troy Vincent gained confidence, we put him on the other team's best receiver, and he would lock him up, shut him down. We didn't have to worry about doubling anybody. That allowed us to put an extra guy closer to the line of scrimmage to stop the run. There were times when Troy was also our best offensive threat as a kick returner.

We could have used a few more players like Davey and Vincent, especially on offense. That was painfully obvious to me during our two-a-day practices leading up to the start of the 1990 season.

At the end of training camp, I'll go over team goals with our assistants. By then, we've practiced enough to know what kind of team we think we're going to have. I demand just one thing from each of them: let's be realistic.

At the end of camp, the players also have their forum to set goals.

"I think we should win every goddamn game," shouted Nick

Polczinski, a senior and starting offensive guard. "Anybody who doesn't agree with me, I'll kick their ass."

I raised my hand.

"I don't agree with you," I said.

A hush fell over the room.

"I've watched you practice as a team," I reasoned. "And two years ago I was with a team that won all of its games and a national championship. Trust me, we're not good enough to win all of our games. So let's be realistic and set some reachable goals."

I can't even remember what goals we set that first year. But it sure as hell wasn't winning all of our games. I didn't want them kidding themselves because that's what they had been doing here for the last three years — pretending they were players when they were not.

***

In trying to create interest and sell tickets, somebody came up with the marketing slogan "It's a Whole New Animal" for the 1990 season.

Too bad that wasn't us — a whole new animal. I knew we weren't going to be much of a different animal from the previous season.

Maybe if we had won our opener against California, we'd have had a chance to win four or five games. I felt like we could have been up 14-0 in the first half against Cal, but we made too many mistakes in the red zone that kept us from scoring. Plus, there was a split officiating crew — Pac 10 and Big 10 — and I felt like we got hosed by the West Coast officials.

A couple of years later, a Big Ten official who was retiring told me that the Big Ten officials got into a big argument with the Pac 10 officials at halftime over some questionable calls against us. The feeling was that the Pac 10 crew was protecting the Pac 10 team.

When John Cooper was coaching at Ohio State, he always said the same thing, and Cooper should know since he also coached in the Pac 10 at Arizona State.

On our first possession, after a Cal turnover, Lionell Crawford is called for a motion penalty that wipes out a touchdown. Instead of 7-0, we have to settle for a field goal.

We knock the ball loose again and recover on Cal's second possession, but we lose momentum because of a holding penalty and have to settle for another field goal.

We should be up 14-0, but instead it's 6-0. That was frustrating because it changed the way I coached the game in the second quarter. I would have been much more conservative — I wouldn't have been throwing — if we had the lead.

What happens?

Just before the half, Tony Lowery throws an interception and Cal returns it 100 yards for a touchdown, and they go up 21-6. That really took the wind out of us, and we weren't strong enough to recover.

The following week, we bounced back and beat Ball State for our only win. We should have beaten Temple but found a way to lose 24-18. So we could have been 3-0 going into the Big Ten.

If that happens, then maybe we win one or two conference games because we have a little confidence. We weren't much better than that because we couldn't move the ball, except at Northwestern, where we scored 34 points and still got beat 44-34.

That was such a low point. Northwestern was terrible, but we were worse. My Uncle John showed up in Evanston for the game because he knew I was in the tank. He used to call me every Sunday and at least once during the week. He could tell I needed support. But what I needed more than anything else was players, Big Ten players.

***

On the night before a game, we got into the habit of taking our kids to a movie. We wanted to give them a break from the preparation and a chance to relax.

What I remember most about our first group is that we had some players who acted like they were still in junior high school. They were throwing popcorn and candy at each other. They were getting up every two seconds and running in and out of the theater.

The last thing on their mind was relaxing and getting ready for a game. It was a circus. And here I was, a rookie head coach, sitting there in the dark, and I was just cringing. "What the hell have I gotten myself into?"

Needless to say, I was relieved when that year was over.

But for all the lows, and there were enough to last a lifetime, we did end on somewhat of a high note. Even though we lost at Michigan State, it was a game that we could have easily won — a wide-open receiver dropped a pass in the end zone — and our competitiveness sent the message to me that the kids were still playing hard.

Going into the game, we were 1-9 and a 29-point underdog, and we had nothing to play for except pride. Our kids went out and played their hearts out, losing 14-9 to a Michigan State team that earned a share of the Big Ten championship.

Had we won, it would have been a helluva way to end the season, and it would have given us momentum going into the following year. Still, I appreciated the effort we got at East Lansing.

We could definitely build on that.

I really appreciated how our seniors played. Davey, Vincent, Polczinski, Greg Thomas, LaMarr White, Bill Williams, Brady Pierce, Dan Batsch and Jim Basten.

"When we go to our first Rose Bowl," I promised them, "I will send each of you a Rose Bowl watch."

Coming off a 1-10 season, I'm sure some of them were skeptical. Some of them probably thought I was losing my mind.

But I believed in what I was saying.

CHAPTER SEVEN
Beginning to Believe in the Plan

Hosea Fletcher, the father of Terrell Fletcher, wanted to make sure I knew something about his son before I left their St. Louis home. As I'm getting ready to walk out the door, Hosea looked me in the eyes and said, "If my son comes to Wisconsin, you're going to win."

I stopped dead in my tracks.

We're coming off a 1-10 season, but that didn't stop me from saying, "Hosea, whether your son comes to Wisconsin or not, we're going to win."

Kevin Cosgrove's jaw almost hit the floor.

Cos was our St. Louis area recruiter, and he had worked his fanny off to get the home visit and keep us in the mix for Terrell. It was coming down to Wisconsin and Ohio State, and Terrell had a close friend going to Columbus, which was not helping us.

And now, because I spouted off, Cos has got to be thinking that I'm going to blow any chance we had of getting the kid.

Hosea Fletcher, though, looked at me and started laughing.

"Coach, I know you will," he said. "I know you will win."

That second year, we signed some good players: Terrell Fletcher, Lee DeRamus, Cory Raymer, Eric Unverzagt, Jason Maniecki and Michael London.

The problem was that Fletcher wasn't quite ready physically as a true freshman — and our offensive line wasn't quite ready, either — but Fletch was one of our only weapons on offense, and we had no other choice but to throw him into the fire.

As he gained experience, Fletcher was really creative. He made some of the most unbelievable cuts I've ever seen. He could make you miss, he could catch it coming out of the backfield, and he could hit a home run anytime he touched the ball.

Fletcher's running style was the perfect complement to the Alley Cat. That's what I called Brent Moss.

You know how an old alley cat will drag itself home after a rough Saturday night, with patches of hair torn out of its face? That's how Moss came back one weekend. A patch of his hair was gone, half of his eyebrow was gone, a patch of his face was gone.

"Where the hell you been?" I asked.

"Went home to Racine," he said matter of factly.

He didn't have to tell me anymore.

He was a tough, tough nut. I never coached anybody who finished every run like Moss did. If you watched him, you would see him get hit at the line of scrimmage, but he would keep his feet moving and his legs pumping until he went down.

I've coached some great running backs during my 16 years at Wisconsin, but if it's fourth down-and-1, Moss would be the one I would want to get that yard.

Moss and Fletcher were really good together because they were so competitive.

During their junior years, Moss didn't want to give up any reps because he knew Fletcher was right on his tail. Moss loved to play, and he didn't want to share. He didn't want Fletch to get more carries.

I'll never forget a hit that Moss took at Purdue. The free safety cornered him on our sideline — right in front of me — and he caught Moss flush on the chin.

Moss' eyes rolled back in his head, and he was out cold before he hit the ground.

Our trainers revived him and got him over to the bench. But two plays later, Moss is grabbing my arm and saying, "Coach, I want to go back in."

"No, you can't go back in," I explained to him. "You've just been knocked out."

"I don't give a bleep," Moss argued. "I want back in that game."

Moss and Fletcher turned out to be a helluva one-two punch. But they both had to grow into their roles, and they weren't alone. Everybody had growing pains the first few years.

Including me.

***

I knew what some of the other head coaches at Wisconsin were probably thinking and maybe even saying behind my back: "Who the hell does Alvarez think he is? And what the hell does he think he's doing? He's only been around here a year, and he's going to call a meeting to tell us how to handle our business? Alvarez has some nerve."

All I wanted to do was to say what was on my mind.

In late March of 1991, the UW athletic board announced it was cutting five sports: men's and women's gymnastics, men's and women's fencing, and baseball. The official vote took place in late April and passed by a 10-7 margin, reducing the number of sports from 25 to 20.

It led to a contentious debate.

Football was isolated from the other sports. We were sitting on an island at one end of the stadium and, as coaches, we didn't mingle very much with the other coaches. We were just grinding away, trying to get over that 1-10 season.

But I'm attached to Pat Richter, who hired me, and he was getting attacked. Our whole athletic program was under siege, and I felt enough was enough.

We had coaches who were running their business through the media. Maybe they were looking over their shoulders, fearing more cuts, I don't know. But almost every memo issued within the department would show up in the paper the next day.

There was tremendous disloyalty within the ranks, and I had never been around something like this before. There was no trust among the coaches. I'm a team player, and I didn't like the atmosphere.

So I called a meeting of all the head coaches.

"We've got to pull together," I said. "Right now, as a program, we look terrible, we look like a bunch of fools, buffoons, because all of our business is on the street. We've got to keep things in-house. If you've got issues, go and talk with Pat. Don't go to the papers, because if you do, it makes us all look bad."

Before the athletic board even took the final vote on cutting sports, I lost a quarterback, Joe Wagner, a redshirt freshman from Adams-Friendship. Just before the start of spring practice in early April, he decided to quit the football team so that he could concentrate on furthering his baseball career as a pitcher.

During the recruiting process, Wagner was seriously considering Arkansas before we came up with an arrangement here allowing him to play both sports. I'd let him work on baseball during the off-season. In the spring he'd practice with the football team, but I'd make him available to baseball on off-days and at the end of spring drills.

I felt like some of the baseball people tried to use Wagner as a pawn when their sport was on the chopping block. One person, Wagner, was not going to make a difference on whether or not the athletic department was going to cut baseball.

All of a sudden, I was being asked to make Wagner available on Fridays and Saturdays in the spring. I reminded the baseball people that we had already agreed on the ground rules and how we were both going to use Wagner. I needed him to scrimmage on Saturdays — I needed him there — because he was going to be our starting quarterback.

"If you can't give him the time off," I was told, "and he can't be with the baseball team on weekends, then he's going to quit football."

My response to that threat was, "If he's not going to scrimmage with us on weekends, then he might as well give it up."

And he did.

I found out later that he had already been shopped around to other schools. Even if I could do it over again — and make some concessions to when he practiced with us and when he played baseball — he still would have transferred. (He ended up at Central Florida and played two years there before being drafted by the Milwaukee Brewers.)

Joe Wagner could have been a helluva quarterback.

He was a real talent. He was smart and tough. He could run, and he had an unbelievably strong arm. He was exactly what you were looking for. He would have been our starting quarterback for the next four years, and he would have gotten better as he went along, giving us a chance to win sooner than we did.

***

We opened the 1991 season with Western Illinois, a Division I-AA opponent, and I knew it was going to be hard to get people in the stands. Since we had to get the word out on our program — to help fill those seats — we sent our graduate assistant coaches to every high school in the state that had a player on the roster.

The GAs were pitching group sales — bus trips to Madison — with the idea of getting the high schools to buy a block of tickets in support of their hometown player.

The first few years, we were constantly selling ourselves in the community and around the state. I was doing two and three speeches a day, and I was gone just about every weekend. Pat Richter was the same way. People kept telling us to slow down, but we never did.

Knowing the students were important, I assigned each of my assistants to a fraternity, a sorority, and a dorm.

Each coach was also responsible for talking to a dean on campus. While they learned more about our football program and goals, we learned more about the system and academics. Once they found out more about us, some deans even helped us in recruiting.

Overall, I wanted to put our stamp on everything we believed in.

Love.

Trust.

Commitment.

Belief.

We were building our program around those meat and potatoes principles. It was nothing original, and I can't take credit, since that's what Lou Holtz stressed at Notre Dame and every other school where he has ever coached. That was his deal. But I believed in it, and I thought we could sink our teeth into it at Wisconsin. If the guys bought it, we'd have some type of substance.

We needed to start somewhere.

During one of our first staff meetings in Madison, I remember looking around the table and seeing everybody wearing a prominent ring on their finger. I was wearing my Notre Dame national championship ring. Dan McCarney had an Iowa Rose Bowl ring. And Bill Callahan and Kevin Cosgrove were wearing Illinois Rose Bowl rings.

That was not the impression I wanted to make on recruits. I wanted to emphasize our future, not our past. So I went out and had University of Wisconsin rings made for everybody on our staff. I thought that was important. I wanted the ring to be a part of our identity.

"Put away the old rings," I told my assistants. "We're all here now, we're all in this together, and we're not going to dwell on where we've been. Instead, we want to establish an identity based on where we're going. This is going to be our program, and this is what we're selling."

I even changed the logo on our helmets, adopting a Motion W. As soon as I saw the design — and we had a bunch of different options — I knew that's what I wanted. It was distinct, it had a clean look, and it didn't vary that much from the old Block W.

I was consistent. I kept the uniform clean, too. Two stripes on the helmet, two stripes on the jersey, two stripes on the pants. I don't like all the razzmatazz.

But you should have seen the nasty letters I got. And I know that I took flack from angry callers on radio talk shows. Why? Because I decided not to put the names of the players on the backs of the jerseys.

When the players asked me about it, I said, "Let's wait until we go to a bowl game. Let's earn the right to wear our names on the jerseys."

I didn't know how long that would take.

Because of that uncertainty, and because I wanted to reward the kids we had just brought into the program — I wanted to do something special for our first three recruiting classes — I jumped at the chance to play a game in Tokyo, Japan.

In the spring of 1992, I was contacted about moving our October 2, 1993, home game against Michigan State to Japan. We'd play the Spartans on December 5 in the Tokyo Dome. I felt like the experience and exposure from such a trip would be priceless.

Sitting here today as the athletic director, it would be hard for me to give up a home game under any circumstances because of the money that is generated. Not many athletic directors would have said "yes" to me in '92, either. But Pat Richter agreed to the move, which really showed how supportive Pat was of me and the football program.

Although I was concerned about giving up a game at Camp Randall Stadium, I knew that we would have the competitive edge on Michigan State for a number of reasons, and I just believed the positives outweighed any negatives.

"I think we should have a real good football game in 1993," I remember saying shortly after we signed the contract to play the Spartans in Tokyo. "It could be a prime TV game (which I was counting on), and it could be a very important game."

Little did I know then how important — or that a trip to the Rose Bowl might be riding on the outcome of a game played thousands of miles away in Asia.

***

"If we can't beat Wisconsin, if we can't beat a freshman-sophomore team in the second year of their program," Iowa State's Jim Walden said before we played, "then there's something wrong with us because we've been building for five years."

In an old-fashioned slugfest, we beat Iowa State 7-6 — the second of three straight wins to open the '91 season. That showed me we had come a helluva long way from 1-10, even though we were still young and not where we needed to be.

The following week, we lost 31-16 at Ohio State, but I felt it was one of the earliest turning points for our program. Our defense continued to give us a chance to be competitive, even in Columbus. Going into the fourth quarter, we only trailed 14-2.

In the final three minutes, we scored on touchdown drives of 66 and 67 yards, with freshmen playing at key skill positions — Jay Macias at quarterback, Terrell Fletcher at tailback, Lee DeRamus at wide receiver, and Mike Roan at tight end.

Fletcher was our leading receiver and rusher against Ohio State. On the second play of the game, he bounced off several tacklers on the line of scrimmage and battled to a 29-yard run. He also picked up 23 yards on a screen pass. He could be elusive.

What really stood out was that our freshmen weren't intimidated by the Buckeyes or playing on the road in Ohio Stadium. Leaving the field that day, I felt really good that these young guys could play in the Big Ten. Given some time to grow, I was thinking, "we're going to be damn competitive pretty quick."

We were really close at the end of '91. We won our last two games, including a rare road victory at Minnesota. That snapped a 23-game road losing streak for the Badgers. That was also my first Big Ten win and Wisconsin's first conference win in the last 20 games.

Those were some ugly streaks.

From the time we took over the program, we were trying to get the players to feel good about themselves. I don't think some of the holdovers believed they could win because they hadn't had success here in the past.

We had to give them confidence. We had to show them how to win. And we had to put them in positions where they could have some success. We did that in 1992.

We should have won eight or nine games.

We should have been a bowl team.

***

Washington, the defending co-national champion, was a 33-point favorite in the '92 season opener at Seattle. We lost 27-10. But the score was deceptive. Our guys got after them big-time, and the Huskies knew that they were in a four-quarter game.

They had unbelievable fire power on offense with Napolean Kaufman at tailback and Billy Joe Hobert and Mark Brunell at quarterback. But we matched up well, and their All-American offensive tackle, Lincoln Kennedy, came up to me afterward and said, "Coach, you've got a good team. We may see you in the Rose Bowl."

I still second-guess myself for not starting Darrell Bevell at quarterback. I don't think they were expecting much of a game from us, and I really think we could have ambushed them, and maybe even beaten them, if Bevell had played from the start. Especially since Washington had trouble covering DeRamus. He was running free all day.

The next week in practice we made the switch from Macias to Bevell. He gave us some stability, and the kids respected him. For two years, we had been scrounging and begging for a quarterback. We needed one so bad, and Bevell filled that void.

He wasn't the greatest athlete, but he knew his limitations, he was intelligent, and he knew what we were trying to do on offense. He always knew where to go with the football, and he would rarely get you beat. Bevell was our catalyst. He tied it all together.

There's something about being a coach's kid — Darrell's dad, Jim, is a high school coach in Arizona — that distinguishes players. Growing up, they live with the game, and they understand what it's all about. They develop a sense of what is important to coaches.

And that's really valuable for a quarterback — like Bevell or Brooks Bollinger, who was also a coach's kid — because they've got their head in the huddle and they're the decision-maker and coach on the field. As a player, Bev thought like a coach.

Hell, he was older than our grad assistants. He was 21 when he signed his tender, just three months younger than Brett Favre, who was starting in Green Bay. I knew Bev would make a good coach some day.

I just didn't know how good of a quarterback he was going to be.

Brad Childress had developed a relationship with Bevell at Northern Arizona, where Childress was an assistant (so was Billy Callahan) and Bevell was redshirting as a freshman. When Chilly joined my staff in

1991, he looked up Bev, who had just completed a two-year mission for the Mormon Church in northern Ohio.

Bevell was hoping to be sent to New Zealand or Australia — where most of his friends were going on their missions. Instead, he wound up in Cleveland.

Bevell liked telling about how going door-to-door taught him that Rottweilers are nothing to fool with, and that if somebody comes to the door with a gun, it's time to knock on another door.

During his exile from competitive sports, he tried to keep his arm limber by throwing a football to his fellow missionaries, but he said most of them quit on him because he threw too hard. Bev? Throwing too hard?

When he first showed up at Wisconsin for winter conditioning, he was in terrible shape. He hadn't been working out, and he pulled every muscle in his legs the first day.

He always used to joke that we reassigned him to the cross country team because he was running laps while everybody else was doing the drills.

Bevell once conceded to me, "Coach, you had to be going out of your mind wondering, 'What kind of quarterback did Brad Childress bring in here?'"

***

Childress was part of that Illinois connection with Cosgrove and Callahan. In the early '80s, they were all on Mike White's coaching staff. Childress went to school in Champaign and worked as an assistant there for eight seasons.

In 1992, I named Childress as my offensive coordinator, replacing Russ Jacques. It was a tough call because I picked Chilly over Bill Callahan, my O-line coach.

Both were strong coaches, and I felt like both would be head coaches. Billy not only took a team — the Oakland Raiders — to the Super Bowl, but he's now the head coach at my alma mater in Lincoln. And I know he will do a good job at Nebraska.

But I had to make a decision on a coordinator, and even though Billy had been with me at Wisconsin two years longer, I felt Brad was the right guy at that time.

Chilly was a good football man. I liked his demeanor and the way he handled people. I didn't think he was a flincher. He was a leader, and I

My mother was big on spit curls. My hair became an issue as I grew older. While everyone else in the neighborhood had flat tops, my hair was too curly and I couldn't get one. I wish I had some of that hair back.

I was 10 here, and getting ready to go into the fifth grade. That bow tie was pretty dapper. Yeah, right. That was the only sport coat I owned. Not that there were a lot of places that called for a coat-and-tie where I was raised.

You're looking at the Burgettstown Lions, my midget football team. I was a starting tackle on both sides of the ball. The following year, I played quarterback in junior high. I was the only one who knew the plays.

Spanky and Our Gang? Not quite. But that's me (lower right) and the fellows chowing down during the middle of two-a-days my sophomore year of high school. Our Burgettstown booster club paid for the lunches at a restaurant that was walking distance of the practice field. My best friend, Jim Nicksick, is on my right.

I was 17 when I graduated from high school. Like most young kids, I went to college not knowing what I wanted to do; beyond knowing I wanted to play football.

As a senior, I was a Mike Linebacker, or strongside linebacker, on one of the better defenses, statistically, in the nation. I played a physical brand of football. You had to be physical to survive in the Big 8. Back then, teams would line up with two tight ends and run toss plays until you stopped them. They weren't spreading you out and throwing the football.

After my senior year at Nebraska, they held a recognition dinner for me in Langeloth. They had a good turnout, too. The people in the community followed my career and were always very supportive even though I never played close to home. That's my brother (left to right), my grandmother, Cindy, mom and dad.

Football was never out of season in Nebraska. There was always something going on for the players. Even after you were done playing. Here we are - Cindy and I - at a party for the seniors at the Falstaff Brewery in Omaha.

Cindy and I were married in the chapel overlooking JFK's gravesite at Arlington National Cemetery in Washington, D.C. At the time, her father was a two-star general stationed at the Pentagon.

That was one of the last pictures of Wella, my grandmother. She was one of the all-time great cooks. She was dynamite in the kitchen and made a terrific Spanish stew. Growing up in the depression, she made you clean your plate, too.

My mother loved people, and loved to talk. She was proud of her sons, and she took pride in my teams. No one supported me more than her. And she would fight at the drop of the hat if she thought I wasn't getting the proper credit.

My son Chad was always right in the middle of everything. At Notre Dame, he would be at practice during the week and on the sidelines during our games. Lou Holtz really liked him. Chad and my dad really got along great. Chad even lived with him for a year.

This was a fishing trip on Lake Michigan with two of my Nebraska teammates, Dan Delaney (far left) and Wayne Meylan, a member of the College Football Hall of Fame. Wayne had a place outside of Ludington, Michigan. His hobby was flying World War II fighter planes in air shows. A year after this picture was taken, Wayne was killed in a plane crash. He was 41.

Before we played West Virginia for the national championship, I had a reunion in Phoenix with my old college roomies. Mick Ziegler (far left) was a running back. Ziggy went to high school with Cindy in Lincoln. Bob Taucher was a big offensive tackle, and a seventh round pick of Dallas in 1968.

John Melton (left) was from Slovan, which bumps up to Langeloth and Burgettstown. John recruited me to Nebraska. Dan McCarney, a great friend, recruited me to Iowa. At least he had as much to do as anyone with getting me into college football, and getting me the job with Hayden and the Hawkeyes. Mac was the first guy I hired at Wisconsin.

Cousin and business partner, Bimbo (aka David Vallina). He's always been like a brother. In the mid-80s, we got involved with a strip mall in Burgettstown. Among other things, we've got a convenience store, a physical therapy gym and Bimbo's Ice Cream.

My uncle John and his wife, Shirley, were in on the surprise - a surprise 50th birthday party that Cindy threw for me. My uncle John was a combination big brother and dad. He always knew when I needed encouragement or a kick in the butt.

Pat McGraw (foreground), my high school coach, was a tough old Irishman, who loved kids and loved to coach. There was only one way to do things - his way. He built pride in a small school and gave everyone the confidence that they could succeed. John Palermo (center) was my defensive line coach at Notre Dame and Wisconsin.

In 1972, Lincoln Northeast won the Nebraska state championship. That's me in the second row, far right. I was in my third year as an assistant coach. We were coming off two losing seasons, but this was a team that had players who knew their roles and did their job. And because they did what they were asked to do, the pieces all fell into place.

photo by Rick 'sulli' Sullivan.

That's me (with the bald head) and my starting quarterback, Mark McManigal, at Mason City celebrating our victory in the state championship game. He was a tough competitor, and one of my favorite players. The story behind the bald look? I promised if we won in the semifinals, I'd shave my head.

Iowa linebacker Larry Station was one of my better players. He was smart and physical and very active. He never got knocked off his feet. My two best linebackers were both under 6-feet. Station and Notre Dame's Michael Stonebreaker.

That's our second Rose Bowl team at Iowa. We had a tremendous leader in Hayden Fry. Many of the guys in this picture, who went on to become head coaches, copied his organizational blue print in building their programs. Every assistant took pride in what they were doing, and didn't want to let anybody down on the staff (from left to right): Bill Snyder, Carl Jackson, Don Patterson, me, Dan McCarney, Bernie Wyatt, Bill Brashier, Hayden, Del Miller and Kirk Ferentz.

Hayden and his posse. We all gathered in New York City for Hayden Fry's induction into the College Football Hall of Fame. That's former Kansas State head coach Bill Snyder (far right), who was Hayden's offensive coordinator, and Bill Brashier, our defensive coordinator, who was from Hayden's home town in Texas. One of the travesties in our business is that Brashier never got a chance to be a head coach.

Hayden Fry was responsible for furthering the development of many young assistants who went on to be successful head coaches. Oklahoma's Bobby Stoops (far left) played for Hayden and later served as a volunteer and grad assistant. To my left are Dan McCarney, who coached the defensive line and Kirk Ferentz (far right), who coached the offensive line. Dan is now the head coach at Iowa State, and Kirk at Iowa.

Hayden Fry was one of the great characters and head coaches in college football. Wherever he went, he turned the program around and was successful, much like Bob Devaney, and Lou Holtz. I learned a great deal about the game from Hayden and used many of his ideas when I got the Wisconsin job. He gave me a chance to get into coaching at the collegiate level. And he was a mentor.

I don't think you realize the tradition or the magnitude of Notre Dame until you get there, and you live through it. The first year I worked with Foge Fazio and I learned a lot from Foge. And, then, to have the opportunity to run my own defense for the first time on the big stage was invaluable to my growth as a coach.

Lou Holtz was a tremendous mentor. And I consider him a close friend. Many of the things I've believed in - the things I've hung my hat on as a coach - are because of his tutelage. I had three wonderful years working for him at Notre Dame.

I was going on adrenaline during my introductory press conference at Wisconsin in 1990. I didn't get more than two hours of sleep after coaching the night before in the Orange Bowl. But I was really excited to be taking over my own program. At that point, I thought I had all the answers, too. I didn't know what I was getting myself into. It was a lot like when I took the Mason City job in Iowa. I really didn't know how bad the situation was. And I really didn't care.

Most Badger fans will forever have this vision of Darrell Bevell holding up the ball after a memorable touchdown run against UCLA in our first Rose Bowl win. You really didn't see him flush out of the pocket very often, but he did on this play. I don't know why he did, but I'm glad he did. As a player, he was an overachiever, who played the game the right way. Football was important to him. He lived it. And now he's having success in the coaching profession for the same reasons.

That was a very emotional post-game celebration for all of us - including Ron Dayne and Chris McIntosh who are pictured here with me - following our 1999 victory over Iowa at Camp Randall Stadium. That may have been the best atmosphere I've ever been around. Ron not only broke Ricky Williams' rushing mark but we clinched the Big Ten championship and a trip to the Rose Bowl. That was a very special day and I've never heard it louder in that stadium. It was electric.

Ron Dayne was en fuego during our second Rose Bowl win over UCLA. They simply couldn't stop him. They couldn't tackle him. He had a lot of great games during his career and that may have been as good as any of them. Even though that wasn't a very good defense, all of Dayne's skills were on display. He was such a patient runner and once he got into the open field nobody caught him.

Stanford's Tyrone Willingham and I celebrated our birthdays on the same day, December 30. And we both got tired of the media playing off that storyline leading up to the Rose Bowl. The day before the game, we both rolled our eyes when they presented us with yet another cake for yet another photo op. I got up and said, "The one thing no one has recognized - and I can't believe no one has researched this - is the fact that Tyrone and I are actually twins separated at birth." I think that was the only time he smiled that week.

Marshall coach Bob Pruitt was on my right while our two players - Chad Pennington and Ron Dayne - were seated in front of us during the Heisman Trophy presentation at the Downtown Athletic Club in New York City. We were all waiting for them to announce the final results and the winner. The network was on a commercial break when this photo was taken. Shortly thereafter, two people ran up to Ron and one was wiping him down while the other was putting make-up on him. Pruitt looked at me and said, "I guess that's a dead giveaway who is going to win."

That's my brother Woody (second from right) and three close friends at Ohio State (from right to left) Tony Canonie, John Flesch and Ted Kellner. I've grown very close with all three guys. Each has a different business and we get together several times each year to talk about different management styles. They've been great sounding boards.

Dating to my days as a high school player in western Pennsylvania, I've always had great respect for Joe Paterno and what he has done at Penn State. He's a college football icon. Whenever I brought one of my Wisconsin teams to State College, there would be someone from Burgettstown or Langeloth sitting behind our bench and cheering for us. On our last trip, we had a late kick-off so Cindy and I took a walk on campus the morning of the game and the people couldn't have been more friendly. Maybe they felt sorry for an old coal miner from the other side of the state.

Pat Richter allowed me to do my job. He was very supportive and never interfered. He entrusted me with the football program and he provided me with whatever I needed. I always felt Pat had confidence in me. Plus, he realized that we had to do well in football for the athletic department to move forward. Chancellor Shalala sent a message that there was support from the top and it just wasn't lip service. That's a step in the right direction when you have somebody like that in your corner; somebody who will take a stand for your program and believes athletics are important.

This was something I had thought about for a long time and when we made the announcement that my defensive coordinator Bret Bielema was going to be my successor at Wisconsin, it was very emotional for me. In the same respect, I was relieved because there was a weight off my shoulders. I feel good about the future of our program. Years ago, Bob Devaney told me that to be a successful head coach in Division I, you have to have a presence, and Bret definitely has that.

Here are some of my all-time favorite Badger fans: my grandsons Joe and Jake Ferguson and granddaughter Scarlett Alvarez (left) and grand-daughter Grace Delzer and her brother Jackson (right).

Cindy and I with the whole group: my son-in-law Brad Ferguson, grand-sons Jake and Joe Ferguson alongside my daughter Dawn, my daughter Stacy and her husband Mike Delzer holding their kids Jackson and Grace Delzer, and my son Chad and his wife Stephanie who recently became parents to the newest member of the Alvarez family, Scarlett.

had the sense he would do a good job. He knew the passing game, which he learned from Mike White.

I had confidence in Chilly. He had a good rapport with the players, and they responded to him. He communicated well. At the same time, he could be tough if he had to be.

In choosing an offensive coordinator, I don't necessarily need someone who is like me, or someone who has the same personality, or someone who thinks along my lines. I tell the coordinator what type of offense I want, and what I want to see, and I let him concoct it.

Before the start of every year, I visit with my staff and go over what I believe in — on both sides of the ball. What's important? What's not important? How do we win on offense? How do we win on defense?

It's important that everyone understands what we're trying to accomplish, and that they recognize that all three phases have to work together.

If you're really good on defense, and you have a good kicking game, you don't want to take too many chances on offense. You want to be conservative.

If you're struggling on defense, and your kicking game is bad, you have to do some different things and take chances on offense. Maybe you throw the ball a little more.

Everybody gets involved with the game plan during the week of practice. But my offensive coordinator is going to call the plays on game days. Of course, everything goes through me.

And if I want something, I'll tell him.

***

On the recommendation of the former Illinois assistants — Childress, Callahan and Cosgrove — I made a change in my game week routine and incorporated something on Thursday nights which had been successful under Mike White.

Each Thursday, between practice and training table, I began meeting with the players for about 15 to 20 minutes in the McClain Facility auditorium.

The game plan was in — the hay was in the barn, so to speak — and I would just come in and shoot the breeze. No rah-rah. Just me and the players in a casual setting.

We've done research over the years and found that Thursday night is the night you really need rest on game week. On most campuses, though, Thursday night is a big party night. That was the case at Iowa, and that's the case at Wisconsin.

So I wanted to get that point across to the kids: Thursday is the night they had to be off their feet, they had to get some rest, because if they didn't, it would show up on Saturday.

On Thursday mornings, I meet with my assistants and they update me on their position groups. Everybody has a chance to tell me what their guys have to do to help us win, and I take notes on some of the things they feel should be addressed with the players.

Armed with that information, I'll meet with the players after practice, and I'll try to leave them with some type of a message. On Thursday, I'm also going to lay out our weekend schedule and cover everything that might come up. I don't want any surprises.

Sometimes, as a change of pace, I might hand out pens and post cards and tell them, "Write a note to your mother or someone special in your life, someone you really care about. Take the time to tell them that you love them."

Mostly, I want to get them ready for Saturday. If we're playing a road game, I'll tell them about the stadium and the turf and the atmosphere and the locker room. I'll tell them about the opponent and what their mindset might be and what to expect.

"They're going to give you their best shot," I'll warn them, "and we have to be prepared for that right away. We have to match their intensity, and this is what we have to do to win — boom, boom, boom — on offense and defense."

The older guys are sitting in the front row, and they're engaged. Or should be. I can tell if they're paying attention or if they're bored with the whole thing and can't wait to get out of the room and head to dinner at training table.

When you're standing up in front of a large group, you're always going to have some young guys in the back of the room who are daydreaming because they're not involved.

I suppose it's like being a teacher in front of a class, only I'm not going to challenge anybody, I'm not going to ask any hard questions. I'm giving out information.

I had never done anything like this before on Thursdays. Devaney hadn't done it at Nebraska. Fry hadn't done it at Iowa. Holtz hadn't done it at Notre Dame.

But I thought it made a lot of sense. The players liked it. And I've always thought it was one of the good things we've done during my tenure at Wisconsin.

***

I motivated players throughout the week, and while I may have taken a different approach to every game, I always tried to find an edge. I didn't care what it was.

When I came up with a theme, I would go over it with the coaches on Mondays, and they were expected to pound their kids with the theme throughout the week of practice.

I'd use others for motivation, too.

The week of the 1992 Ohio State game, I had the Rev. Jesse Jackson talk to the team after our Tuesday practice. He had spoken to our players at Notre Dame and I was impressed.

If someone influential is speaking on campus — and Jackson was speaking later that night at the UW Field House — I want to put him in front of the players. I want to give them an experience they normally wouldn't have.

Jackson talked to our guys about being confident and seizing the moment.

Whenever I speak to a group, I tell the story, which has been embellished over the years, of how one of our players wanted to know how Jackson got his Mr. October nickname and how he felt when he hit those three home runs in the World Series against the Dodgers.

That's always good for a laugh; the notion that someone had mistaken Jesse Jackson for Reggie Jackson, the former New York Yankee slugger.

Unfortunately, after beating Ohio State 20-16 — our first big win, and Wisconsin's first win over a ranked opponent since 1985 — we won only twice more that season.

Not that we weren't close. We had seven games that were determined in the final two minutes. And we lost four of them by a total of 11 points. That was no laughing matter.

A 13-12 loss to Illinois was really hard to swallow. It was a game that we should have walked off as a winner — we were kicking their ass — and we walked off a loser.

I vaguely remember ripping my clothes off in the locker room. My cousin, Bimbo, was a house guest that weekend, and he cut short his visit and jumped on a plane and flew home after the game. He told Cindy that he had never seen me that mad and frustrated.

At 3 a.m. I couldn't sleep, so I got up and started writing notes. By the time I was done, I had four pages of notes. Sometimes you have to take a look at yourself and what you're doing and make an honest evaluation.

The following Saturday we're playing at Michigan State and ABC is doing the game. After one of our practices, I met with Dick Vermeil, the former NFL head coach, who was working for the network as a color analyst. He had just watched the Illinois tape.

"If you stick with that formula," he instructed me, "you'll lose some games like that. But you'll also win most of the games that you're suppose to win."

That was a helluva point, and sometimes you need to hear it from somebody else. I've always believed in the same formula — play solid defense, don't turn the ball over, outrush your opponent, and win the kicking game. We had won some close games that way. We beat Northern Illinois, Ohio State and Purdue by a total of eight points.

But as the season wore on, those close games began to add up, and, emotionally, they took a toll on a young football team. From week to week, the players were elated after a close win or drained and gutted after a close loss. None was more gut-wrenching than the Northwestern loss in the final game of the regular season.

You win that game and nobody is asking when you're going to turn it around, or whether you can turn it around at Wisconsin. Instead, you're one of the hot programs on the rise. You're in a bowl game three years after you've taken over a rock-bottom program. And that would have been unheard of.

The night before the game in Evanston, I had the Independence Bowl people in my hotel room. They really wanted us in Shreveport, and I committed to them on the spot because I was determined to get our team to a bowl, any bowl, I didn't care.

These kids had worked hard for three seasons, and I wanted to give them a reward. I wanted to give this group of players more practice time, which you get when you're bowling. I wanted to get them ready for the next season because I knew we could be even better.

"If we beat Northwestern, we're yours," I assured the people from the Independence Bowl that Friday night, "we're going to Shreveport."

The next day, Pat Richter comes down on the sidelines during the fourth quarter and says, "Barry, I'm sitting with the Freedom Bowl people, and they want to set up a rematch of the 1963 Rose Bowl between Wisconsin and Southern Cal. If we win, we'll accept."

I told him I had already committed to the Independence Bowl.

"Don't worry, Pat — this is a good problem," I said. "If we win, we'll just go flaky on the Shreveport people, make up something, and we'll go to California."

There was a problem.

We did everything we could to lose the game, and we succeeded — losing to Northwestern 27-25. People want to focus on Jason Burns' fumble in the final 49 seconds that cost us a chance to kick a game-winning field goal.

But it went far beyond just one play. We missed field goals of 40 and 25 yards in the first half. We blocked a punt and didn't recover it. We did some crazy things. We might have been worthy of a bowl, but we threw it away.

Lou Holtz called on Monday and encouraged me, "Hang in there. Learn from the loss, but put it behind you. Concentrate on recruiting, and move forward."

Our players were all coming back, and they just had a taste. They had a taste of the big crowds, the big wins. They had a taste of what could have been. And they were hungry. More than anything, they realized they could play with anybody.

"If everybody gets better and stronger," I said to the players, "if everybody improves a half-step, we can take a huge jump."

That was our emphasis afterwards. We were close to being a good team, close to an eight or nine-win season, but we were still learning how to win.

At our team banquet, I said, "A year from now, instead of talking about maybe going to a bowl, we want to be talking about which bowl we're going to."

We were done playing everyone close and not winning.

"If everybody takes care of their business," I reiterated, "we will be a winner."

Everybody went into the off-season knowing that.

Bevell confirmed as much.

"The Northwestern loss laid the ground work for the turnaround —

it was our springboard in learning how to win," he said. "Everybody saw how close we were, and we realized the coaches weren't just feeding us coachspeak. We had a chance to be good, and the way we lost that final game made everyone hungrier. About 75 to 80 guys stayed in Madison that summer and made a conscious effort to take that next step."

That same summer, Joe Panos came into my office. He was upset.

"Hey, coach, I've got a situation here," he said. "I threw a party for my teammates. I welcomed everyone to my house — walk-ons, starters, whites, blacks. There were no labels, only Badgers. After the party, we all went out on the town.

"When we got back home that night, we found out that we had been robbed. One of my teammates had stuff taken out of his room. I think it was a Camcorder or something like that. I didn't want to get you involved, coach. And I don't want the police involved.

"So, I'll take care of this on my own. I did some recon work and found out who did it — a couple of my teammates — and I'm calling a Code Red on those guys."

I warned him about taking the law into his hands.

"Joe, you've got to be careful about how you handle this," I said. "You can approach them and you can talk to them, but then you tell me who they are and I'll take care of the rest."

A few days later, Joe Panos returned to my office. He was in better spirits.

"I had a team meeting and I called the guys out," he told me. "I didn't name names, but I stood in front of the group and let everyone know how I felt.

"I said, 'You guys know what kind of team we have. You guys know what kind of team we want to be. We want to be a family. But two mother-(bleepers) from this team just came into my home — which I had opened to everyone — and stole from me. There are two people in this room who don't want to be a team, who don't want to be a family.'"

And that was the end of that. Panos came back to my office and identified the two players, and I suspended one and the other left the program.

It was important to have someone like Panos handling anything that might come up — off the field — because all the kids looked up to him and respected him.

He was a natural leader and the best captain I've ever had.

Here was a tough kid who didn't get much traffic from the college recruiters when he was playing high school ball in Brookfield. So he goes to UW-Whitewater and starts a few games as a true freshman, and winds up transferring here as a defensive lineman.

But we were so thin on the offensive line, we moved him there. He never complained while playing three different positions: guard, center and tackle.

As he matured, you saw that he had great leadership skills and tremendous pride. And through hard work and toughness, he turned himself into one of the best linemen in the Big Ten. In preparing for the 1993 season, he really took hold as a leader.

Panos kept reminding everyone, "We were 5-6 (in '92) because we didn't know how to put teams away, we didn't know how to win the close games. But we were only a few plays away from being 8-3. We know we're going to be good. We just don't know how good."

The kids listened to his every word and followed him.

Joe Panos became our Pied Piper.

CHAPTER EIGHT

Living the Dream

I'll never forget the advice that I got from an assistant high school principal, Jack Anderson, when I was coaching and teaching in Lincoln. He was conducting a battery of tests and one of the questions was, "Is it important for your players or students to like you?"

Most people would probably say no and maybe add something like "It's not important for them to like me, but they have to respect me."

I was an assistant at Northeast High School — my first coaching job — and that's not how I answered. "It IS important for them to like me," I emphasized.

Anderson, who had a son on the football team, said, "That's pretty good. Saying 'no' would have been the wrong answer. You're asking your players to do quite a bit, so they better like you, or they won't do the things you're asking them to do."

That doesn't mean compromise. You have to treat your players like they are your own kids. If they do something wrong, you have to punish them. But you also have to give them guidance, and show them that you care — sincerely care about them.

You definitely have to give them direction. I really believe kids want rules. They also want to know they have a chance to win and that you have a plan for them.

Going into a game, I've always wanted my players to feel like I've coached them better than the other coach and that they are better prepared than their opponent. Whether they really are coached better or are better prepared doesn't matter — as long as they believe they are.

In this context, your players have to trust what you're saying.

"Whatever I'm telling you is the truth," I'll remind them. "I'm not blowing smoke, and I'm not going to sugar coat it. If you have a question — and you're not afraid of the answer — then don't be afraid to ask that question."

Give them some credit. Kids can read a coach, and they know if he's being an imposter or a phony. That's going to surface and that coach is going to be exposed.

Hayden Fry always used to say, "I don't like telling lies when I recruit because I'm not smart enough to remember them over the course of time."

***

After the 1992 season, I was an assistant coach for a college all-star game that was played in Japan. Not all of the top college players were there, but many of them were, and I'm looking at them and thinking, "Shoot, we've got better guys at every position."

That stayed with me.

During our 1993 training camp, I stood in front of our players and I didn't mince words, I didn't hold back. I told them, "I can honestly say we're as good as anybody in the Big Ten in the offensive line, at running back, at wide receiver ...."

I went right down the list, position by position. "This is where we are — and we're as good as anybody we're going to play," I repeated for emphasis.

For the first time, we had a mature team on both sides of the ball. That meant physically we were finally good enough to stand up to the people — the Michigans and Ohio States — who had proven themselves in the conference, year after year.

We had enough speed and enough weapons on offense to allow us to be balanced between the run and pass. On defense, we had filled holes in the secondary with junior college transfers Donny Brady and Kenny Gales, who redshirted in '92.

We also had great leadership from our co-captains, Joe Panos and Lamark Shackerford. We really didn't have any glaring weaknesses any-where. That's why I thought it was important to let the players know that we had high expectations.

They could read what was being written about them in the preseason magazines. The general consensus from around the country was that we were really close to being a damn good football team. We had been telling them that — we just weren't blowing smoke — and it was good for them to see that other people were thinking the same way.

We had laid the groundwork, teaching them how to win and how to stay focused. We emphasized keeping all distractions to a minimum. As a team, we weren't going to worry about how many games we won or count the wins as we went along. We just wanted to improve each week. That was our focus: the task at hand.

"We're going to be a good team — how good depends on the chemistry," I lectured the players during two-a-day practices. "Don't worry about how many games you win. Don't worry about a bowl. Worry about getting better. Don't let anything break your focus. Everything will take care of itself. The wins will come, and we'll get enough of them."

Our 23-year-old sophomore quarterback, Darrell Bevell, had added 15 pounds to his skinny frame during the off-season. There was something else different about Bevell. He had gotten married. He had met his wife, Tammy, during their Mormon mission together in the Cleveland area. They were the only married couple on the team.

Darrell Bevell was on his own mission. I remember reading a story in a Madison newspaper in which he quoted John F. Kennedy, "Once you accept second place — when first place is available — you have a tendency to do it the rest of your life."

His dad had used the quote to motivate his high school players, and it was something that Darrell was using to motivate himself. He wasn't about to settle for second-best.

From a maturity standpoint, there was no better person to speak to the plan that we had outlined for the players. "When we came to training camp, we talked about team goals," Bevell said. "The one and only goal we had was to get to a bowl game, and win. It was never about the Rose Bowl. Our tunnel vision was by design."

One of the biggest things we had to deal with when we took over the program was convincing our kids that they were as good as anyone else and that they could be winners.

I felt we had reached the point where we could compete with people, so I wasn't concerned about setting the bar too high. Or the pressure that comes with higher expectations. Pressure? We put plenty of pressure on ourselves. And I wanted to set the tone.

***

Before the start of the '93 season, I called a meeting of the support staff at Wisconsin — anybody who touched Badger football — and we filled the old W-Club room.

I had been working so hard with the players and my assistants that I felt like I hadn't spent enough time with the people in the business office, or the people in the ticket office, or the people in the equipment room, or the trainers, secretaries, and custodians.

I tried to explain how important it was to maintain an open line of communication and how important each one of them was to our success as a football team.

"We have a chance to have a good team," I pointed out. "And I want to make sure everybody is on the same page. Everybody needs to pay particular attention to their own job so we can get it done, and we'll all be rewarded with a good season.

"We need to communicate, and we need to get along with each other. Be positive about the program. Be positive about the direction we're going. Sell the program."

All it takes is one person to create a problem. If someone in the ticket office is not cooperating with a player and making it difficult to secure tickets for his parents, that's a distraction. If a player feels like he's not being treated right in the equipment room, that's a distraction. It can be the littlest thing but it can turn into a big deal.

That's why I wanted to make sure that everybody knew their roles and exactly what was expected of them. In Jimmy Johnson's autobiography *Turning the Thing Around*, he wrote, "As head coach, or CEO, it's my job to put everybody who is in the organization in an environment that allows them to be the best that they can be."

That was my objective for calling the meeting. To paraphrase Johnson, you also have to create a sense of urgency with your people so that they know if they don't play their role, the job won't get done. But when they execute their responsibilities, they will share in the accolades. Not only must you show support and loyalty, but you must provide the structure and guidance for them to make the decisions that, essentially, you want them to make.

As an athletic director, I want to do everything I can so my coaches can coach. I don't want them worrying about anything else. I'll handle the administrative end. I'm going to give them direction and tell them what I want, and then I'm going to give them the latitude to make decisions and move forward. Whatever job they have, I expect it to be done well.

But let's not get too far ahead of ourselves.

Let's stay focused on what we have to get done today.

WIN.

What's Important Now.

At Notre Dame, we had just taken over as the No. 1 team in the nation, and we sat down as a staff and talked about the dangers of moving up to No. 1 and all the accompanying publicity. There's a tendency to reflect on what happened in the past, leaving yourself vulnerable. If you're not focused on the present, you can get ambushed.

You see it happen all the time. You put so much into one game, and you're zapped emotionally for your next game. Or you're distracted by having celebrated too long.

When Pat Riley was coaching the New York Knicks, he wrote a book in which he talked about the "Disease within me." His point was that once a team has some success, the guys can start worrying more about "me" than the team. And that can fester.

That's how we came up with the slogan at Notre Dame.

The acronym: WIN.

Does being No. 1 change anything? Do you get more points for a touchdown? Do you have to go only nine yards for a first down? Of course not.

What you want to be is No. 1 at the end of the year, and to do so, you had better prepare and you had better focus on what's important now.

When I hired Bret Bielema as my defensive coordinator at Wisconsin, he had his own phrase. No matter the record or what had happened in the previous game, he always focused on one thing: "Let's be 1-0."

That's exactly the same as WIN.

Stay focused on what we have to get done today.

It's something I've always fallen back on as a head coach, and now, as an administrator, I'll go into a meeting and say, "We've got to address these issues. This is what's on the table. Let's get it done, and let's not worry about anything else."

It goes back to what Lou Holtz always said about taking a problem, breaking it down to its simplest form, and coming up with the solution.

From a management standpoint, that's what our chancellor, Donna Shalala, had done in dealing with a football program that was losing and an athletic department that was in debt.

Donna had her fingers on everything, and when I took over as the head coach, she wanted me to be involved on the campus. Whenever she had a dean's reception at her house — a cocktail party or dinner — she always included Cindy and me.

By the same token, if I had recruits on campus and asked her to stop by, she didn't hesitate to come over and visit with them. Whatever it was, she was willing to help.

In June of 1993, the school's management team had a change at the top, with David Ward taking over as the new chancellor. Donna Shalala left the university to become the Secretary of Health and Human Services in the Clinton White House.

At his introductory press conference, Ward said that he was determined to "let good people do their jobs instead of constantly second-guessing them."

I appreciated the elbow room.

Like Donna, he had only one request; implied, if not stated.

Win.

***

Since our 1993 season opener fell on Labor Day weekend, I was hoping to stage a night game at Camp Randall Stadium. I thought playing under the lights might help attract a bigger crowd. But our first opponent, Nevada — coached by Jeff Horton, who would later become one of my assistants — balked at moving the kickoff.

Not that I was overly concerned about our drawing potential, especially knowing the type of team we might have. During the 1992 season, we averaged a little over 61,000 for the six home dates, and that was a big jump from the 49,000 we averaged in '91.

Going into the '93 season, we expected another spike in attendance since we had already sold out our allotment of student tickets (12,000).

"Pretty soon, they're going to be selling season tickets in the end zone," I boasted. "That's what you want. You want to do what Nebraska does. You want to sell out your stadium with season tickets and let the people fight for them."

After a convincing 35-17 win over Nevada — Bevell set a school record with five touchdowns passes — I knew the crowd would not be an issue at SMU. Crowd? What crowd? They were expecting less than 20,000 in Dallas. But I had plenty of other concerns.

Like playing a night game on the road.

Our road win at Minnesota in 1991 was the school's only road victory in the last seven years. Or since a win at Northwestern in 1986.

There was no getting around it, since that's all they were writing about in the Madison newspapers — the Badgers were 2-31 in their last 33 road games and hadn't defeated a non-conference opponent on the road since 1985.

But we had something to build on because we had played so competitively on the road at Washington in our 1992 opener. We lost three other road games by a total of 10 points. I wanted to make sure our players knew we had done a thorough job researching the road situation, and I wanted them confident about how we were approaching it.

I had visited with Green Bay head coach Mike Holmgren, a former NFL assistant with the San Francisco 49ers. I wanted to know how the 49ers handled their travel logistics because of the length of most of their road trips, especially when they were traveling east.

I also talked with Penn State's Joe Paterno, who never practiced at or went to the opponent's stadium the day before a road game. "Get everything done you can on Friday at home," Joe told me, "and leave as late as possible."

That was designed to keep everything as routine as possible for the players before leaving on a road trip. And that's where we came up with our philosophy.

All coaches are paranoid to begin with, and they're always worried that someone might be spying on them while they're working out in somebody else's stadium.

That's a part of the advantage of doing everything at home on Friday. We tried to make our road games like our home games, the only difference being instead of taking the players to a Friday night movie, we would get on a plane and travel.

My most pressing concern was playing a night game on the road. I still had bad memories from a loss at Minnesota when I was on the Iowa staff.

In 1983, we beat the Gophers 61-10 in Iowa City. The following year, we're playing them in the Metrodome with an outside chance of still going to the Rose Bowl.

We sat around the hotel all day and went out that night and got beat 23-17. You talk about sleepwalking? It was ridiculous.

That's why I knew SMU would be a challenge. Don't get me wrong.

They weren't very good, and if we played the game in Madison, we'd probably win by two or three touchdowns. But it was a totally different environment in Dallas.

SMU plays its home games on campus in a 23,000 seat-facility — Owenby Stadium — which had the atmosphere of a high school field.

The visiting team dresses in two separate locker rooms in a recreation building less than a mile from the stadium. It's a decent walk, and they hold up traffic before the game to allow the players to cross the street.

So, you start piece-mealing your people through a parking lot, across a highway and onto the field for pregame and when you look around — we have more people in the stands for a spring game — you start to wonder, "What the hell are we doing here?"

In Dallas, they were still talking about the SMU program in terms of it being 5 A.D — five years since coming off the "Death Penalty" when they were forced to cancel the 1987 and 1988 seasons because of NCAA sanctions.

SMU coach Tom Rossley, who was later the offensive coordinator for Mike Sherman in Green Bay, talked about being forced to play freshmen immediately because the numbers were down in the program, and he couldn't afford to redshirt anybody.

The irony is that SMU had more time to recover than Wisconsin did — since the Badgers were coming off the equivalent of their own "Death Penalty" in 1990.

When we took over the program, we inherited a small number of legitimate D-I players. Like SMU, we were starting from scratch, too. With the exception of our safeties — Scott Nelson and Reggie Holt — the '93 team was made up of the players we recruited.

Were they ready to win?

We were going to find out because there were plenty of distractions at SMU, and we were at an early crossroads in our season.

It was a bad atmosphere. It was hot. When we stepped outside, it was like a blast furnace. It was 94 degrees at kickoff.

Worse yet, we fell behind, 13-0, at halftime. We weren't sharp and I sensed the kids were frustrated when we didn't get on the board.

But there was no reason to go into the locker and yell and scream at them. I just wanted to get their attention. I didn't want to make them more uptight than they already were. I wanted them to walk out for the third quarter with some confidence.

"Don't panic," I told them. "Just stick with your knitting, and we'll be fine. They haven't stopped us yet, and we can play better defense than we have. There's a long, long ways to go in this game. Be patient. Nobody panic."

Nobody did. We rallied for a 24-16 victory, and I can remember how relieved I was afterward. A game like that can really help you mature as a team.

Our senior linebacker, Yusef Burgess, was speaking for his teammates when he said, "Everybody was talking about how Wisconsin can't win on the road. Well, this is a new Wisconsin. And we're building a new tradition starting now."

That Sunday, we were ranked No. 24 in the Associated Press poll and No. 25 in the *USA Today* coaches poll. That was the first time a Wisconsin team had been recognized nationally in the Top 25 since the 1984 season.

I made the comment that the polls are nice for all of the alumni who pick up the newspaper in the morning and see their school ranked — they can beat on their chests all day at the office, and that hasn't happened in a very long time at Wisconsin.

Expectations and rankings are two different things. We don't talk about rankings. But it was no secret that I had high expectations for this team, and I stressed that if we kept improving from week to week, the rankings would take care of themselves.

Nonetheless, breaking into the Top 25 after the SMU victory was good for our players from the standpoint that it showed them they had some credibility and respect — both of which had been lacking.

***

"Why not Wisconsin?" Joe Panos fired back at the interviewer after we won our Big Ten opener 27-15 at Indiana to run our record to 4-0. "We haven't shown a reason yet that we can't play with the big boys. Anything can happen. Why not us?"

Panos was the first one who had enough guts to say something like that. And that was an eye-opener for some of his teammates who started thinking, "Why not us?"

What prompted Panos to make such a statement? "I was getting irritated," Joe said. "I kept getting the same questions over and over again. Do you think you can beat Michigan? Do you think you can beat Ohio

State? What do you have to do to beat those teams?

"Finally, I turned it around on them and asked 'Why not us? What do those teams have that we don't have? Do they have an All-Big Ten running back? We've got the best running back in the league in Brent Moss. And we've also got Terrell Fletcher.

"Do they have better offensive linemen then we do? We've got three All-Big Ten linemen. And nobody is better than Joe Rudolph and Cory Raymer.

"Do they have better defensive linemen? I know they don't have anyone better than our nose guard, Lamark Shackerford. And there's nobody better in the conference than our two tackles, Carlos Fowler and Mike Thompson.

"So, why not us? Why not Wisconsin? Is it because we don't have tradition? Well, we're going to make tradition.'"

I am not sure Joe thought that quote would have the legs that it did. But it fired everybody up, including the fans. According to Tim Van Alstine, the ticket director, his office received 58,000 calls following our win at Indiana. During a one-hour period, Van Alstine said that there were 152 contacts on his secretary's private telephone line.

It was simply overwhelming.

So was our running game. Indiana's defense was ranked No. 6 in the nation, and we rushed for over 350 yards — Moss had almost 200, Fletcher had almost 100, and our fullback, Mark Montgomery, had over 50. On average, we were rushing for over 255 per game, and for the fourth straight week, we had more than 400 yards of total offense.

Brad Childress did a helluva job as our offensive coordinator. He called all the plays, and we had a great balance, almost 50/50, between the run and the pass.

We just had so many weapons.

We had a tight end, Mike Roan, who could catch. We had a really fast receiver, Lee DeRamus, who could beat you deep, and a solid possession receiver, J.C. Dawkins.

We had a tailback, Moss, who would just wear you out and keep moving the chains and getting first downs. And we had another tailback, Fletcher, who could catch the ball and go the distance on any single play. Our fullback, Montgomery, could catch and block.

Our quarterback, Bevell, ran the show and knew where to go with the ball. We were just as effective throwing as running, which made our play-action game so dangerous.

When we were lined up in a pro set to the right, we could do a lot of things. We could run power, stretch or isolation behind our first really tough offensive line.

These guys were nasty tough — Mike Verstegen, Joe Rudolph, Cory Raymer, Steve Stark and Joe Panos — and they'd chop your legs and really get after it.

When we'd run power, we'd pull the backside guard, so we always ran power to the right. We never ran to the left because Rudolph was our left guard and our backside puller.

Michigan State and George Perles were running zone in 1987 with Lorenzo White, so it wasn't anything new. But defenses in our league still hadn't caught up with the zone. George's offensive line coach, Pat Morris, was good friends with Jim Hueber who was running zone with Darrell Thompson at Minnesota.

In '93, Huebs was our running back coach, and he meshed his knowledge with Billy Callahan, our O-line coach. Billy used to say, "With (Darrell) Thompson, they would read the play-side, see what bodies were covered up, see what bodies weren't covered up, and they would break it back. That's essentially what we were doing, and that's where some of the biggest running plays come from — the backside."

In zone blocking, you're basically track-blocking. Instead of worrying about blocking a defender in any one of three directions — outside, head-up, or inside — you're taking him in one direction. We were usually zoning the play-side gap.

Our linemen were confident, aggressive, and physical.

"If your backs can read the covered linemen," Billy used to preach, "and if there's an uncovered lineman — or he's not blocked properly — the tailback can cut off that block. If we can get them covered up, we can puncture a hole on the play-side and keep it there."

They were all confident guys. Some of them gained confidence as they went along. But they had personality, and they had a leader like Panos who could direct them. When they practiced, they practiced hard. But they also had fun.

Most importantly, they liked one another and respected one another. And the one thing they would all do is compete — they weren't intimidated by anyone.

"Those kids take tremendous pride in chemistry," Billy Callahan used to say, "and they help keep everyone on the team close and on the same page."

***

Following the Indiana game, we had a bye in the schedule — October 2 — and that gave us a chance to scout two future opponents. Callahan was sent to the Illinois-Purdue game in West Lafayette. We drew the Boilermakers in two weeks and the Illini in mid-November.

After the game, Billy is checking out the sight lines from the visitor's box in Ross-Ade Stadium, and he pulls the Illinois kicking depth chart off the wall.

Pretty harmless stuff.

Or so we assumed.

The next thing we know the Big Ten office is calling and telling us that a complaint has been lodged by Illinois coach Lou Tepper and it fell under the conference's new ruling for unsportsmanlike conduct, which meant a one-game suspension or a $10,000 fine.

It should have never gotten to that point, but Tepper was so paranoid — he felt so threatened by Wisconsin — that he turned us in to commissioner Jim Delany.

We should have fought the league harder; we should have appealed. There was no way that merited a suspension. But I didn't want the school paying that penalty.

Instead, we took the hit.

And that's where I made a big mistake, a fatal mistake. Billy coached his position group the entire week right up to our Minnesota game. But on the morning of the game, we told the players that Billy had been suspended and Jim Hueber would handle the offensive line.

I violated my own rule: no surprises.

I learned a valuable lesson. Instead of waiting until game day, I should have told the kids earlier in the week how everything was going to play out. I handled it wrong.

Minnesota wasn't as good as we were, and I thought we'd beat them anyway. But we had created our own distraction — with the Big Ten's assistance.

The Gophers had an extra week to prepare for us, and they used it well. They got a jump in the first quarter, and before we knew it we were trailing 21-0 at halftime.

We finished with over 600 yards of total offense — Darrell threw for over 400 yards — but we also had five interceptions and a lost fumble, and Minnesota hung on 28-21.

That loss might have cost us a chance for a national championship.

Despite everything that went wrong, I felt this group of kids would bounce back, especially since we were returning home to face Michigan.

***

On a Friday night, I'll sometimes think about what I'm going to say to the team before the kickoff. Or I might write down some notes on Saturday morning or before I walk into the locker room. I've had some very emotional pregame talks. Everyone is different.

There are times when things will build up during the week or you feel very strongly about something, and you don't have to write anything down. You don't need notes. It just comes out, like it did before the Michigan game. I was ticked.

During the pregame warm-up, some of Michigan's players were dancing and woofing on the W-logo in the middle of the field at Camp Randall Stadium. One player, Walter Smith, began taunting our kids about our lack of tradition and our lack of success.

I played that card — that they were really disrespecting us.

Before the kickoff, I got real emotional. I knew I could get their attention with what I had to say. They know when I'm excited — or mad — because my voice rises and I talk louder. I just thought it was time to do that and I really got our players cranked up.

We played with emotion, too.

Our defense shut down their running attack, Moss rushed for nearly 130 yards, Fletcher scored the only touchdown on a draw, and our walk-on kicker, Rick Schnetzky, nailed a couple of field goals. The 13-10 win was our first over Michigan since 1981.

After my postgame press conference, someone told me that some kids had gotten hurt as the result of a stampede in the student sections. They said there had been a human tidal wave, a surge of bodies from the top rows to the bottom, and hundreds of students got trampled along the railing and chain link fence below Sections O, P and Q.

We had players crying as they came back into the locker room — guys like Panos, Rudolph, Moss, Mike Thompson, Brian Patterson and Tyler Adam thought that they had just helped carry off dead students. I remember walking back down the ramp and looking out on to the field and seeing all the emergency medical squads and ambulances.

It was scary. I thought it looked like World War II or Sarajevo. It looked like someone had set off a bomb. Although more than 70 had been injured, we were very lucky that nobody lost their life.

My daughter Stacy had been sitting at the bottom of the student section. Cindy couldn't find her immediately after the game, but I knew Stacy was out of harm's way because she was one of the first people to hug me at midfield.

Then you start thinking as you're driving home how some parents would have felt if they didn't know where their child was. I imagined myself in that situation, and kept thinking about the students in the hospital. I was hearing so many different things about their condition, and I was trying to get as much information as I could.

That game became very secondary — and that win, as big as it was, also became very secondary — when you're talking about injuries and possible fatalities.

Mike Brin, a walk-on wide receiver, was the focal point of national publicity — ABC's Person of the Week — after Brin pulled two students from the scrum of bodies. I remember Brin telling a reporter about riding an emotional roller coaster, going from an "incredible high" after beating Michigan to an "incredible low" during the postgame rescue efforts.

Everyone experienced that same ride — from the highest of highs to the lowest of lows. On Monday, we brought in counselors and made them available the entire week to all of our players.

We had to be smart as a coaching staff. Everybody was emotionally spent, and we needed to give them some space and time to rejuvenate and recharge. We put in the game plan for Ohio State, but I really didn't say much until later in the week.

At a Thursday night pep rally, I cut loose. I brought up our 20-16 win over Ohio State the year before and how "Ohio State is now talking about revenge." Working the crowd, I said, "Let me say this to you — they were damn lucky that the game was that close."

ESPN's Lee Corso said that he was going to pick us to beat Ohio State again until he heard that I was giving the Buckeyes some "bulletin board material." Corso had too much respect for them.

And not enough for us.

When he was coaching at Indiana, he was intimidated by Michigan and Ohio State. That's why he never beat them, along with the fact they were a lot better than he was.

That Friday night, we showed our players the film *Rudy* and to top it off, we had the real Rudy — Dan Ruettiger — speak to the team.

I sold the game as "big on big." And that's how it unfolded during a 14-14 tie. Overall, I thought we outplayed the Buckeyes. We had given up the lead in the fourth quarter, but we still had one final chance.

Before the start of our final possession, I got on the headsets with Brad Childress in the press box and said, "Get us to the 20 and we'll kick to win."

With seven seconds left, we had the ball on the Ohio State 15. That's when we screwed up. The kick was from the left hash, and we should have gone with an unbalanced formation to the wide side of the field, which would have put an extra blocker on the right edge.

Had we lined up that way, Ohio State's Marlon Kerner would have had to run an extra yard and he would have never blocked the kick. But he did a helluva job, and both teams had to settle for the tie.

On Sunday, I got a phone call from Joe Moore. We had coached together at Notre Dame. "Barry, did you see the Ohio State bench after they blocked the kick? They were all jumping up and down," he said. "You ought to show that to your kids. That's supposed to be the No. 3 team in the country, and they're tickled pink to TIE you."

All I knew was that we had another open date on the schedule, and it couldn't have come at a better time. We needed to clear our heads, relax and come back fresh.

***

Michigan upset Ohio State and we took care of business at Illinois, which meant that if we beat Michigan State, we were going to the Rose Bowl, ending that 31-year drought for the Badgers. Even though our "home" game was being played in Tokyo — over 6,000 miles from home and Camp Randall Stadium — all the intangibles were in our favor.

People talked about the distractions flying to Japan. I'm not so sure we wouldn't have had more distractions if we were playing in Madison, with everybody calling about tickets for a potential Rose Bowl. In Tokyo, we had total control of the players and their environment.

We also had two weeks to prepare, while Michigan State had to jump on a plane after playing Penn State. I knew their players weren't going to be right until midweek.

Since there was a 15-hour time difference, our trainer, Denny Helwig, researched how to best handle the jet lag. He consulted with a couple of UW professors whose specialty was sleep disorders, and they helped develop a plan for the players and travel party.

These professors had been consultants with NASA, and I think it reassured everyone that we were getting the same care and treatment as the astronauts in the space program.

Our kids really thought that they had a big edge on the Michigan State players. Plus, we had more at stake than the Spartans, and we were the better team. That was the bottom line. We were better, and we went out and proved it, 41-20.

I was euphoric afterward. I was in a trance. I couldn't stop smiling. It was one of those special times that you always talk about and dream about. You shoot for the stars and you hope someday it will be a reality. But it had still been a dream until now.

When we first got to Wisconsin, we put up a sign above the doorway in the McClain Facility, "The Road to the Rose Bowl Begins Here."

You have to believe in something. You don't just show up in Pasadena. And every day for four seasons, we talked about winning and doing things the right way, and all of a sudden we're there, we've reached the mountain top, we're going to the Rose Bowl.

The most gratifying thing was knowing where we had started — at the bottom — and knowing how hard we had fought to keep believing and keep dreaming until we got to the top. I know people back in Madison were pretty damn excited about what was going on.

When we returned home from Japan, I remember addressing the rally at the stadium and saying, "I don't know about you, but we're going to Disneyland — Pasadena and California will never be the same after Wisconsin gets there."

***

I had no trouble finding an edge against UCLA. I played the "home team advantage" card. During the regular season, the Bruins play their home games at the Rose Bowl and their coach, Terry Donahue, asked me if he could keep his players in the home locker room instead of moving them out. C'mon, do you really think I'm going to let them do that?

We're going to take the home locker room, we're going to dress in red, and we're going to make them as uncomfortable as hell about the whole deal. I started telling the kids, "The Rose Bowl is going to be all red, and we're going to be playing at Camp Randall West."

As we got closer to the game, I had a former UCLA student body president — who was chauffeuring us around town — tell me that UCLA fans were scalping their tickets. You couldn't get a ticket for less than $750 and UCLA people were unloading them.

That also played to our advantage — their fans weren't loyal.

Their team was having some other issues. Their athletic director was trying to save some money, so he had the players stay in the dorms for the first week before relocating them to a hotel in Pasadena. That made it less of a treat for their players than it was for ours. And I could just sense it wasn't that big of a deal to be playing us in the Rose Bowl.

I played that card, too.

I poor boy-ed it because I thought we could set them up. They were a good football team, very talented. But they had no respect for Wisconsin. I'm sure most of their players felt like they could just go through the motions and win the game.

Their starting strong safety, Marvin Goodwin, was the younger brother of Duer Sharp, who played two years for us in '90 and '91. "Goodwin turned us down," I told our players of Wisconsin's attempt to recruit Goodwin. "He disrespected us."

You could see where I was going with all of this.

At the Rose Bowl luncheon, the master of ceremonies got up and started talking about UCLA and he never stopped talking about UCLA. We had three of our players there, and he couldn't even get their names right. I was steamed and when it was my turn to talk, I was still fuming. I said, "I'm really sorry if I'm interrupting a UCLA pep rally."

That played into my "no respect" theme. I knew our guys would be really fired up for the game, but I had to make sure they weren't overwhelmed when they took the field.

There's nothing like the Rose Bowl. It's the prettiest stadium I've ever seen. It's the type of venue that gives you goose bumps.

When you come out of that players' tunnel, and it's dusk, and you can see the palm trees rising above the scoreboard, it takes your breath away. And if you're not prepared, you can play the first quarter with your mouth open.

I went through all of that with our players during the pregame. We even went out 15 minutes earlier than normal so they could walk around and get a feel for the atmosphere.

"Get it out of your system — we have to start fast," I warned them. "Remember this is not UCLA's home field. The Bruins rent this place. Where do we play best? At home. Look around, it's going to be all red here today. We're going to have 70 percent of the people rooting for us. This is our home field, this is our home game."

This was our game to win, and it would have been a blowout if they throw the flag in the third quarter on UCLA's Donnie Edwards for being off-sides — which he was — on a fourth-and-short run from the Bruins 9. We couldn't block Edwards and he tackled Moss.

If we had scored on that series, it's 21-3 and the game is over, because they're getting ready to quit. Right after that defensive stop, we lose two of our best players — DeRamus and Montgomery — after they got into an altercation with Goodwin and Donavon Gallatin. All four players were ejected and it affected us more than it affected them.

In the fourth quarter, though, Darrell Bevell had the most unlikely touchdown run you'll ever see — from Darrell Bevell. But that wasn't my favorite run. Their quarterback, Wayne Cook, flushing and running with no timeouts left, may had been the greatest run I've ever seen because it ended the game and sealed our 21-16 win.

I remember reading Jim Murray's column the next day in the *Los Angeles Times*. Murray, one of only a handful of sportswriters to ever win the Pulitzer Prize, had some great lines about how the rubes from Wisconsin rode their hay wagon into the Rose Bowl, baited the city slickers, set them up, and walked out a winner.

That's how Murray saw it, and that's what we did.

To this day, I can't go anywhere in Wisconsin, or the United States, without running into somebody who wants to tell me what they were doing when we won that first Rose Bowl.

That game gave everybody credibility. It gave our fans bragging rights. It showed them that hope was alive. That game put our program on the map. We were legitimate.

CHAPTER NINE
Then Along Came Ron

Following our Rose Bowl win, I got everyone together in the locker room and thanked the seniors "for a great job of leadership and for pulling everything together."

Then I singled out the returning players — specifically the younger ones — and planted the seed for the 1994 season.

"We have a majority of our people coming back, a great group coming back," I said. "But how good we're going to be as a football team depends on how you lead — the type of chemistry you have — and how you develop as a team."

I asked them, "All the stuff we've accomplished this year — the tremendous experiences that we've had — is it worth all the hard work?"

We had gone from worst to first, and from being one of the bottom five teams in the Big Ten to being one of the top five teams in the nation. Now, we're going from the hunter to the hunted.

"We can handle this," I said. "But next season we'll be a new team with new roles and a new chemistry, and we'll have to establish our own personality."

I really thought we'd have a heckuva team.

I thought we'd win the league and go back to the Rose Bowl.

We were losing Joe Panos, but we had all of our skill players returning on offense. We also had a number of players coming back on defense, though I didn't expect us to be much better than mediocre on that side of the ball, average at best.

My mistake was not spending more time talking to the players about dealing with success. As soon as everyone returned for the second semester, I should have called a team meeting and dealt with the issues. I should have been tougher on them during the off-season. I didn't do a very good job of preparing them.

Some of our guys got lazy and complacent. Some lacked discipline. They were feeling too good about themselves. They were treated very well on campus, and it went to their heads. They thought they had it made, that they had arrived.

All of the things that they had worked so hard to get? They had them. And they were under the false impression that they could maintain the status quo and not have to prove themselves all over again. Or work even harder to stay where they were.

Teams that win championships are faced with new challenges because everybody is gunning for them. The players are going to be treated differently because they are getting more attention, but also because there are suddenly people jealous of their success who are looking for flaws, chinks in the armor, or evidence of guys cutting corners.

As a head coach, you try to be proactive instead of reactive. You try to anticipate things happening, try to recognize signs and address issues before they become problems. You need to identify the potential pitfalls that come with success.

I could see it coming with Brent Moss.

In the middle of the summer, I got a call from a Madison police officer who notified me that they had been monitoring heavy traffic near Brent's apartment, and they felt there might be some drugs involved. So I called Brent and his dad into my office.

His dad was very good. He tried to stay on top of things, but Brent was off on his own. So I confronted him with the police reports and the suspicion of drug use.

"If you're messing with drugs," I said, "you need to go out right now, you need to enter the NFL's supplemental draft because I don't want you back on this team."

Moss denied everything. "It's not true," he said. "I'm not involved."

I made sure the officer kept me abreast of what was going on, and I told Moss, "The word is out. I'm looking at you, and the police are looking at you. If there is any truth to the matter, you'd better be smart enough to back off, eliminate it, and get yourself straight."

***

I was standing in the middle of the field and the play was coming right at me. Lee DeRamus was running a "dig" route, a deep square-in, a 17-yard route. Darrell Bevell threw a pass that came in low and short.

The defensive back, Dwayne Cuff, a redshirt freshman, was in position to make a play on the ball because it was thrown right at him.

But he didn't know what to do, and he backed off. At the last second, Cuff stepped forward to go for the interception, and he got there exactly at the same time as DeRamus.

This was near the end of a Thursday practice, two days before the 1994 season opener against Eastern Michigan. We were practicing in shorts, shirts, and helmets. No pads.

The players were constantly reminded to stay on their feet during these drills to avoid injuries.

On contact — Cuff slamming into DeRamus — DeRamus went down in pain, clutching his left leg. He didn't get up. I turned to my son, Chad, who was standing next to me on the field, and said, "There goes our season."

DeRamus broke his leg in two places, the tibia and fibula bones. He had surgery in mid-September, and he never again played for the Badgers.

DeRamus was our starter at X or split end. He was our deep threat. Going into his senior year, he was 13 catches away from breaking Al Toon's record for career receptions.

Green Bay Packers general manager Ron Wolf later told me that DeRamus would have been their No. 1 pick, if he hadn't been injured.

(DeRamus still had a year of college eligibility remaining but chose to enter the 1995 draft. He dropped all the way to the sixth round and went to the New Orleans Saints.)

After DeRamus was sidelined, we still had some possession receivers, J.C. Dawkins and Keith Jackson. We also had some young guys, Tony Simmons and Reggie Torian, but they weren't ready. Without DeRamus, defenses started loading up on the run.

What we missed as much as anything was DeRamus' personality, his charisma. He was always happy. He always had a smile on his face. He was loosey-goosey.

He was nicknamed "Babe" because he was the baby in his family. Two of his older brothers went to college on track scholarships, so there was no lack of competition at home.

Babe really competed, too. And he didn't lack confidence. Before he ever played a snap for us, he was predicting to a writer that Wisconsin would be in the Rose Bowl. That was the Babe. We couldn't replace his swagger. Or his speed. Or his competitive nature.

Throughout the '94 training camp, DeRamus talked about playing against Colorado and matching up against their *Playboy* All-American cornerback, Chris Hudson. He really wanted to play against Hudson, and then he breaks his leg in that stupid practice incident.

Without Lee DeRamus, we couldn't throw the ball. It was no coincidence that our leading receiver in 1994 was Ron Johnson.

He was our fullback.

***

That might have been one of the hardest years I've ever gone through as a coach. There was never any continuity. The adversity began in late June when a former player, Nick Rafko, was killed in an auto accident near his hometown of Monroe, Michigan. Nick was only 23 and had gotten engaged just a week before his death.

Rafko was a backup linebacker and one of the fifth-year seniors on our first Rose Bowl team. He was such a fun person to be around because of his sense of humor. He was the guy who made everyone laugh with his Bill Murray impersonations.

In the coaching profession, there are so many things that hit you. My successor, Bret Bielema, is just starting to find out the magnitude of what you have to deal with. It's not just football, it's not just grades, it's not just recruiting. There's always something that comes up, and you never know what that something is going to be.

Like the tragic death of one of your most-liked players.

How are we going to deal with it? How are we going to present what has happened to the team? How are we going to show respect? In the end, we chartered a bus and about 40 of Rafko's former Badger teammates went to the wake and funeral in Michigan.

That was the second time I had been touched by the death of a member of my football family. My first year as an assistant coach, my favorite player was Ron Anderson. I also coached him in wrestling at Lincoln Northeast.

His dad later told me that Ron's goal was to be a football coach someday. I would have definitely hired him — he would have coached for me in high school — and I would have brought him along in the business. Except I never got that chance.

After his freshman year at college — the University of South Dakota

— he was killed in an accident. That might have been the first funeral I ever attended, and I didn't know how to respond to his death.

I had never been through it before. Death had not been a part of my life at that particular time. It was very difficult then, and it was very difficult with Rafko.

*****

The lack of continuity was really noticeable in the fall. You have the injury to DeRamus. You have some personnel questions. You have some growing pains. As a team, you lose some tough games and you don't live up to expectations. That bothered the hell out of the media, and people began piling on.

They were calling the '93 season a fluke. They were calling us a "flash in the pan," and they were zinging us, "From Rose Bowl to no bowl."

They jumped the gun, and I shouldn't have let it bother me.

But it did.

On top of that, every week, it seemed, we had something happen to a player off the field. And it was always different things. I can remember Terrell Fletcher coming up to me and rolling his eyes. What next? It was embarrassing. People were having fun at our expense.

Moss wasn't himself as a senior. There were many outside distractions. He still played hard on Saturdays, but he wasn't as intense, he wasn't as hungry. And when you're not focused, it's difficult. In early November, with two games left in the regular season, he was arrested and charged with cocaine possession, and I had to kick him off the team.

There was some second-guessing of my decision about how to handle Moss' case, including some racial inferences. But the rules were set. This wasn't a straw vote. He had been warned in the summer and we had a policy in place: if you're involved with drugs — using or selling — you're done. That was a team rule and there was no discussion.

It still frustrates me. Moss was one of my favorite players at Wisconsin. I loved coaching him, and we had a very good bond.

Even when a player gets into trouble, you don't forget about that person once he's gone or his eligibility is up. You want him to be successful. You want him to live a quality life, contribute to society and be a productive adult.

Whenever Moss came back on campus, I talked to him about getting his degree. I told him we'd pay for his schooling, and finally, almost 10 years later, he took me up on the offer.

We made arrangements for him to work for his room and board and we covered his scholarship, and he got his degree. But he still couldn't avoid getting into trouble. It seemed like every time he took a step forward, he took two steps back.

Besides Moss, we had several more issues with drugs during the '94 season. There were some young players who were smoking dope and not going to school. They had bright futures, but I eliminated them from the team.

It was a hard lesson to learn. We had too many young guys who were spoiled and taking short cuts. And I had taken some things for granted on how they were living.

During the recruiting process, we tell parents that we're going to look after their sons when they get here. From that point on, I insisted, "We're going to go into their apartments and we're going to go into their dorm rooms. And we're going to check and spot check periodically. If we suspect someone isn't living right, we are going to address it."

Maybe if Joe Panos had still been around in '94, he would have confronted those guys who stepped over the line. That was the kind of captain he was. He probably would have handled it — in his own way — and it may not have even gotten back to me. Coaches don't always know everything that is going on. The players do.

That's why I advise my captains, "It's easy to tell people, 'Do this or do that.' But you've got to live right off the field. The other players know what you're doing, and if you're not doing it right, they're not going to listen to what you have to say."

They listened to Panos.

In December, I addressed the overall situation, again. "I don't care what it is," I told the players, "if anybody gets arrested for anything, you're done, you're off the team."

No ifs, ands, or buts.

What happens? We had two players get picked up for shoplifting, and I suspended them for the Hall of Fame Bowl in Tampa.

Despite the ongoing distractions, we rolled over a good Duke team — Fletcher rushed for over 240 yards in a 34-20 win — and that helped salvage our season. I was extremely proud of how the players rallied to get us into a January 1st bowl.

After we lost a home game to Minnesota in late October, we were 3-3-

1 and going nowhere. Not many people gave us a chance to win many more games. But we went on the road the following week and won at Michigan — with Bevell nursing a shoulder injury — and we ended up winning four of our last five.

***

I got to know Donnie Duncan while he was working at Iowa State, and now Duncan was the athletic director at Oklahoma and looking for a coach to replace Gary Gibbs who had resigned the week of the 1994 Nebraska-Oklahoma game. In early December, Duncan contacted me, we sat down and talked, and he offered me the Oklahoma job.

I knew they had some great players. Frankie Solich was an assistant on the Cornhusker national championship team that season, and he told me that Oklahoma was the only opponent that could stay on the field with them and compete with their athletes.

Cindy didn't know anything about Norman, Oklahoma, and she didn't want to find out. "There's no way I'm going to Norman," she said.

Duncan stayed after me pretty aggressively to take the job. And maybe I should have at least checked out the campus and facilities. But I just wasn't interested.

Duncan wound up hiring Louisville coach Howard Schnellenberger. (Schnellenberger lasted one season before the Sooners made another change and brought in John Blake.)

But it didn't end for me with Oklahoma.

A few weeks after our Duke win, I got a call from Miami athletic director Paul Dee, who wanted to interview me for their opening. Dee was looking to replace Dennis Erickson, who had left for the NFL's Seattle Seahawks.

"Barry, you'd love it down here," Dee said.

"Paul, I know I'd love it — I really like Florida, I really like warm weather," I said. "But I originally wanted to go to college at Miami, and my mom wouldn't let me. And now I'd love to take your job, but my wife won't let me."

Cindy wasn't interested in uprooting the family.

Sometimes when you talk with other coaches and reflect a little bit — especially when you're among old friends who were high school coaches with you — it makes you think back to when you started out in this profession, and how there were certain jobs that if you ever have an opportunity to take them, you would just take them.

Oklahoma and Miami were probably two of those jobs. It was very flattering to be in the position to be offered them — when I was — but I never looked back. I wasn't thinking, "I'm not going to get another chance."

And I never wondered how my life might have changed if I had made a different choice. That type of thing just never entered my mind. As a coach, you can't afford to think that way. You worry about the job that you have, and that's all you concern yourself with.

But it didn't end for me with Oklahoma and Miami.

In January, I coached in the East-West Shrine game. Dennis Erickson was the East head coach and I was his assistant. At the time, Philadelphia Eagles owner Jeffrey Lurie was putting together a short list of candidates to replace Rich Kotite, who had been fired.

Lurie had contacted me prior to the Shrine game, and when I had visited with Erickson, he said, "Barry, I really like Lurie. I think he's going to be a great owner."

Cindy and I went out to dinner with Lurie on the West Coast. Jeffrey and I continued talking, and we made arrangements to talk again at the Super Bowl in Miami. We got together, and Lurie offered me the Eagles job. I really gave it serious thought.

I called Joe Panos, who was with the team, and I got kind of a scouting report from him on what was going on in Philadelphia. I wanted to know what the facilities were like, what they lacked as far as personnel, and so on.

I liked Jeffrey Lurie. And I agreed with Erickson: I thought he was going to be a good owner. He didn't have much of a track record yet, but I was impressed with him. I liked his aggressiveness. I thought he had a feel for Philly and what the Eagles meant to the city.

As I made a list of the plusses and minuses of taking the Philadelphia job, I always came back to the same things: I know college football and I love college football. Even though I'm a fast learner and I felt like I could go into the NFL and learn what I needed to learn, when push came to shove I didn't want to do it.

Lurie hired Ray Rhodes, and I stayed at Wisconsin.

Again, I was flattered to be considered, but I was also really worn out. Our season had taken a lot out of me. I followed that up with recruiting and I was zapped emotionally.

I wasn't looking to leave Wisconsin, either.

I thought that we were going to have a little bit of a slip in 1995, and I wanted to get over that hump. I didn't want to abandon the program or Pat Richter. I wasn't going to hang him out to dry.

After building it up to the level where we had just won back-to-back January 1st bowl games, including a Rose Bowl, I didn't feel like I should leave at that time.

I didn't have concerns about our direction as a program. We knew how to win, and we still had good young players. We had a good nucleus coming back, too, and we had Bevell. There were some question marks. But I still thought we could be decent. I didn't think we would drop off that much or to the extent that we wouldn't go to a bowl.

***

During my first year as a Big Ten coach, I had the opportunity to sit down with Penn State's Joe Paterno. Growing up in western Pennsylvania, I always respected Paterno and what he meant to the game. He stood for college football.

"Coach Paterno, do you have any suggestions for a new head coach?" I asked him.

"You've played for one of the best, Bob Devaney," he said. "You worked for two of the best, Hayden Fry and Lou Holtz. Take the lessons you've learned from them — because those guys know how to win — and apply it to what you're doing at Wisconsin."

Since I had his ear, I threw out another question.

"How have you survived as a head coach for all those years in Pennsylvania?" I asked. "Football is so important for people in the state that they take it to a different level. Everyone thinks they know everything there is to know about the game. Everyone has an opinion on how it should be played. So how have you survived?"

Paterno said, "The one thing I told them when I took the job was, 'You're going to have to trust me. You've given me this job, you've entrusted me with this job, now you have to trust me. I need your support, particularly your financial support.

"But I do not need your advice. Don't tell me what plays to call and who to play. Support me, instead of questioning me...and I do need your money.'"

When I was a high school senior, Joe Paterno was the guest speaker at an all-star banquet in Pittsburgh, and I always tease him, "I thought you were old THEN."

Penn State never recruited me. "Alvarez, you were a fat ass," Paterno still likes to say whenever we get together. "You were slow. That's why I didn't recruit you."

We have fun jabbing each other.

Joe has always had access to so many good players. He's had plenty to choose from, and I've always respected the type of football that he has played. He recruits tough kids. They're not going to be fancy, but they're going to be sound in everything they do.

Watching Paterno in his 40th year as a head coach, it's mind-boggling what he has done for the school. Joe Paterno IS the school. He put Penn State on the map. I liken it to what Knute Rockne did at Notre Dame. What's even more amazing is that Joe has spent all those years — well over 50 years — at the same school. That's not easy.

Lou Holtz used to say, "Don't stay any place longer than seven years because the fans are going to get tired of you." Spike Dykes liked to say, "You lose 10 percent of your supporters every year." Even Bobby Bowden has coached at different schools, and somewhere other than Florida State, where he will retire someday.

At Paterno's age — he'll be 80 in December — it's so impressive that he's still coaching on the field every practice. I know how much coaching takes out of you, physically and mentally. The stress is 24/7, especially for someone like Paterno who can't go anywhere without being recognized. But he's still sharp today and outspoken as ever.

Any time we beat Penn State, it was a good win, and it was very gratifying for me because of my Pennsylvania roots, and the fact that I knew they had so many good players.

For my family and friends in Burgettstown and Langeloth, a Badger win meant bragging rights for a year.

As a head coach, the first time I beat the Nittany Lions was during the 1995 season. They were ranked No. 6 and had the longest winning streak, 20 games, in Division I-A. But we upset them in Beaver Stadium, 17-9, behind Bevell's 18 of 22 passing.

That was our Big Ten opener, one of the few highlights from the season. As long as we kept getting better, I thought at the time, we would be fine. We didn't get any better.

We were close to being a bowl team again. But we had trouble running the ball consistently, and our placekicker, John Hall, was inconsistent. He kicked a 60-yard field goal at Minnesota. But he missed a 36-yarder in a 24-24 tie at Stanford, and he missed a 29-yarder in the final game of the season, a 3-3 tie against Illinois.

We finished with a 4-5-2 record. Some people wanted to blame Bevell. But he was never a quarterback who was going to win games by himself.

One of the low points was a home loss to Iowa that eliminated us from bowl contention. We ran the ball 20 times for minus-18 net yards.

That weekend we had a recruit on campus — a highly-touted running back out of New Jersey. Most schools were recruiting him as a fullback. We wanted him to play tailback.

I asked him, "Do you like carrying the ball?"

He nodded his head and grinned.

"Well, I'll give you the damn ball as many times as you want it."

I kept my promise to Ron Dayne.

***

When I first saw Dayne on high school film, I saw him lining up as a fullback about a yard or two behind the quarterback. He would take two steps, get the ball, and kind of disappear at the line of scrimmage. And then you'd see the pile move.

There were times when he would line up much deeper in the backfield, and you could see that he had great vision and patience. Most big runners are just going to try and run through the pile. Not Ron. He would allow things to develop.

Once he got into the secondary, you could tell that guys weren't crazy about tackling him, and he had the speed to outrun people. That's when I said, "He can play tailback."

That was one of our recruiting pitches. "We're not just going to put you at the position and forget about you," I said. "You're going to get your shot to be our tailback."

He liked that.

What wasn't there to like about Dayne? He had vision, strength, and burst. He used his size to his ability and nobody caught him when he came out the back end.

As the game wore on, he got stronger. And he loved to play in the winter, he loved to play when it was cold. I couldn't have drawn it up any better.

Bernie Wyatt recruited New Jersey for Hayden Fry, and he really worked his contacts with the high school coaches and administrators in the state. One of his first catches was Leroy Smith, who was an All-Big Ten defensive end for the Hawkeyes.

When Bernie joined the Wisconsin staff, he kept the pipeline open to New Jersey by signing Lee DeRamus, who went to Smith's high school, Edgewood Regional.

Bernie's lead contact was Ron Hopson — a counselor, principal and Dayne confidant. Bernie had always looked after Hop's kids in Iowa City, and Hopson knew that if Dayne came to Madison, he would be treated right.

Ohio State was also recruiting Dayne hard. But the publicity and the prestige of the Ohio State program wasn't going to sway Dayne. It was all about where Ron Dayne felt comfortable. Hopson felt all along that Wisconsin was the best fit.

Dayne trusted Hopson, and Hopson trusted Bernie. "Ron just needs some attention," Hopson told me, "and a big hug when he gets out there."

He was such a nice kid; so laid-back and really quiet. But he would open up with me — that was the type of relationship that we had over his four years here.

I remember when he first showed up on campus, he had just won the discus title in a national high school meet on the West Coast. He was built along the lines of Larry Station, the linebacker I coached at Iowa. They were the same height, but Dayne was much bigger.

I never worried about Dayne's weight. He was really thick as a freshman — 270 pounds — but he handled it well. John Dettmann, who coordinated our conditioning, said Dayne was beating the other tailbacks by a step-and-a-half in the five-yard sprints.

***

Dayne dwarfed cornerbacks.

Aaron Gibson dwarfed Dayne.

We really didn't know what we had with Gibson. As a freshman, he was academically ineligible to practice. We knew this much — he was huge, over 400 pounds.

As a sophomore, Gibby had "trimmed down" to 378. The first time I saw him work out — I watched him bend and go through some lineman drills — I turned to our offensive line coach Jim Hueber and said, "Huebs, he's special, really special. Let's use him."

Since we already had two quality Big Ten tackles — Chris McIntosh and Jerry Wunsch — we decided to use Gibson as a tight end in a "Jumbo" formation.

I'll never forget when we unveiled Gibson. We were playing at Ohio State, and we sent him on the field with the play, and he's running out there with his arms up in the air. You should have seen the looks on the faces of those defensive players.

In addition to using Gibson as a tight end in the Jumbo, we shifted McIntosh to the right side with Wunsch, forcing the Buckeyes to make some adjustments.

Gibby was fun to watch. He was like a cub bear. With his big paw, he would just whack people and knock them down. You had no chance if he got his hands on you.

During the 1996 season, we got quite a bit of mileage out of Gibby, who helped create some big running seams for Dayne. Even as a freshman, Dayne was a special tailback, a special kid, and we were going to ride him. I knew Sammy — quarterback Mike Samuel — wasn't a great thrower, but he could run. We built everything around that.

Four games into the Big Ten season, though, we're 0-4 and reeling from some really tough losses: 23-20 to Penn State, 17-14 to Ohio State, and 34-30 to Northwestern. That was one of the toughest losses I've ever been through, and I've never gotten over it.

That was a game that we had in the bank, a game we're going to win. We're leading Northwestern 30-27, with 1 minute and 33 seconds left, and we've got the ball on our 38.

No one will take a knee faster than me. But we couldn't run out the clock. We had to run the ball and get a first down or line up and punt with time remaining. And the percentages are better handing the ball off than snapping for a punt on fourth down.

After Ronnie gained seven yards on a first down run, what we should have done is run a quarterback sneak with Samuel. We could have probably run two sneaks and gotten the first down instead of handing it to Dayne on second down.

But we missed a block, somebody flashed right in front of Ron, he flinched, and he never got the ball in his hands. You can't believe your eyes when something like that happens. Northwestern recovered the fumble, and two plays later scored the game-winning touchdown. And it's over. Just like that. It's over, except for the criticism.

ESPN's Gary Danielson challenged my strategy, criticizing me for poor time management and not taking a knee. Lee Corso comes on and says I should be fired.

That really upset me.

That's a former coach, making a statement like that on national TV, and he doesn't even have the facts: I couldn't have taken a knee and gotten out of the game. It was irresponsible on Corso's part. I don't care if you're trying to make a name for yourself on television or not, that's just not right, and I later confronted Corso about it.

The following week, Danielson's play-by-play partner, Brad Nessler, apologized for any critical remarks and for second-guessing my decision. I appreciated that.

Nessler admitted that he and Danielson were packing away their charts and spotting boards, thinking that the game was over, when Dayne fumbled. Danielson looked up, saw how much time was remaining on the clock, and made a statement that wasn't accurate.

He wasn't right. But, unlike Nessler, he wasn't willing to back down.

Michigan State coach Nick Saban also came to my defense, pointing out that if we had taken a knee on three straight snaps, we still would have been punting the ball to Northwestern with about 30 seconds on the clock. Saban agreed with me; there was a greater risk from a high snap or blocked punt than a quarterback-tailback exchange.

In my post-game press conference, I said, "If I had to do it over again, I would have run the same play and given the football to the same kid."

Ronnie thanked me for the comments.

I think he bounced back quicker than me.

I know he did.

***

A couple of weeks after that frustrating Northwestern loss, Dayne rushed for over 240 yards in a win over Purdue. During that game, a Big Ten official came over to our sideline, laughing about Gibson. "Barry," he said, "the Purdue defensive end wanted to know if there was a weight limit for tight ends in this conference."

Gibby could be overpowering.

So could Dayne.

"Quite frankly, I'd rather tackle a Ron Dayne than players who dance around because I could never grab them," I told a reporter who asked if I would have been a match for Dayne during my playing days as a linebacker.

"I wouldn't mind the collision," I went on. "Whether I'd get him down or not is another thing. I've got short arms. I don't know if I could wrap him up."

With Dayne, we changed our landmarks on some of our running plays — like the stretch and outside zone — to take advantage of the type of runner he was.

Terrell Fletcher was a speed back, and that's what we wanted on the stretch. We wanted him running at full speed to stretch the defense, which meant Bevell would have to go as hard as he could, and reach as far as he could, just to get the ball to Fletch.

Dayne didn't have that type of initial burst. He was probably a half-step slower than Fletcher, and his landmark was a full man inside. Dayne was more patient. And while he could take it outside or cut it back, most of his big runs were off-tackle, where we'd create a seam. By sealing everything inside, we made the safety come up and tackle him.

Some of our players thought Minnesota's defensive backs were "short-arming" Dayne. At times, it looked like they were scared to tackle him — explaining why we gave the ball to him 50 times and he rushed for 297 yards and three touchdowns against the Gophers.

In my post-game press conference, someone wanted to know what Dayne was going to do for an encore after rushing for 541 yards against Purdue and Minnesota.

"He's just starting to get lathered up," I assured them. "All you have to do is look at him to know he's special. He's very mature, very strong. He's an overpowering kid. He's pretty durable and he's dishing out a lot of punishment himself. You know what the best thing is?

"He's got plenty of playing time left, plenty of years left, plenty of great days in him."

Plenty of great nights, too. Like the one he had at Hawaii.

We had to win to get to a bowl, and I was a nervous wreck beforehand. One of our boosters, Tom Wiesner, a former Badger running back, was at our practice the day before the game, and I remember telling Tom, "I don't like the look in our freshman's eyes."

Dayne looked distracted. We were going through our script of 15 openers, and we were on play No. 12 when I jumped the offense and made them start over from No. 1.

I had them repeat everything because I wanted to get their attention, especially Dayne's. It must have worked because he rushed for 339 yards in THREE quarters. He had 250 at halftime, and he could have had 500. I had never seen anything like it.

The Hawaii defense was like a bunch of little kids trying to tackle a grown man — Dayne — and they wanted nothing to do with him.

Every time I go back to Hawaii, I'll have at least one person thank me for taking Dayne out of the game when I did and not embarrassing them more.

Their defensive coordinator said afterward that trying to tackle Ron Dayne was like trying to stop a Mack truck with a pea shooter.

No freshman has ever done what he did.

He rushed for over 2,000 yards.

"And he will only get better," I predicted.

I'm not sure anyone believed me.

***

When you have a running back like Dayne, you have to have a quarterback who isn't worried about his numbers, his statistics. Mike Samuel was perfect.

In the 1996 Copper Bowl, we beat Utah 38-10. Dayne rushed for 246 yards, Samuel attempted six passes, and a receiver ran the wrong route on one of the completions.

When we recruited Mike Samuel out of Philadelphia, we knew that he could play some positions other than quarterback. But I've always liked quarterbacks who can run, and I really liked Sammy's toughness. He was as tough of a competitor as we've ever had.

Ask the kids, "Who on this team would you walk down a dark alley with?" Mike Samuel would be the No. 1 choice.

He was serious and all business. Not that I didn't get upset with him. Every practice, he would do something to upset me when he tried to pass. I've never seen the football come out of anybody's hand like it did Mike's.

It wasn't like he wasn't trying. He just couldn't throw very well. At least not consistently. That was the irony. When you needed a big throw, he could make it.

He was clutch, not pretty, but clutch.

And we played to his strengths. We won three games during the '97 season that we had no business winning, and it was because of Mike Samuel.

Boise State has us beat. They had a corner blitz on a third down play — third-and-long — and the guy whacks Samuel. The game should be over. But Mike won't go down. He flushes out of the pocket and scrambles 28 yards to keep the drive alive.

I had benched Mike earlier in the game. He threw two interceptions and lost a fumble, and he heard the boos from the home fans. But he was there for us when we needed him: Samuel scored the winning touchdown on another third down run.

In our Big Ten opener, we're getting beat by a bad Indiana team. But they can't close us out, and we got one final possession. On fourth-and-15, Samuel completed a 22-yard pass to Tony Simmons, setting up Matt Davenport's game-winning field goal.

The next week, we're getting beat at Northwestern and that game looks like it's over, too. But the Wildcats lose the ball on a fumble, and we take over on our own 4. On the final drive, Samuel has a 23-yard run and a 28-yard pass to Simmons on third-and-7. And that led to another game-winning field goal from Davenport.

Clutch, like I said.

We needed someone to take the pressure off Dayne, someone who could burn people when they went to their blitz package. That someone was Samuel.

People would come up to me and say sarcastically, "Great coaching job — you just hand the ball to Ron Dayne. We know your next play before you're going to run it."

True. We were like Woody Hayes and his "three yards and a cloud of dust."

It wasn't hard to figure out who was going to get the ball. But you still had to tackle Dayne, and you had to deal with Samuel when we ran the option.

"Why don't you throw on first down?" I was repeatedly asked.

"I don't like second-and-10," I answered.

We did what we had to do to win.

***

In mid-December of 1997, while we were getting ready to begin preparations for the Outback Bowl against Georgia, there was some breaking news at Nebraska. After 25 years as the Cornhuskers' head coach, Tom Osborne announced his retirement at a press conference. Frank Solich was going to be Osborne's successor.

Someone from Lincoln had called and tipped me off. "Tom is getting ready to retire," he said. "You need to get ahold of someone right away and get your name on the list."

Things happened too quickly for that: Frank was named that same day.

I was never officially contacted by anyone connected with the school. But I would have been interested in returning to my alma mater. I'd be lying if I said otherwise.

I've always had a soft spot in my heart for Nebraska. You had everything there you needed to be successful. We loved the people, and we still had friends in the city.

But I was very happy that Frank Solich got the job.

The Nebraska line of succession — Osborne handpicking Solich — was very much like what I did here with Bret Bielema. And it was set into motion years earlier.

I was aware of that because Solich had committed to being the offensive coordinator on my first coaching staff at Wisconsin. I had Dan McCarney for the defense and Solich for the offense. Frankie was all set to come to Madison. His family was fired up.

But he decided to stay in Lincoln. It sounded like Tom Osborne may have promised him then that he would be the next head coach when Tom eventually retired.

What if Nebraska had called and offered me the job?

It would have been very difficult to say no.

CHAPTER TEN
History in the Making

The play is still painfully vivid in my mind. On third-and-short, Georgia quarterback Mike Bobo turned and pitched the ball to his tailback, Robert Edwards, and Edwards raced around the left end untouched to the end zone.

I had never seen anybody do that — run outside of our flank — against one of our defenses. I looked at my D-line coach, John Palermo, and said, "What the hell just happened there?" John shrugged and said, "I don't know."

That's the way it went for us in the 1998 Outback Bowl, and it was reflected in the final score, 33-6. That was a national championship-caliber Georgia team, and one of the most talented opponents that I've played against in my 16 seasons at Wisconsin.

Edwards was a first-round draft choice and rushed for over 1,000-yards during his rookie season before having his pro career shortened by a knee injury. His backup, Olandis Gary, was also a 1,000 yard rusher in the NFL.

Hines Ward was Georgia's leading receiver, and we all saw what he meant to the Super Bowl champion Pittsburgh Steelers. Offensive tackle Matt Stinchcomb was a first-round draft choice, as was cornerback Champ Bailey. And two freshman defensive tackles, Richard Seymour and Marcus Stroud, matured into high draft picks.

After the bowl, people were knocking us because we were beaten so soundly. They were writing that we needed to go out and recruit better athletes and more speed, but that's not what beat us. Georgia was just better than us. We really weren't in their class that year.

The bottom line was that we were still young at many positions. Our three starters on the interior offensive line — Bill Ferrario, Casey Rabach, and Dave Costa — were redshirt freshmen. On defense, Ross Kolodziej, John Favret, and Jason Doering were freshmen.

All things considered, we maxed out the 1997 season to win eight games with that team. Especially to win as many close games as we won — five by a total of 11 points. And even though we didn't play well against Georgia, even though we were overmatched, we were still playing in a New Year's Day bowl, which has always been one of our goals.

I remember saying afterward, "We're doing it with kids who are going to be playing with this program for three more years. It's a helluva accomplishment for them to get here, and we'll get a lot of positives from this game."

What I didn't expect to hear is what our sophomore offensive tackle, Chris McIntosh, had to say after the Georgia loss. "I didn't come to Wisconsin to go to the damn Outback Bowl," he said with conviction and passion. "I came here to go to the Rose Bowl."

Here we had just gotten our ass beat and he was talking about the Rose Bowl. That was impressive, especially coming from such a young player. I like it when somebody has the grit and confidence to stand up and make a statement like that.

Now you've got to back it up. McIntosh, though, was a team leader, exactly like Joe Panos. Sometimes you get guys who are spouting off in the locker room, and everyone is looking at them like they're crazy. They're just making noise, and nobody is listening.

But they listened to Mac, and his comments set the tone. Our two senior captains, Cecil Martin and Bob Adamov, came up to me during our 1998 training camp, and said, "Coach, we came here not just to go to bowl games. We'd like to go to the Rose Bowl."

I smiled. "Enough said. That's our goal."

We had some question marks. Jamar Fletcher, for instance, was such a skinny kid — barely above 150 pounds — and I didn't know if he was physical enough to be our starter at corner. But he had to play. You'd like for him to hold up, but you didn't know.

Our philosophy hadn't changed. Our focus was on improvement, about each individual getting a little stronger and faster. If that happened, we would get better as a team. We had a good nucleus coming back, and we were solid at almost every position. We just needed some young players to come through starting with our season opener at San Diego State.

That was a game much like our 1993 road game at SMU — a potential ambush. They were pointing to us and looking to get off to a fast start by knocking off a Big Ten opponent, and we were going into the game not knowing if we would have Ron Dayne.

During a preseason practice at Camp Randall, I was going to blow the whistle fast but I wanted to see Fletcher tackle in the open field. I let the play go and somebody came in late and rolled up on Dayne's ankle.

Dayne tried to go in warm-ups, but his ankle was still too tender, and we had to scratch him and start Eddie Faulkner against San Diego State. Then we lost Faulkner with a shoulder injury in the first half. So we were down to our No. 3 tailback, Carlos Daniels, a redshirt freshman, and Daniels gave us a lift by rushing for over 100 yards.

But it was quarterback Mike Samuel who really saved us. Early in the fourth quarter, trailing 14-13, Samuel took off on a 47-yard touchdown run. He just wouldn't let us lose.

After we had escaped with the victory, I remember saying, "Sammy is one competitive son-of-a gun and I'll tell you what — for those people who still want to criticize Mike Samuel — I'll fight them right here and now."

Rallying for a win on the road showed character, and we gained confidence from it. Our freshmen corners, Fletcher and Mike Echols, each had an interception. And I thought our defense played lights out, particularly in the second half.

But after we walked out of there with a 12-point win, I wrote in my game notes, "We're in trouble at a couple of positions." Fletcher and McIntosh got hurt.

In the second quarter, Mac jammed his thumb against a defensive lineman. He kept playing, thinking it was only dislocated because it fell out a few times and he just clicked it back into place. But when the offense came off the field after the series, Mac sought out a trainer and learned he had broken his thumb.

At halftime they put a cast on the thumb, and he went back out and played. After the game, we feared McIntosh might need surgery and miss the next three or four weeks. Or longer.

But they didn't operate, and he kept playing. Offensive linemen need their hands. Both hands. And even though McIntosh had a cast on his right hand, which made it tough to control pass rushers, he never complained or made excuses.

"He'd play blind if he had to," our defensive end, Tom Burke, said of

McIntosh. "On the sidelines, he'd just ask you, 'Where's my guy?' and he'd step out and block him."

That was Big Mac.

He'd speak his mind.

And he was tough.

***

McIntosh, Martin, Adamov and Donnel Thompson were our four captains that season. Mac took the role of captain very seriously. During the offseason, he even talked with Panos and asked for some ideas.

Panos explained his thinking. "Don't change who you are — stay who you are — don't change your personality," Panos said. "Sometimes people will become captains and think that all of a sudden they have to be a different person, and they start treating others differently. Don't change, just try to set an example for everybody else."

On Mondays, we had a captains' roundtable, where I would sit down and discuss team issues. It was something I started during the 1993 season because I wanted to get the players' voice. I used reps from each class. I chose the older ones, while the freshmen voted on their representative. I didn't plan a roundtable every year, using it based on need, the type of team, and the type of captains.

Food always seemed to be an issue.

McIntosh, Martin, Thompson, and Adamov met regularly during the '98 season. Mac couldn't make it one Monday because he was having his thumb X-rayed, so he sent word through Adamov that there was a concern among the offensive linemen. The concern? The time allotted for eating dinner on the night before a game.

They didn't think 30 minutes was enough time to eat. They wanted 45 minutes so they could really sit down and digest their food and get themselves mentally ready for the movie. They had 45 minutes last season, and they wanted the 15 minutes back.

I told them, "Hell, if they keep playing good football on the offensive line, we'll get them cigars and Courvoisier afterward, whatever is right."

After our Northwestern win, we gave our team award — the Most Valuable Player on offense — to the entire line. It's not a token award. The kids all sit in as we grade the film. They know who's playing well and who's not, and they know who's making mistakes and who's not. When you can give the MVP award to a group of players, that tells you they're all playing really good football.

You could say the same thing about us — as a team.

On offense, we had a Pro Bowl wide receiver (Chris Chambers) and a Heisman Trophy tailback (Ron Dayne) running behind an NFL offensive line: two first-rounders at tackle (Chris McIntosh and Aaron Gibson), a third-rounder at center (Casey Rabach), and a fourth-rounder (Bill Ferrario) and free agent (Dave Costa) at guard.

We benefited from hidden yardage and some outstanding specialists. We had a great punter (Kevin Stemke), placekicker (Matt Davenport), and kick returner (Nick Davis). And our defense was really good.

Tom Burke had a motor and created things rushing off the edge. He was hard to block. Our inside linebackers, Donnel Thompson and Chris Ghidorzi, weren't as talented as some we've had, but they were very smart. They studied tendencies and understood the game.

Thompson and Ghidorzi were the catalysts. They brought the whole group together. On Thursday nights, Ghido's parents would drive down from Wausau and fix dinner for the entire defense.

Fletcher and Echols were young, but they were confident. Fletch didn't have great speed or strength, but he had a great mind for the game and anticipated well. The best way to recruit a corner is to recruit a good athlete. You want to watch him run track or watch him play basketball and see how he moves his feet.

Echols was a no-brainer. He jumped out on film. Lanky, long arms, fast. Fletcher, on the other hand, was a high school quarterback.

Whenever we're recruiting a player for one position — and he may want to play someplace else — I tell him, "To start with, we're going to give you an opportunity to play wherever you want. And I won't move you to another position without visiting with you first. But we want to play our best players, so getting them on the field is the bottom line."

I knew Fletcher and Echols would keep getting better. I also knew they would get the challenge of their life against Purdue and Drew Brees. We prepared them for what they were going to get — not that anyone could anticipate Brees attempting 83 passes. But I had coached in games like this before at Notre Dame against Miami and Stanford.

We went into the Purdue game with a plan: don't let them catch it over your head, don't give them anything easy, and don't get discouraged when they complete passes. Let's just make sure we come up and make the tackle when they make the catch and we limit their yards after the catch.

Brees completed 55 passes. But we knew that if we stayed patient, the closer they got to the goal line, the harder it would be to throw because we were dropping more people. It was a long, tedious game — because of all the completions — but we were leading 31-17 when Purdue finally scored again in the final 22 seconds. The plan had worked.

Fletcher had the defensive play of the year when he picked off Brees and returned the interception 52 yards for a touchdown, breaking a third-quarter tie. The play unfolded right in front of me.

Fletch likes to sit on receivers, and he sat on the out cut. I thought he played well the whole game as far as contesting throws. When I was asked about him afterward, I said, "Right now, he's a good corner. Someday, he may go into the 'really good' category."

***

We won nine straight before finally losing at Michigan. We weren't nearly as sharp or focused as we had been, and we didn't do a good job handling some distractions. Ghidorzi pulled his hamstring and missed the game. His replacement, Roger Knight, broke his arm in the first half, and we ended up playing Nick Greisen, a true freshman.

Without Ghido, who called the defensive signals, Donnel Thompson had to take on a new role. As a defense, we were out of sync, and Michigan capitalized, rushing for over 250 yards. That was shocking.

We had five times as many mental errors in that game as we did in the two previous games combined. There were times when Michigan would run its counter play, and we had three guys stacked up behind one another instead of being spaced.

It really shuffles things up when your signal-caller (Ghidorzi) goes down because now somebody else (Thompson) can't just go out and play. He has another burden and other things to worry about.

That wasn't the only distraction.

During the week, the local media was quick to point a finger at Mike Samuel, who had been involved in an altercation outside a State Street bar the previous Saturday. Some people jumped to conclusions about Samuel without knowing the facts. His brother was the one who had thrown a punch. Charges were later dropped against Mike.

Sometimes you're not going to play well on defense, and that's the day when the offense has to step up, but ours sure didn't at Michigan. We couldn't get anything going. It was like banging your head against a wall. We had put in a new audible system for the game, and our quarterback and tailback went the wrong way at least three times.

Despite the loss, we were still in the running for the Rose Bowl. "But we don't control our destiny anymore," I told the players. "We handled winning well. Now we have to handle a loss. We're still sitting here at 9-1, and we still have a lot of things to play for."

For everything to work in our favor, we needed Ohio State to beat Michigan in Columbus, and we needed to beat Penn State at Camp Randall. All I wanted was our brand of football back. That's what we talked about all week. If it's good enough, great. If it's not good enough, that's fine, too. But I wanted to play old school football, and that's how we played.

The Buckeyes beat the Wolverines, and we beat the Nittany Lions to create a three-way tie atop the Big Ten standings. Better yet, we had the tie-breaker and the trip to Pasadena. McIntosh got his wish. We weren't going to another damn Outback Bowl.

***

After the 1994 Rose Bowl, I never even thought about getting back. I tried to stay focused on what we had to do to get better. I tried to stay in the present. That's because at Wisconsin, you've got to be lucky in recruiting. We're not in the same position geographically as some of the Top 10 schools that are sitting in recruiting hotbeds.

We have to leave the state, especially for the skill positions. And the farther away from home you go, the tougher it is to recruit.

Over the years our average has been 50 percent — of the players that we've recruited about 50 percent pan out. We could still be consistent and competitive. But we had to have the right fit with our personnel and the right team leadership and the right timing to separate ourselves from the pack.

The '98 team may have been my best team.

Through 11 games, we led the nation in points allowed. And we were also one of the top defenses against the run and the pass. On offense, we were efficient and disciplined, and we led the country in turnover margin. We didn't win with fluff. We weren't fancy.

UCLA was the sexy team with the high-powered offense, so we took a beating in the press, even though we were 10-1. I always look for an edge going into a game, and I didn't need help finding one. CBS analyst Craig James came out and called us "the worst team I can remember playing in the Rose Bowl." The worst team, ever? Really. That was a lay-up.

I also knew UCLA was upset about playing in the Rose Bowl because the Bruins had their hearts set on playing for the national championship. No one had slowed them down all year. With Cade McNown at quarterback, they were averaging over 40 points. But they couldn't slow down anyone, either. They lost 49-45 to Miami in a rescheduled game that cost them a chance at playing Tennessee for the title.

I knew the Bruins weren't taking us seriously. Nobody was. On a players' tour of Universal Studios, Jamar Fletcher got really upset when the tour guide said, "We'd like to congratulate the two Rose Bowl teams. We have UCLA and the other guys."

During one of the press conferences, UCLA coach Bob Toledo mistakenly referred to Tom Burke as Tom Barnes. Burke handled it well. When the media came to him for a response, he said, "I don't say much with my mouth. I talk with my pads."

At a black-tie event, William Shatner, who was the Grand Marshal for the Tournament of Roses parade, got up and rooted for UCLA to beat us. This was at a function involving both teams, and, damn it, you can't do something like that. I was ticked.

The next day at a luncheon, Shatner walked up to me and handed me his autographed picture. I didn't ask for it, and I didn't want the damn thing. So I crumpled it up and threw it at his feet and walked away. Knowing what I know today about Shatner's character in a TV series, there were only two words to describe the scene.

Denny Crane.

Shatner didn't say a word to me.

Not that I blamed him.

I tend to get wound up.

At the same luncheon, they introduced one of UCLA's big defensive ends, and I turned to our chancellor David Ward, who's very scholarly and soft-spoken, and let him know we were going to do everything possible to make that Bruins' life miserable. "We're really going to get after that guy's ass," I said.

David did a double-take.

I don't think anyone thought we could win a shoot-out with UCLA.

But I knew they weren't any good on defense, and I knew we could run the ball on them. But not like we did.

***

"List all the reasons why you like it here," I said. "List your feelings. What did you come here for? What did you come here to accomplish?"

That was the best advice I could give Ron Dayne, who was weighing the pro's and con's of returning for his final year of eligibility.

I personally contacted over 10 teams in the National Football League on Dayne's behalf, and a majority of them responded with written evaluations of Dayne's draft status.

"If you go pro, this is what the people who make those decisions are saying about you," I said, showing him the results. "And if you come back and play as a senior and polish your game a bit, mature more, and improve on specifics, this is where you can be in next year's draft. You can move up the draft ladder considerably."

We put the facts on the table. We had all the information, and I didn't feel like there was any reason to drag it out because Ron was starting to get questions on what he was going to do. Every day, people were asking him about it and speculating on his future.

But it was still all about Ron Dayne and what was best for him.

Ten days before the Rose Bowl, he announced that he would be coming back for his senior year at Wisconsin. "I have great fans," he said, "and I don't want to leave them yet."

He talked about the "family" atmosphere on the team, and he talked about staying in Madison for another year so he could be near his 13-month-old daughter, Jada, and Jada's mother, Aliah. He talked about being closer to getting his degree. And he talked about some things that he still wanted to accomplish. Like catching Ricky Williams and becoming the NCAA's all-time leading rusher. Like winning the Heisman.

"But it's a team sport," he reminded everyone at his press conference. "If the team doesn't do good, I'm not going to do good. I always look at my team first."

For him to make the decision when he did was settling for me — I don't like distractions or outside people interfering with our business — and settling for him.

Especially him.

Ron Dayne may have had his best game ever against UCLA in the Rose Bowl. Our guys up front blocked well, but the Bruins couldn't slow him down, they couldn't tackle him. In outscoring UCLA, 38-31, Dayne ran for 246 yards and four touchdowns. Man, was he good.

He gave us some big runs. We've seen runs like that before, but it had been a while. I felt like he'd be physically OK for this game. But you never know. He didn't practice much in December because of a torn pectoral muscle, and he played with pain.

Whenever he came out of the game and we gave the ball to Eddie Faulkner, they stoned him. Ronnie gets back out there, and it's like a man playing against boys.

At one point, an official came up to me and asked, "Barry, where did you get all of this team speed?" I laughed and said, "It's the same guys that played against Georgia."

I had to listen to that nonsense for a whole year — that we couldn't compete with the better teams nationally because we didn't have enough speed and skill players.

We got the last laugh.

That's the one thing about this group of players, they never flinched.

That was our motto.

In the locker room after the game, I thanked the older guys for their leadership, and I challenged the young guys to stay hungry. We had gone to school on what happened after the 1994 Rose Bowl, and we were not going to let them become fat cats. You can't get complacent and have a chance to survive, especially in the Big Ten.

I realized that nobody had ever won back-to-back Rose Bowls. But I didn't use that as motivation for the players. I didn't think it was important. I never considered the history behind doing something like that. Others may have, but I can't control somebody else's expectations. And they weren't going to affect how I go about my business or how we go about setting goals and standards for this team. We'll do that ourselves.

I knew we'd be a good team again. But I was concerned about quarterback. Samuel brought a tough, hard-nosed competitive spirit to the offense and our kids fed off Mike because they saw someone who never backed down and never showed a sign of weakness.

He never flinched.

***

When I talked to Dayne about coming back as a senior, I promised we would have a plan for his Heisman Trophy campaign. If he was going to win the Heisman or break the NCAA career rushing mark, I wanted it to be within the context of the game.

Our sports information director, Steve Malchow, came to me during training camp with a list of things we could do as a school to promote Dayne for the Heisman.

"A good, solid, no-gimmick campaign is our best approach," Malchow said. "My goal is to get Ron to New York with the finalists for the award presentation. The rest is out of my hands. I feel the incredible Big Ten television exposure will carry us.

"The only issue is team success. I know Ron will get too much credit if we win, and too much blame if we lose. But I think 10 wins will get us to the Downtown Athletic Club."

In the season opener, Dayne rushed for 135 yards in the first half against Murray State, and I decided not to play him in the second half. It was just a gut feeling based on how things were going, just common sense. The game was already in hand.

But I took heat for not playing him more. Someone said, "The only person who can stop Ron Dayne from breaking Ricky Williams' record is Alvarez."

If I had left him in the game, he would have rushed for over 300. But I just didn't feel that was the thing to do. That would have been humiliating for him and humiliating for Murray State. And would the record have meant as much?

I said afterward, "There's a lot of football left. There are going to be games when he's going to be carrying the ball in the fourth quarter. You don't want to panic. Ron will get plenty of touches. But the record is not going to be a distraction. It's still about winning."

After four games, we were 2-2 and winning back-to-back Rose Bowls was the farthest thing from our minds. We were just trying to get on a winning streak of any kind, especially after losing back-to-back games to Cincinnati and Michigan.

That Cincinnati loss still ticks me off.

I hate to see officials steal from the kids.

Nick Davis had an 81-yard punt return for a touchdown wiped out because of a questionable blocking-from-behind penalty on Michael Bennett.

Then, on our final series of the game, Scott Kavanagh completes a touchdown pass to Lee Evans, but the play is nullified because of an illegal motion penalty against tight end John Sigmund. The flag was thrown after Evans made the catch. Ridiculous.

It was the worst homer job I've ever seen. Even the Big Ten supervisor of officials, David Parry, said he couldn't believe his eyes when he was reviewing the tape. He thought it looked like the game officials were getting excited about throwing a flag against us.

"We've enjoyed a lot of wins," I stressed to the players. "We've got to learn how to handle defeat. Nobody likes it, but we've got to deal with it and bounce back."

I felt like we did bounce back against Michigan in our Big Ten opener. We didn't win the game, but we uncovered a starting quarterback in the fourth quarter.

Brooks Bollinger led the offense on an 80-yard scoring drive, and he showed so much composure that I knew there was no question he had to be our guy.

Right after the Michigan game, I talked with my quarterback coach, Jeff Horton, and I told him how I felt about Bollinger. Jeff really did a good job explaining our decision to Scott Kavanagh. That was a tough situation.

Kavanagh had waited five years for his chance to be the starter, and now we were going to move a redshirt freshman ahead of him. Jeff talked to Scott, then I talked to Scott.

And I thought he really handled it well. Scott accepted our decision. He could have been bitter or disruptive. Some kids today would have just quit the team. But he hung in there.

I'm glad he did, too. Kavanagh ended up being a grad assistant on my staff, and he's now coaching in the Ivy League. He's going to be a very good coach.

Bollinger just brought more to the table. He was a fierce competitor. I can't say there was anyone who competed harder than Brooks in my 16 seasons.

I love combination quarterbacks who can beat you throwing or running. Plus, he had all the intangibles. He showed leadership in the huddle. He did all the right things on the field and off. He was a guy's guy. The players respected him.

As it was, we had some weapons. It was going to be hard to stop Ron from running the ball, and we also had Chris Chambers as a receiving threat. But now we had a quarterback who could run the ball. How are they going to stop our offense?

The week leading up to the Ohio State game, I felt so good about what we had seen in practice with Brooks running the team that I told a reporter on Thursday, "We're going to win this game in Columbus. And it might not even be close."

Even though we fell behind 17-0 in the first half, they couldn't stop us, and we scored on six straight possessions against the Buckeyes — 42 unanswered points.

I enjoyed the hell out of that Ohio State game.

As we were getting ready to pull out of Ohio Stadium, some fans were raising Cain with me outside of our locker room. I can't believe this has happened very often to an opposing coach in Columbus, but they were upset with me for running up the score. That was one of the greatest compliments I've ever had.

I needed something to raise my spirits.

On Monday, I checked into the Mayo Clinic.

***

My right knee first flared up in March. I had been having some trouble with a torn meniscus and really bad arthritis. I had already had it scoped three times. In the middle of the night, I got up and caught my foot in the sheet, twisting my knee. That would not be a big deal to anybody else, but I was in such pain, I was on the floor crying.

The next day, I saw a doctor who suggested that I was going to need a knee replacement. He said he would take one more shot at cleaning the knee of spurs. But he was honest with me. He didn't think it would work.

During training camp, I felt a sharp pain in the knee, and I could feel it fill up with fluid. It got to the point where I was using crutches and having trouble getting out of bed. I started using a golf cart at practice, but I was walking again by the week of our season opener.

Right after we got to the stadium on game day, I was stepping off the team bus, and I felt more piercing pain in the knee. It filled up with blood again, swelling my knee to almost the size of my head. I went straight to the training room, and Dr. Ben Graf used a syringe to drain the knee. Draining and squirting, draining and squirting.

This was right before I talked to the team prior to sending them on the field. I spent the first half on the sidelines. But we were routing Murray State, 42-7, at halftime, and the doctors recommended that I spend the second half in the press box.

I was also having trouble sleeping. It didn't matter if I was laying down or sitting up, in a bed, on the couch, or in my favorite chair. The pain was so excruciating that it wasn't unusual for me to break down and cry in front of Cindy.

The breaking point was right after the Cincinnati game. We were flying home, and after the plane took off, I unstrapped my seat belt and stood straight up. I was in so much pain I was forced to stand during takeoff.

"You're going to Mayo," Pat Richter ordered.

That Sunday, I had 150 cubic centimeters of blood drained from the knee, and I was able to sleep for the first time in weeks. That Monday, I met with the players in the morning and skipped my weekly noon press conference. Instead, I flew to the Mayo Clinic in Rochester with Cindy and our team trainer, Denny Helwig.

We were on a fact-finding mission.

The doctor examined me, and said, "You've got an angry knee."

The knee was worn out, degenerative arthritis. He gave me some options: a two week hospital stay to quiet down the knee or more arthroscopic surgery. But he kept coming back to the inescapable conclusion — I needed an artificial knee.

"There has to be a finality to it all," I agreed with him. "It's time to get down to common sense and do what I have to do."

The surgery was scheduled for Tuesday, October 5, three days after the Ohio State game and the week of the Wisconsin-Minnesota game in the Metrodome.

I returned to Madison and addressed the media on my condition. It was tough to get the words out because I was pretty choked up emotionally.

"I've never been sick a day in my life, never had surgery, never had a stitch until I came here, never missed a game or practice," I said. "It's very difficult when you can't go out there on the field with the people you love and work so hard for."

I knew I had a good football team, and I didn't want to screw it up. I didn't want to be the center of attention or a distraction to the players.

I briefly toyed with the idea of using a three-wheeled cart on the sidelines, similar to the scooter Don Shula used after tearing his Achilles tendon. But I rejected the idea. I didn't want to turn our team into a side show.

When I had first checked into the Mayo Clinic — on the Monday after our Cincinnati loss — I was scared, but I thought the worst was over. I was wrong. I didn't realize how sick I was.

After they opened up my knee, the medical team couldn't follow through with the scheduled procedure because my knee was too infected. They cleaned out some spurs and cysts but had to delay the knee replacement surgery until the end of the regular season.

I felt helpless. I was stuck in a small hospital room in Rochester, Minnesota. I was away from my team, and I just felt so helpless.

I taped a video message that was going to be shown Friday night to the players at the team hotel in Minneapolis. I didn't want to get real emotional with them because the kids had been through enough already. I just encouraged them to play our brand of football.

The day before the game, I got a call from the Big Ten. Minnesota coach Glen Mason was questioning whether I would have an unfair competitive advantage by watching the game on television. He was worried that I would have multiple screens and would be relaying information to my team. He assumed I had some elaborate, sophisticated technology.

What I had was the room at the end of the hall with the custodians' carts and mops right outside my door. What I had was a 22-inch television and a cell phone that would allow me to talk to the assistants. Cindy chuckled when she heard Mason's complaint.

"The hospital room was so small," she said, "that a friend who was visiting had to leave because he's claustrophobic."

I called Mason on Friday.

"Glen, listen, if you want to come up here on Saturday," I said, "you can have the same situation as me. Bring a 12-pack, I'll give you a telephone just like I have, and we can watch the game together. How's that sound?"

He didn't take me up on the offer.

Sports Illustrated's Rick Reilly called and wanted to be in the room with me during the game. It might have made a good column, but I turned him down. I didn't want anybody else around. It was just me and

Cindy watching what turned out to be a stressful game.

We were down 7-0, 14-7 and 17-14. But we rallied for a 20-17 victory on Vitaly Pisetsky's field goal in overtime. I wasn't much help to the team.

I really couldn't see the defensive schemes, and I never knew what camera angle I was going to get from play to play. It was frustrating. If I needed to talk with someone, a coach, I could. And Cindy said that helped my morale more than anything else.

The nurses came into the room a few times during the game because Cindy and I were screaming. They told me to quiet down and watch my language. Ten minutes after the game, they took my blood pressure and it was off the charts.

I talked to quite a few of the players afterward — Brooks and Ron and Big Mac. I talked with each one of my assistants and thanked him for the job he'd done. Bernie Wyatt got on the phone and, all of a sudden, he says, "OK, see ya, bye."

And he hung up. We had gone from the excitement of a big win to silence. Cindy and I looked at each other and shook our heads. That's when I called my doctor and asked him if I could have a bourbon. He said yes, so Cindy went down to the hotel and brought back a glass of bourbon for a victory drink.

***

I was anchored to the press box the rest of the regular season, starting with our game against Indiana, my first game back. Brian White was our first-year offensive coordinator, and I sat next to Brian and tried to help him in terms of thinking ahead in his play selection.

Let's say you've got a play called for first-and-10. Now, you have to move on to second and long, or second and medium, or second and short. Let's get to your next call.

You're going play-action and taking a shot?

All right, now let's have your third-and-short ready — in case you don't pick up the first down — and have a first-and-10 call ready, too.

Always anticipate. Have your personnel groupings in mind. Have your next play call ready to go. Don't sit there and worry about your last call, don't procrastinate about what you should have done or worry about why it didn't work. We'll correct it later.

From where I was sitting, I tried to look at the big picture. I could definitely see the game better. But I've always felt that one of my strengths was getting a feel for the kids on the sidelines. Who's playing with confidence, who's not? If someone had that deer-in-the-headlights look, I could get him out of the game and get him straight.

But I had no other choice but to be in the press box.

I had to make it work.

Indiana was not much of a test. We won 59-0. At the half, it was 38-0, and Dayne already had close to 170 yards. He didn't play in the second half. Ron accompanied me to my postgame press conference and someone asked him, "At halftime, did you ask to go out?"

I stepped in and said, "We take a vote. We give everybody a slip of paper. Should he go out? Shouldn't he? We collect the votes, count them, and go from there."

I'm not sure everyone knew I was being facetious.

"Listen, I run the team and make the decisions," I said. "This is not a democracy. I know when I make those decisions, everybody has an opinion. Rightfully so. I have no problem with that. But once you make a decision, you move forward.

"We think things out. We talk about it as a staff. Nobody loves Ron Dayne or wants him to break that rushing record more than me. Yet I have some concerns. I want to make sure he's healthy. I've got a responsibility to this football team and Ron."

It would have been foolish for me to put him out there in the second half just to get his yardage, just to put another 100 yards on the board, especially with the games coming up.

Dayne had his own personal motivation — taped and hanging from his locker. *Sports Illustrated* had called him the sixth-biggest disappointment in college football, and Dayne clipped out the article. He wasn't about to forget their words. Neither was Malchow.

I could tell he was getting frustrated.

He told me so.

"The items they were putting forward were falsehoods and the conclusions that were drawn weren't accurate," Malchow said of the national press. "One Saturday night, I was watching a college wrap-up show on TV, and an analyst said something that was absolutely wrong. As I was sitting on the couch, I started drafting the 'Truths & Myths on Ron Dayne.'"

The feedback was positive.

"I didn't think the idea was all that special," Malchow said, "but the gist of the story ran on the banner of the *Chicago Tribune* and earned praise from a New York City paper as the most unique and simple Heisman campaign in history."

Near the end of the season, Malchow got Ron's girlfriend Aliah (who's now his wife) and their daughter Jada involved. He invited the national writers to Madison.

"And a whole new 'Ron Dayne' image emerged," Malchow said, "from a picture of Ron, Aliah and Jada that ran in *USA Today*. We also ran a video of Jada raising her arms, saying "Touchdown Daddy" after one of his scores. That was priceless."

***

But it still came down to the basics, what Dayne did on the playing field. He had a huge game against Michigan State and their No. 1-ranked rush defense. He followed that up by outshining Drew Brees at Purdue. That game won him the Heisman Trophy.

Dayne added an exclamation point to his season by breaking Ricky Williams' rushing mark in the Iowa game. That was probably the best atmosphere I've ever seen in Camp Randall Stadium. On top of the history being made, we clinched the Rose Bowl.

What a magnificent day. You couldn't have scripted it, couldn't have planned it better. That was just the damnedest thing I'd ever seen.

Throughout the season, we tried using Ron's breaking that record as motivation for our linemen — turning an individual award into a team award. How better to be recognized as a lineman than if your tailback becomes the NCAA's all-time leading rusher?

Everybody felt like they were a part of it. That included our tight ends, Dague Retzlaff and John Sigmund; the tackles, Chris McIntosh and Mark Tauscher; the guards, Bill Ferrario and Dave Costa; and the center, Casey Rabach.

Tauscher was one of the most unsung members of the team, along with safety Bobby Myers, who was a heckuva player, but was overshadowed by Fletcher, Echols and Doering.

As a fifth-year senior, Tauscher was going to finish up his eligibility at Youngstown State. He wanted to be a teacher and coach. He had been recognized on our Senior Day and got his ring at the banquet.

But in the spring, I saw some of the guys who were auditioning to replace Aaron Gibson at right tackle, and I said, "We better get Tauscher back here."

While we were finishing up spring drills, Tausch was living the life — which included a visit to Churchill Downs and the Kentucky Derby. I kidded that he had turned into a cigar and wine aficionado. He denied being a wine drinker.

But he agreed to return to Madison.

After the first scrimmage in the fall, he moved up to No. 1, and he played so well we never noticed him the rest of the season. He was very athletic, his feet were as wide as hippo feet — you couldn't knock him off balance — and he was strong and smart.

I remember Green Bay general manager Ron Wolf taking a look at Tauscher on tape and saying, "That kid playing tackle opposite McIntosh had a helluva year."

Dayne had a helluva year, too.

And it was capped by his Heisman Trophy acceptance speech.

Before the start of Dayne's sophomore year, we were in New York City to play the Kickoff Classic against Syracuse in the Meadowlands. So we took Dayne and all of his teammates for lunch at the Downtown Athletic Club.

I led the players on a tour of the portrait room.

I had played against Oklahoma's Steve Owens, who won the Heisman in 1969. I was coaching in Lincoln when Nebraska's Johnny Rodgers won the Heisman in 1972. And I was an assistant at Notre Dame when Timmy Brown won the Heisman in 1987.

Every coach dreams about having a player who wins the Heisman Trophy. And you feel like you've got something invested in them when they do win. This is the guy you recruited, coached, and nurtured. You feel like you've got a small piece of it.

Ron Dayne joined an elite fraternity, and I told him that he won't realize what this really means until years from now. No matter what he does with his life, he will always be known as a Heisman Trophy winner, and he'll be a part of college football history.

The doctors recommended I limit my travel because I was still in the early stages of rehabilitation after having knee replacement surgery on November 16. But nothing was going to prevent me from being in New York City. Or in Langeloth.

On Tuesday, three days before the Heisman ceremonies, I attended the funeral of my Uncle John. He was 72.

***

With all the problems I had physically, you don't know how grateful I was to have a wife who was there looking after me 24 hours a day and helping me get through this. While I was fighting the infection with antibiotics, Cindy gave me shots three times a day. She had to come down to my office at noon for one of the shots. I didn't drive for four months.

Professionally, I was grateful for having a coaching staff that I could rely on unequivocally to accomplish our plan. And I was really grateful for having such a great group of players who did what we asked them to do and believed in us. To accomplish what we did, you have to have a team that buys into everything 100 percent. And these kids did.

The rehab from the second surgery, the replacement surgery, was a little depressing at times. I would have swelling and seem to regress. I had gone so long without walking that I couldn't bend my knee 90 degrees, and I was scared that I wouldn't be able to walk again.

But the doctors assured me that I was making progress.

Funny story: On Friday nights before games, I always have a hotel room stocked with treats. I don't want any of my coaches going to a bar. But after our player meetings, if they want to have a drink, they can come up to the room and we'll have some snacks and visit.

The night before one of our games late in the season, the assistants were still meeting with the players, and I was in the room, lying on the couch. Father Mike Burke was standing right next to me when a bowl scout walked in. He took one look at my color — I was anemic — and he thought Mike was giving me last rites.

I can laugh about it now.

But I didn't realize how sick I was.

***

I was planning on coaching from the press box in the Rose Bowl. My knee was still temperamental and acting up. Not that I'm superstitious, but since missing the Minnesota game, we were 7-0 with me upstairs.

The night before the game, I'm in my room making sure I stay awake until midnight. Since we were on the brink of the new millennium, I'm waiting for Armageddon.

If the world is going to end, I want to be up for it. So I've got my leg in the air — my knee is packed in ice — and I'm watching some live TV reports from the East Coast as midnight approaches.

Locally, they break in for a sports update, and the anchor is reporting that two of Stanford's best players — wide receiver Troy Walters and defensive tackle Willie Howard — were expected to play against Wisconsin in the Rose Bowl. Earlier in the week, both players had been ruled out of the game because of injuries.

I knew what Stanford coach Tyrone Willingham was up to. "He's trying to jack his guys up," I thought to myself. "The hell with it. I'm going to coach from the sidelines."

I needed a cane, but I was down on the field with my team.

Not that this was the same team that ended the season. We hadn't played for six weeks, and we were lethargic, sleepwalking in the first half. I wanted to keep everyone healthy for the game, so I protected the players and didn't scrimmage. It was much like Auburn getting ready to play us in the Capital One Bowl. Only the roles were reversed.

We were Auburn. Stanford was Wisconsin.

At halftime, we trailed, 9-3, and I was so upset, I went straight to the kids in the locker room, which I've done maybe eight times in 16 years. I grabbed the damn cane, and I was holding it like a baseball bat, and I'm beating and slamming a garbage can.

I was going nuts, beating that sucker and screaming, "We're going through the damn motions; you've been reading your press clippings. But Stanford doesn't give a crap that you're the favorite. You have to go out there and play on the field."

In the second half, we were a much different team, and we made history by becoming the first Big Ten team to win back-to-back Rose Bowls.

Thing is, I thought my best team was coming back.

Until we had the rug pulled out from under us.

CHAPTER ELEVEN

Coping and Moving On

Notre Dame's Rocket Ismail was probably the best player I've ever been around. Iowa's Ronnie Harmon was right there with him. Rocket was not only fast, but he could wiggle, he could make a tackler miss in space. Harmon was the same way.

That's what they both had on Michael Bennett — more wiggle. Bennett was unbelievably fast, though. Wow, was he fast. He could explode with that sprinter's speed.

So, we lose a Ron Dayne — the NCAA's all-time leading rusher and the Heisman Trophy winner — but we've got a Michael Bennett to play tailback. For Bennett, the sky was the limit.

I felt the same way about the team that we had returning.

We had put ourselves in a position to do something no one had ever done in the Big Ten. No one had ever won two Rose Bowls in a row, and I thought we had a chance to win three. Some people were even picking us as a contender for the national championship. We were ranked No. 4 in the country to start the 2000 season.

Watching the team practice during two-a-days, you could see the kids had confidence and chemistry. I remember thinking, "Boy, we've come a long way as a program because we can do this thing again — we can go back to the Rose Bowl."

That was my impression. And I felt that way even after our best wide receiver, Chris Chambers, was injured in training camp. Chambers was expected to be sidelined anywhere from four to six weeks with a stress fracture of his foot. But we still had Nick Davis and Lee Evans, and I was optimistic that we would get Chris back for the Big Ten season.

Lou Holtz thought if you had at least five great players — and you surrounded them with players who wouldn't hurt you — you had the makings of a title contender. Holtz developed that formula as an Ohio State assistant under Woody Hayes. In 1968, the Buckeyes won the national championship with a team that was centered around sopho-mores Rex Kern, Jack Tatum, and Jim Stillwagon, and offensive tackles Dave Foley and Rufus Mayes.

In 2000, we had the players to make that formula work at Wisconsin. As a head coach, you always worry about your corners, and we had two cornerbacks, Jamar Fletcher and Mike Echols, who had already played against the best receivers in college football. We also had Jason Doering at free safety and Wendell Bryant at defensive tackle.

On offense, we had Brooks Bollinger at quarterback and no shortage of quality skill players — Bennett, Chambers, Davis and Evans. We had Ferrario, Rabach and Costa returning on the offensive line and veteran kickers in Stemke and Pisetsky.

I didn't try to shield our players from the expectations.

On media day, I said, "My guys are like anyone else — they read papers, they see rankings, they have visions. And that's the way you should be. If we didn't have visions, we would have never gone to the Rose Bowl."

But nobody could visualize what was coming.

***

A week before the season opener, I got called into the office of Melany Newby, the vice-chancellor for legal and executive affairs. She went through all the details of an in-house investigation of players accepting extra benefits and credit arrangements from a discount shoe store, The Shoe Box, in Black Earth, about a 30-minute drive from Madison.

She was going to recommend a certain number of players be suspend-ed for the Western Michigan game. Some would be suspended for three games, some for one game. Her decision and plan for how we were going to deal with this was shocking to me.

"I'll just forfeit the first three games," I said. "We've got a good enough team. We'll forfeit the first three nonconference games against Western Michigan, Oregon, and Cincinnati. We're playing Hawaii in late November, so we'll just play the Big Ten schedule and Hawaii."

I was serious.

I didn't know how to do it any other way. The players who were going to be suspended were older, and I didn't know how to put that many freshmen on the field with just one week of preparation. Nobody does.

When I left the meeting, as I understood it, we were going to recommend that five players — who hadn't paid anything on their outstanding accounts — would be suspended for one game or two games or three games, depending on what their bills were.

The morning of the Western Michigan game, we had six of our players interrogated by the NCAA via a video-conference call at our team hotel. We pulled them out of their rooms — including Chambers, Davis, and Fletcher — and they told their side of the story.

One of our own faculty reps was present and talked about how her son was a high school coach and had negotiated for shoes at The Shoe Box. Listening to the feedback, there was the sense that the people in the room had an understanding of the situation.

But, then, all of our eyes were opened when one of the NCAA subcommittee members shot back, "Wait a minute. We're not trying to decide whether this is right or wrong. Wisconsin has already admitted that this is a violation."

I thought we were building our case — not appealing it.

Obviously, we had already rolled over.

***

As you look around the college landscape, you see how other people deal with something like this. They hire somebody independent of the athletic department to come in and conduct the investigation. There's no rush to judgment.

Why weren't we trying to build a case for our players? Let's find out how many kids on our campus actually went out there and got discounts on shoes. How many fraternities went out to Black Earth and bought shoes? If there were some issues, then we'd address the issues, but what was the big hurry to get it done?

Did I know my players were going out there?

Hell, they were wearing Shoe Box T-shirts.

But there was no intent on their part to do wrong.

They did not get free shoes.

If you wanted tennis shoes, you'd go there because you could get a good price. Want to take a flight on an airplane? You get on the Internet and find the best price. Buying a new car? You negotiate it down. You don't pay what's on the sticker.

That's what people do.

We lived in Middleton for a long time, and my son would go out to The Shoe Box with his entire high school football team and get shoes at a discount. One of my former assistants, Bernie Wyatt, would go out there all the time and negotiate for shoes.

From the start I didn't think the Shoe Box issue was handled correctly. And I don't see it any differently today as the athletic director. I'm still upset. We got in a hurry to pass judgment, and I don't know anybody else who would have handled it like that. But we had set ourselves up because we had handled some other things poorly in the past.

In March of '99, the NCAA cited the school for a major violation after we had turned ourselves in for "unauthorized spending" of booster club money. An internal audit determined that staff members had been improperly reimbursed for allowable expenses, such as travel, lodging, and meals. Our system wasn't in compliance with the NCAA.

In my case, I followed the policy I was ordered to follow.

If I needed something from our booster club, the Mendota Gridiron Club, I would get permission from my sports administrator, Joel Maturi. I would also get signatures from Wayne Esser, the Mendota executive director, and Pat Richter, the athletic director. That was our checks and balances system for approval: four signatures, including mine.

The oversight, according to the NCAA, was that the reimbursement check had to be written by the university, not the Gridiron Club. But that wasn't required by the system that was in place at Wisconsin.

It wasn't a malicious violation. Everyone was following policy, and it should have been viewed as a secondary violation because we were slow, as a department, to comply with the NCAA. I don't think you roll over and say you're at fault. Now, it looks like we're trying to get away with something which was the furthest thing from the truth.

Because it was such a technicality, the NCAA later changed the rules.

But it didn't erase all the bad publicity. I got a letter from my mother with a newspaper clipping — the headline was "Alvarez, Richter receive illegal payments" — and attached was a note from her, "Are you doing something wrong?"

I was so upset, I went in and saw Chancellor Ward.

"All I'm doing is following the policy within the department," I said. "And my mother wants to know if I'm stealing. There are stories in papers around the country making us sound like crooks. That's tarnishing our program and school."

In the early '90s, some anonymous sources had turned us in to the Big Ten for alleged violations, and the school reacted by assigning a UW law professor, Frank Turkheimer, to conduct a three-month investigation of our football program.

He used a fine-toothed comb — nearly 100 interviews — and came up with three secondary violations. We hadn't done what people were saying we were doing. Turkheimer and Chancellor Donna Shalala, in turn, congratulated us for running a clean program.

Some people were nervous, back then, that we were making strides. We were getting better, my staff was really aggressive, and we weren't going to be held back.

Some people wanted to maintain the status quo. When you've got somebody down, you want to keep them down. You want that win every year from a Wisconsin.

And they were worried because they could see we weren't going to be satisfied with that status quo — it was changing — and we were going to get the job done.

You can imagine how nervous they got when we started winning.

***

The Western Michigan game was played on a Thursday night. That morning, we had the two-hour conference call with the NCAA. That afternoon, we were going through our routine at the stadium — a little shake-out with the players — when Pat Richter called me.

The NCAA had made its ruling: 26 players had been suspended, 11 for three games and 15 for one game each. The suspensions had to be served within the first four games.

I felt like I had been ambushed. A week earlier, I thought they were going to recommend that five players be suspended. Now it was 26. And we got to that number on appeal because originally they had wanted to suspend 47 players.

How do you break that to the team? How the hell do you tell somebody that has just gone through two-a-days and is getting ready to play a game that he's not playing?

I called an emergency team meeting — some four hours before kickoff.

"We're going to overcome this," I promised the players. "We have to accept this — we have no other choice. We just need everybody to rally."

I got very emotional.

"We've got people shooting at us. We've got people who are afraid we're going to be too good. We've got people who are trying to sabotage us. But we'll overcome this."

I wanted to get their attention. I tried to rev them up. I wasn't going to stand up there and mope around because they'd all go into the game moping around. I was trying to get them excited and ticked off — ticked off that somebody was sabotaging us.

There was disbelief on their faces. Nobody could believe something like this could happen. How the hell does this happen on the day of a game? It didn't make any sense.

But we were going to move forward.

These were the cards that we were dealt.

"We always talk about dealing with adversity," I told them. "This is how you find out whether you're leaders. Guys need to bow their necks and not feel sorry for themselves."

We had to decide who we were going to play, who we were going to hold out. We had to rearrange our whole game plan and decide on what we could run offensively.

Just think about the mental gymnastics we put those kids through. Imagine going through that yourself. After preparing and game-planning for two weeks, you're preparing to play and then you have to sit out and somebody else — who is a back-up and isn't geared to start — has to play.

Our experience has to be unprecedented. That has never happened to anybody in the history of the world. And that may have been the longest day I've ever had to go through in coaching.

That's why I was thrilled with the win.

It was really hot and humid, and we beat a good Western Michigan team, which had won the league title the year before. But because we were playing some guys who weren't ready to play, Brooks Bollinger almost got crippled in that game.

The following week, at least, we knew what we were dealing with as far as the suspensions, and our players responded with a great win over Oregon. Michael Bennett had some really long runs, rushing for a total of 290 yards. You could just see him get a little more patient and let things happen and then accelerate instead of putting his head down once there was a little congestion. "He may have just grown up to be a great running back," I said.

We had spent three weeks of training camp preparing for the season. But now, with the suspensions, everything was makeshift. We reshuffled the entire offensive line going into the Oregon game. We started Al Johnson at center and moved Casey Rabach to guard and had Dave Costa shift from guard to tackle. I knew that the lack of continuity was going to catch up to us and have an impact on the team as we went along. It's impossible doing it that way.

But we got to 3-0, and I thought we may have survived the worst.

With the exception of Chambers and Fletcher, we had everybody else back for our Big Ten opener against Northwestern. We had a chance to put away the game in the third quarter. We were leading 16-7 and driving for another score when they knocked the ball loose from Brooks — picked it out of the air — and ran for a touchdown. Once we lost the momentum, we couldn't get it back, and we wound up losing in double-overtime, 47-44.

Nick Davis hadn't played in the first three games, and you could tell he was out of sync. He dropped a touchdown pass in the end zone and lost a fumble. It always hurts you as a coach when you lose a game that you know you should have won. We beat ourselves.

We never realized our potential as a team that season.

We couldn't.

We were never as good as we were the week before we played our first game against Western Michigan. For us to win eight games during the regular season was pretty good. It could have been a total fiasco and a bust season, and it would have been a tragedy if that team didn't go to a bowl.

If I had to do it over again, I would have taken a different approach in the summer with the chancellor and Pat on how the Shoe Box issue was going to be investigated and how we were going to respond to it. That's more of an administrator's responsibility than a coach's responsibility. But I would have gotten more involved.

Can you learn from this? Absolutely.

But it was so frustrating. I was looking at some examples where schools were getting competitive advantages. They were paying players or there was academic fraud. And they were not getting punished or their punishment was so far after the fact that it didn't have an impact. Our sin? We had athletes getting discounts on shoes.

And it wasn't just football players, either.

But our program got the black eye.

There were over 40 athletes from other sports who were part of the extra benefits investigation. There were other coaches involved, but I was the most vocal — especially about the way the NCAA mishandled Mike Echols' appeal — and I ruffled some feathers.

I was so disgruntled, so upset with the way the 2000 season went down, I was thinking about getting out of the coaching business. I was even in the process of talking to some people about doing broadcasting. I was that close to checking it in.

But I kind of played through my frustration. We won the bowl game — we beat UCLA in the Sun Bowl — and that got me cranked up and ready to go again.

For a while.

***

Over the years, I had been contacted by different job search people, representing the NFL or college teams. In some instances, I was contacted, by alums or boosters who were close to a specific program, and they would ask, "Are you interested in so-and-so?"

None of the jobs really interested me.

But when Miami contacted me — in January of 2001 — I was still upset with the way the Shoe Box suspensions had been handled, and I was vulnerable and ready to leave.

I was serious about the Miami job, particularly knowing Donna Shalala was going to be taking over as the school president. She hadn't officially started yet, so she stayed out of the negotiations. But I knew I would be working for her if I made that choice.

My agent was Neil Cornrich out of Cleveland. Still is. He's very highly respected in his profession, and his client list is impressive. Among others, he represents Iowa's Kirk Ferentz, Minnesota's Glen Mason, and my successor, Bret Bielema.

Cornrich entered into talks with Miami athletic director Paul Dee. Dee wanted to move quickly and name a new head coach to replace Butch Davis, who had left for the Cleveland Browns, before the recruiting signing date in February.

Dee was still addressing me as "Mr. Big," which dates back to my 1995 job interview with Miami and the exchange I had then with Dee.

He said something to the effect that I'd really like it in Miami, and I responded, "I'd be big in Miami."

I was getting a second chance, and had everything fallen into place with the contract, I would have gone. But my agent said, "I can't let you do this right now. With this language, we don't have enough time to work it out."

In hindsight, maybe we should have said, "Let's do the deal and we'll clean up the contract language over the next few months."

It was all happening so fast.

It had to be one of those, "I'll take the job. It's done. Send a plane."

But I had too much invested in Wisconsin, too much invested in the business. If you're a successful football coach, the work is very lucrative, and you've got to be able to trust somebody else — an agent — somebody who deals with contracts for a living.

So, what's wrong with this picture?

I'm talking with Paul Dee, and he said, "We can pay you $1.4 million."

And I said, "I'm thinking a little north of that number."

I couldn't believe I said that.

Dee said that he would have to get back to me.

When we were done, I had to talk with somebody because I was frustrated, so I grabbed a graduate assistant coach who happened to be outside the office.

"I can't believe what just happened — listen to this," I said. "I grew up in a house that is smaller than this atrium here. I'm a football coach, and I just told somebody that $1.4 million wasn't enough money for me to coach maybe the best football team in the country.

"Not only would I be coaching the best players, I would be coaching in a location — Miami, Florida — that I love and for a school president — Donna Shalala — that I know and respect. There's something wrong with this picture."

There's one thing you learn in this racket, though. You don't second-guess any of your decisions. You make them and move on.

Some people, including Paul Dee, thought I was trying to use Miami for leverage on my contract at Wisconsin. I wasn't. I was very serious about that job.

But I'm happy with the way things ended here.

During the negotiations, I still remember Pat Richter and Chancellor John Wiley coming out to my house in Madison and visiting with me and Cindy. And I remember what the chancellor told the press about our meeting: "I laid it out real straight and direct. That's sort of the way I deal. We talked about the opportunities here and what the future might hold."

He showed me that he understood the business and wanted us to be competitive in the market. He also showed me that he was going to be very supportive of the program.

I would compare Chancellor Wiley to former Chancellor Shalala in that he's not afraid to make decisions and move forward with them. He's not a fence rider. Like Shalala, he understands the importance of athletics to the total university and the alumni. Chancellor Wiley is someone I can trust, and, like Donna, someone I've enjoyed being around socially as well as professionally.

The first time I interviewed with Pat Richter — when I was still a Notre Dame assistant — Pat asked, "Where do you see yourself some day? Where do you want to end up?"

"I want to do what my college coach, Bob Devaney did," I said. "When I'm finished coaching, I want to step into the athletic director's job."

When Miami was courting me, Pat brought my exit plan to John Wiley's attention. The topic of taking over as the athletic director some day was first broached during that meeting at my home, though nothing was promised. Chancellor Wiley didn't say, "You're going to be my next AD." But he did say, "I'll give you serious consideration when that time comes."

That's all I wanted to hear.

***

Finishing 5-7 and not making it to a bowl in 2001 was very disappointing. It felt like a setback because we had grown accustomed to playing in bowls. It also was reality.

Take a look around at some of the great football schools.

Oklahoma played five seasons without a winning record and went through three head coaches before the fourth coach, Bobby Stoops, stopped the losing.

Southern Cal won more than six games just once during a six-year span, and went three consecutive seasons without a winning record before Pete Carroll turned it around.

Prior to the 2005 season, when Penn State won a share of the Big Ten championship, the Nittany Lions had lost more games than they had won in four of their last five seasons.

What made 2001 a little more frustrating was the fact that Miami won the national championship that season with Larry Coker as its head coach.

"What were you thinking?" Brooks Bollinger asked me. "Here we are struggling and we don't get to a bowl, and you had a chance to coach a team that won the national title."

Everybody has to deal with a bump in the road, and that's what I was thinking. The '01 season was a bump, but only a speed bump. Our program was on solid ground — we were right back in a bowl the following season — and we were doing a better job of recruiting.

We may have gotten a little complacent in our recruiting for a while. I'm not sure. I know we didn't do as good a job as we could have and that all comes back on me. Did I oversee well enough? Were we not thorough enough in our evaluations? Did we work hard enough?

I don't know.

All I know is we didn't do a good job.

Winning back-to-back Rose Bowls didn't help us. I thought, "Hell, you've just won two BCS games, you ought to be able to go out and recruit better."

But I didn't feel it gave us an advantage.

It didn't help to lose some assistants, including Brad Childress, who went to the NFL's Philadelphia Eagles. For one thing, if Chilly would have stayed, I believe we would have gotten Walter Payton's son, Jarrett, who ended up at Miami.

We went after some high-profile kids, particularly running backs. We got our foot in the door. We got them on campus. But we couldn't close the deal and often came in second.

When you start making mistakes in recruiting, you're going to have challenges down the road because you're going to have holes in your classes. One year, we were at the end of recruiting and still had some spots available, so we just started taking guys.

We would have been better off saving those scholarships. At Wisconsin, if we make a recruiting mistake, we rarely have the opportunity to get a junior college player to plug in.

It all adds up.

During the '99 season, I couldn't go out and recruit because of my knee. That may have been a factor. Normally, I'm on the road seeing every kid.

Did the Shoe Box have a lingering impact? You'd like to say it didn't affect you, but it did. I'm sure we lost some recruits because of the negative publicity.

We also lost scholarships and that definitely had an impact. You don't know how much, though we tried to deal with it the best we could. At the time, I didn't want to give anybody the satisfaction to say, "Yeah, it's going to affect us."

But it did. Sure it did.

Wisconsin is always going to be a tough place to recruit. You have to deal with the weather, you have to deal with the distance. Our academic standards are difficult, too. Prospects may see us on TV every week and they may have seen us play in the Rose Bowl, but they're not standing there with their hand up waiting to come here.

If you recruit a kid on the East Coast, he goes through almost every Big Ten school before he gets to Madison. Distance is a factor. Families want to see their kids play.

Look at the top recruits, the top 100. Where do a majority of them go to school? They stay close to home and go to a school nearby. The sexy schools with the big names — the USCs, the Miamis, the Florida States, the Michigans — will throw out a line and get kids from all over the country. But for the most part, kids stay close to home.

Why can't we get "Five Star" players to Wisconsin? Look where those Five Star players are — warm weather states, Ohio, and Pennsylvania.

I always felt we were a developmental program. You have to know who you are. That's not saying we're throwing our hands up and not taking a run at people. You always have to take a run at them, particularly within a 250-mile radius. And you need to keep building relationships with coaches and contacts because you need to get one or two special players.

You have to get a Chris Chambers and when you do, you can get a Lee Evans. Because of a connection, you get a Ron Dayne. Because of a tip, you get lucky on a Nick Davis, who was recommended to us late in recruiting. Nobody was recruiting him.

The good players in the state of Wisconsin can play anywhere. But there's another group of kids who, if they stay with the program and develop, can take a position on the field, play with the right attitude, and they won't hurt you. Those are the walk-ons.

I can't say walk-ons were an original idea. I stole that from Nebraska.

But I felt that was one way we could compete and overcome our mistakes in recruiting. If you go back and look at every Rose Bowl team, at least one of the captains was a walk-on: Joe Panos, Bob Adamov, Donnel Thompson, and Jason Doering.

I'm very proud of the walk-ons that we had in our program. Many of them not only earned scholarships, but they were really good players. In sum, they were guys who liked football, who were hungry, who played for the right reasons. They loved Wisconsin, and they conveyed a sense of pride in playing for the state university that was contagious.

We were among the first to identify preferred walk-ons. We would actively recruit them, telling them, "Nobody is going to get special treatment. It doesn't matter if you're a scholarship player or a walk-on, if you play the best, you are going to play. And if you move up the depth chart, if you get into the two-deep, you're going on tender."

Panos was one of the original walk-on success stories, and you could always go back and use him as a reference point.

Jimmy Leonhard was the same way.

I remember watching Jimmy during our summer camp. I didn't know much about him except that he was a wish-bone quarterback who ran about a 4.4 in the 40. But the one thing that stood out was his nose for the football. At the end of every play, he was going to be around the ball.

He was very smart, and he was always where he was supposed to be. He jumped out at me during two-a-days which is hard to do for a true freshman. After Jimmy established himself as one of our better players and was getting a lot of accolades, I got a letter from his grandfather, who talked about how proud the people were back home in Tony, Wisconsin.

He wrote a P.S. — "Jimmy can play quarterback if you need him."

We never took him up on that. Maybe we should have.

***

In 1990, when I took the Wisconsin coaching job, John Mackovic held the dual title of football coach and athletic director at the University of

Illinois. Before I embarked on that same path — holding down two positions — I contacted Mackovic and talked to him about the challenges and logistics of combining the responsibilities. I also contacted John Robinson, who was doubling as the head coach and AD at UNLV.

I wanted to hear their insights.

And I took notes on a yellow legal pad.

Mackovic asked me, "What's your first impulse? What's your first inclination?"

I told him, "I'm excited."

"Then you need to do it," he said.

Robinson asked me, "Barry, how old are you right now?"

"I'm 56," I said.

"Hell," he replied, "you could take that job as AD, pump gas part-time, and coach — you could do all three."

I respected Robinson as a coach and friend, and he left me with one other piece of advice: "Don't lose your identity as the head football coach."

Both Robinson and Mackovic stressed, "You'd better have someone on the administrative side who's bright, and you better have people as associates you can trust."

In mid-February of 2003, Pat Richter announced that he would be retiring, effective April 1, 2004, and I would take over as athletic director while continuing to coach.

To be honest, I didn't know many of the administrative workings of the Big Ten nor the many issues that crossed the AD's desk. How would I know any of that?

I had to learn on the fly. What was beneficial was having a year with Pat Richter and Jamie Pollard, my deputy athletic director, to lay our foundation with my senior staff while I was getting my feet wet.

In late February of 2002, the Camp Randall Stadium renovation project had come to a halt because of some financing concerns. That was one of the reasons that made it easy for me to make the decision about the athletic director's job.

We were asking people for money and looking for a lead gift, and with Pat retiring, those people weren't going to make those donations without knowing who was in charge. The chancellor expressed confidence in me and reassured our donors, "Barry is in charge."

When the chancellor asked me, "Do you think we can do it?" I said,

"Yes," not knowing whether we could or not.

I just wanted the project to move forward.

***

The first time I had a conversation with Bret Bielema was during Bernie Wyatt's retirement party in Madison. Bret was then an assistant on Kirk Ferentz's staff at the University of Iowa. Kirk attended the function, along with Bobby Stoops. (Ron Dayne came back for the party, too.) Bernie had been Bret's first position coach with the Hawkeyes. Bret and I visited for about 10 minutes and found we had some mutual acquaintances in Iowa City.

From a former player's perspective, Bret had noticed a dramatic change in the Wisconsin program from the first time he played here in 1991 — "That was a team that was beginning to learn how to win and didn't know how to finish the game," he observed — to 1999 and the Dayne celebration game when Ronnie broke Ricky Williams' record.

"That day," Bret said, "you saw a team walk onto the field with confidence. The players had put themselves in a position to have success based on what they had learned."

After Bernie's retirement party, I had everybody come over to my house.

"What I saw was a head coach who cared about his people," Bret said. "I saw that in the way Ron Dayne reacted to you when he came into the room."

A few years later, at the National Coaches Convention, I was having breakfast with Bobby, Mike, and Mark Stoops. Bret was there, and we talked a long time. He wanted to know whether he should leave Iowa and go to Kansas State as a co-defensive coordinator.

"You've got to go," I said.

I remembered when I took the Notre Dame job and how hard it was for me to leave Iowa City. My family loved it there and I had a secure job. In this business, there aren't many of those. I told Bret, "Had I not left Iowa when I did, you wouldn't be coaching linebackers there now because I'd probably still have that job."

My advice was, "You've got to go someplace where you make the decisions."

That's what he did — he worked under Bill Snyder for two seasons at K-State, sharing the defense with Bobby Elliott. When Kevin Cosgrove left my staff to become the defensive coordinator at Nebraska, the first name that popped into my head was Bret Bielema.

I talked to both Kirk Ferentz and Bill Snyder about Bret, and they both said the same thing about him: they liked him. He can be tough, but he's fair and the players like him. They respond to him. And that was all very important to me. He was sensitive to people.

When I'm hiring a coach, I like to let him talk. And from some of the things that Bret said to me, I thought he was ready for the job. I was looking for someone to run our defense. Cos had been with me for so long, I wanted somebody I could feel comfortable with right away.

I thought his personality would be a good fit. His youth appealed to me. I can't say that's why I hired him, but as your staff matures, you want to make sure you hire young assistants so you can bridge the gap between senior coaches and your athletes.

"I want you to come here and put your name on our defense," I emphasized to Bret. "I'm a lot like Hayden Fry. I let people do their jobs, and I'll let you coach your position. Lou Holtz was the same way with me. These are the principles I want coached. Take care of these and you're not going to have any problems with me."

I really hadn't thought about who was going to succeed me as head coach when I hired Bret. That didn't play into it. He had a job to do and he knew I was going to let him do it.

"I was confident that what I had been told was the truth," Bret said. "I was excited to run my own show, and I knew the head coach wasn't going to be the type of guy who jumped into the middle of the defense and tried to tell you how to run things.

"My whole thought process that first year was to coordinate a defense to the best of my ability — blending some of the stuff they had done in the past with some new things — and I wanted to learn to work with a bunch of coaches I hadn't been around before."

I saw something in Bret during that first training camp that really confirmed to me that I had made the right decision in hiring him.

They printed his salary in the paper, so everyone knew he was going to be making more than some of the senior coaches. Even though he was taking a pay cut from his previous job at Kansas State, it could have been an awkward situation.

Bret came up to me and said, "I think this could create some problems."

He hadn't coached a down yet, but he was willing to take a cut in salary — even though the money was owed to him — because he knew the potential for some coaches to be critical of what he was making and he didn't want to disrupt the staff.

Bret wasn't going to force the issue and that sent a strong message. Most guys wouldn't do that. They'd take the money and run because that's what they were promised, and they wouldn't care if anybody else was upset.

From the start, I thought he was sensitive to a veteran staff. He didn't get pushy. He just went about his job. And I saw how the kids really liked and responded to him.

***

Going into the 2004 season, I could see during two-a-days that our defense was going to be outstanding. Our D-line was dominant. People didn't know anything about Erasmus James, and he was ridiculous coming off the edge. We've had some good defensive ends, but I don't know if anyone was as dominant as James was during the first half of the season. Up until he hurt his ankle at Purdue in the seventh game, nobody could block him.

It was hard for people to move the football on us, and although we struggled on offense, we had some weapons so we could afford to be more conservative. That's where you try to win as a team, knowing people aren't going to be scoring many points against you. Unfortunately, by the end of the season, we ran out of tailbacks.

Once Anthony Davis became injury prone, we missed him.

Davis rushed for more yardage than anybody in the nation during the 2001 and 2002 seasons. After he picked up nearly 250 yards in the 2003 opener, I said, "We've been around a lot of good backs, but I don't know if we've ever had one playing as good as Anthony is playing right now. Ron played at a pretty high level for four years, and I'm just saying Anthony is every bit in that category. He's truly special."

But he twisted his ankle in the third game of that season and the injuries held him back. If he had finished his career strong, I think he could have been a pretty high draft pick and he would likely be playing in the NFL today. A.D. played really fast. He was short and hard to find, and he was really powerful in the hips and thighs.

Losing at Iowa was frustrating because we had a chance to earn a trip to the Rose Bowl, but we didn't have any running backs. Anthony didn't play. Booker Stanley had a bad toe. And Matt Bernstein hurt his knee on the first series. Iowa beat us. But the really frustrating game was the week before when we lost to a bad Michigan State team.

We started 9-0 and finished 0-3.

Even when we were unbeaten, Cindy noticed that I wasn't enjoying the wins as much as I had in the past. Steve Malchow mentioned the same thing. "Coach, your highs after wins weren't as high," he said, "and your lows after losses were lower."

He was right.

Something had changed.

And it was time to acknowledge it.

CHAPTER TWELVE
A Last Hurrah

I was in the middle of a conversation with a good friend, Tony Canonie, when I turned to him and said, "I'm going to tell you something I've never told anybody."

The blank look on his face told me he had no idea where I was going with this.

"I'm really thinking about giving it up," I said.

That was back in 2000. I hadn't lost my passion for coaching, but I still hadn't gotten over the way that season had played out. It was probably fair to say I was bitter.

"Barry, let me tell you something — don't do it too soon," Tony advised me then. "I retired, gave up my business too soon, and I will always regret that."

It was good advice, and I took it.

People always say, "You'll know when it's time to leave."

I knew.

Little things start bothering you — they start wearing on you.

I was so involved in coaching football for so many years that that's all I thought about — 24/7 — because that's all you CAN think about. It's all encompassing. It's every day.

You're engulfed by the job.

But everything changed in 2003 when I took on the added responsibilities of being the athletic director. Although it was still an ongoing transition to the position, I had other things to think about, and I could see that my thought process was different. I didn't like that.

I definitely didn't want to cheat football, and I was fortunate that I had somebody like Jamie Pollard who could run the day-to-day operations of the athletic department. That allowed me to focus on football. Still, there were many issues in other areas coming across my desk and I had to deal with them. So now I was multi-tasking.

For as long as I can remember, I have started my preparation for football in July. I've done all my reading, I've got my theme for the year and I take maybe a week to write all my notes for our preseason coaches and players meeting on what's expected of them, my beliefs, and the approach we're going to take for a given season.

Once July arrived, it was all football, with the exception of weekends. Cindy would say, "I know it's football season because you don't hear anything I'm saying."

I have always been single-minded. But when I was doing both jobs — coach and athletic director — my mind was wandering. Even in July.

And I felt guilty because I couldn't do football 24/7 — I just couldn't — and that wore on me. That put me at risk because I knew I was competing against excellent coaches in a tough league.

"The constant is that you have so much self-pride you would never let the job you're doing slip," Cindy reassured me. "Your competitiveness is what has enabled you to win."

But she could tell the enjoyment wasn't there during the 2003 season. "You struggled that year personally with your future and where you were going," Cindy suggested. "Why didn't you enjoy it as much? You had to answer that question."

Nobody can handle things better than Cindy.

She babysits me and runs the house. When the kids or the grandkids have issues, they go to her and she'll spoon-feed me with what I need to know. She has been an unbelievable partner. From the time I was a high school assistant, she has helped me get through this business. She always knew where I wanted to go and what I needed.

During training camp, Cindy went to Langeloth to check on my parents. She came back and told me that she believed my dad had dementia. My mom was not doing well, either. She had cancer. Not too long after Cindy was there, my mom had surgery, but they couldn't remove all the cancer and she didn't want to go through chemotherapy.

I went home — back to Langeloth — during an open date in the schedule. My brother had called and said my dad had fallen and suffered a mini-stroke. He was slurring his words.

I had some close friends who really helped us. They pulled some strings to get my dad's name moved to the top of the list so we could get him into an assisted living facility.

The more I read about President Ronald Reagan's battle with

Alzheimers, the more I saw the same characteristics in my dad. Fortunately, he was still able to recognize me, but the conversations were very difficult.

That was really hard, emotionally, to see my dad that way. Especially since I was in the midst of dealing with the stress of a football season. That was a tough, tough year.

***

There's no denying that Pat Richter had a presence as the school's athletic director. He had a high profile in Madison and the state, and it seemed like he made appearances everywhere. That was one concern Chancellor Wiley and the administration had with me.

In my dual role as a coach and AD, they were afraid I wouldn't have a presence on campus or in the community or at various alumni functions.

I tried to alleviate their fears by doing more. On a Friday night, I left our team dinner and talked at a W-Club reunion in Madison. I was even hitting functions on the morning of games. The night we played Ohio State at Camp Randall, I was talking to a group at noon.

I wouldn't have thought about doing something like that in the past — to leave my team and hobnob and shake hands on the night before a game or on a game day.

Don't get me wrong. I liked what I was doing as an athletic director. That's what I wanted to be doing. But the time spent trying to be in two places was wearing on me.

"You talked the entire 2003 season about quitting," Cindy reminded me. "You'd come home after games, whether you won or lost, and you were just defeated. There was no joy, no spark. I can remember you saying, 'I don't want to do this anymore.'"

Cindy wasn't ready for me to retire, and she didn't think I was ready. But I was really down, and I was truly in the tank after we lost to Auburn in the Music City Bowl.

"That game was the culmination," Cindy said. "I just thought you were depressed and down and not happy with what you were doing or where you were going. And because I was so worried about your depression, I went and talked to somebody about it."

I could understand her concerns. But I snapped out of it.

According to Cindy, I said, "I'm going to dot every i and cross every t and I'm going back to the basics — what was successful for us in the

'90s. I'm going to re-energize and reapply myself to coaching football."

"I think you felt like you had let some things slide," she added, "and you were determined to get more involved as a head coach again."

She was right. I had my own questions. Where have we lost it? How can we get better? I felt we weren't a physical team anymore, and that's what we had built our program on.

I came up with a plan — to get it corrected — while walking the beach.

From the time the players got back for the second semester, they competed every day. Different ways, different things. But you had a winner and a loser and the loser paid a price.

In the spring, when we were in pads, we finished every practice with some type of competition. We also incorporated a number of different physical drills to start practice.

We had one-on-ones with the defensive backs and receivers.

We had one-on-ones with the offensive and defensive linemen. Our Badger Drill.

Mount Union College coach Larry Kehres was in town to speak at our clinic, and he came out and watched practice. "I haven't seen a practice this physical in a long time," he said afterward.

This was from a guy coaching a program that has won eight Division III national championships in the last 13 seasons. That was our first day of spring ball, too.

I had to do some new things to get us to be more physical. I felt we had lost our toughness and competitive edge. Did the extra work pay off? Obviously, it did. We won a lot of close games. Hell, we won 19 games over the next two seasons.

How did we lose the toughness? We started taking things for granted, we got a little softer, we changed practices, little by little. We used to go 20 minutes every day with our inside drill. Then we got down to running six plays, eight plays, and we lost the edge.

We're simply not going to recruit as well as Michigan, Ohio State, Penn State, and maybe Michigan State. Iowa is going to recruit as well as us. So how do we win? The only way we can win here is to play with great fundamentals, and we've got to be tougher.

***

That summer, the summer of '04, my mother died. She was 79. She had fought the good fight against cancer but lost the battle. We were prepared for it.

She would never complain about the pain, and that was a little misleading to the people close to her. Whenever I talked to her, I could feel her losing more and more strength.

At my mother's funeral, I was able to reconnect and reminisce with some people in the Burgettstown and Langeloth communities. That was touching and meaningful for me.

But when you go to a wake or a funeral home for the first time, there is a finality that you can't prepare yourself for. That was the hard part, knowing I couldn't talk to my mom again, knowing that my greatest fan wasn't going to be there for me.

While I was grieving, I talked with my former assistant — Iowa State coach Dan McCarney — whose mother passed away a day or so after Alvera. We were going through many of the same things, feeling the same emotions. It was good to share our thoughts.

When I returned to Madison after the funeral, I told a local reporter, "I still love football. I still love working with players and developing a team and all the things that go along with it.

"I'm getting excited about the 2004 season — excited about starting coaches meetings and two-a-day practices. I've always said I'll know when it's time to get out of football, but I still have the goose bumps and the excitement for starting a season."

Maybe more than anything I was energized by the progress made in the Camp Randall Stadium renovation. I wanted to make sure that we took this next step — especially after the project was temporarily stalled — and we were now moving forward with a first-class facility that ranked among the finest in the country. It was something to be proud of.

Cindy said she could see a change in my demeanor and attitude. She could see what I was trying to do and how I was trying to re-apply myself to coaching.

But it didn't last very long.

"Even when you were 6-0, it still wasn't that exciting for you," she said. "Then when we lost some games, you went back to telling me, 'I don't want to do this anymore.' And I'm working the whole time on getting you to stay, stay, stay."

After we lost to Georgia in the Outback Bowl, Cindy and I were walking on the beach in Florida when she said it hit her. She felt like I had lost my passion to coach.

I disagreed. But I knew I felt differently about things.

Cindy and I had been talking about retirement over the years, so it wasn't like all these feelings suddenly materialized. I did tell her, "I think this is it."

She wasn't crazy to hear that.

But I felt it was time.

That day on the beach we started planning for my retirement. We began putting together a timetable and made a pact that we would tell absolutely no one.

We met with money managers, stock brokers, investors. We choreographed everything. We didn't tell the children until two weeks before the official announcement in late July.

Cindy said that she never quite understood why I felt the way I did, but she supported me. Over the last year, as she has read about other men in high-profile positions talking about losing their passion, she says that she has gained a different perspective.

"How does Joe Paterno handle the stress for so many years?" she asked.

It's true, the stress in a job like this is constant. You're always on your guard, and you have to learn to live with the stress. It just becomes a part of your life.

"You don't know how to do stress-relief," Cindy said. "You don't have a hobby. You don't have an escape or release. You never learned how to turn it off."

I don't know if you can do that — turn it off — in this profession. I couldn't.

"You didn't have another outlet," she went on. "Maybe if you had or maybe if you were a different type of personality, maybe you could have lasted longer."

***

When I took the athletic director's job, I wanted to make sure I had the opportunity to name my successor. Chancellor John Wiley agreed and said, "Nobody has invested as much in the program as you have, and you should have that right."

During the 2004 season, I watched the way Bret Bielema handled things, and I started thinking, "This is a guy who's going to be a head coach. He has an air about him."

If possible, I wanted to hire somebody from my staff. I thought it would be easier on the players — as long as it was the right guy and I felt it was somebody who could be successful at Wisconsin. Potentially, you could protect more coaches that way, too.

This is a state and university where you have to have the right person in place. You'll have a problem if that person doesn't understand the nuances of how things work here. You'll also have a problem if that person has a personality that doesn't fit or if there isn't a chemistry with the people. I thought Bret Bielema was the right fit.

I have always kept a short list of coaches, and I would occasionally put them in a pecking order. Every year the list would change because my hottest guys were moving on.

The Fiesta Bowl annually plays host to a golf scramble, and I like playing in it because it gives me a chance to visit with coaches from around the country. I might hang around the pool and talk with different guys — just to see what they're really like.

I can see a coach's record on paper and I can read what other people are saying about him. But I want to see how he carries himself and how he handles things. I'm always on the lookout for coaches who have been successful and are moving up the ranks.

It's funny, but when Randy Walker came into the Big Ten, we butted heads. At least our staffs did. As time passed, I could see how innovative he was on offense. He gave everybody fits and really changed the game. I thought he was an excellent coach.

I knew Randy was very loyal to Northwestern. But if I didn't have the right person in place here — when I was ready to make the move and name a successor — I felt he was someone that I had to talk with just to see if he would be interested in the job.

I knew it would be hard to make a move from school to school within the Big Ten. But that's how impressed I was with him. I thought he did a lot with a little. He never complained about having a shorter stick. He maximized his personnel.

It was a tragedy that Randy Walker died at such a young age. He was only 52.

It never got to the point where I actually talked to somebody else. I saw everything I needed to see in Bret Bielema. He was a very progressive thinker. He was very passionate about his work. He was a guy who lived it 24/7. And he knew how to win.

I have been asked if I saw myself in Bret.

Yeah, I did.

But I wasn't looking for that. Some things are different, some things are similar.

Being around me in certain settings and environments, Bret has said as much. "From the way he attacks a golf game," he said, "to the way that he socially interacts and cares about people, I noticed a lot of similarities, too."

I had some things that were important to me in a head coach. One of the most important was having a presence. If you don't have that, you're vulnerable. Bret has a presence as well as an ability to look at the big picture. Not many assistants do.

Most assistant coaches worry about their own world. When you discuss issues and you're trying to make decisions for the program, most assistants are going to make recommendations that are self-serving because it fits them better — it fits their personnel and what they want to be doing — even if it may not be best for the overall program.

In all of Bret's recommendations, in all of the things that he brought up and talked about, he was always focused on the big picture and winning — as a program. He was also very perceptive. He saw what was going on — for the most part — and he watched how I handled my dual responsibilities.

"I saw someone who had a lot on his plate — things coming at him from the athletic director's point of view, along with coaching, and all that entails," he said. "I saw a guy who genuinely cared about doing things the right way.

"As that first season unfolded, I began to appreciate how much detail he paid to all the things beyond the football program. In the back of my mind, I was thinking, 'How long can one man do both of these jobs and put himself in a position to have success in both?'

"Along the way, Barry gave me certain decision-making responsibilities. He put me in charge of the secretarial staff. He asked me to be involved when we hired a new football trainer. He asked me to be involved when we hired a new video coordinator.

"He was nurturing me. That's the greatest sign of a leader — if he can get you to do things without you knowing it. Those hires, the new trainer and video coordinator, are now on my staff and he was making sure I got the right people around me."

It was all a part of helping Bret transition from an assistant to a head coach. I had a chance to visit with Purdue athletic director Morgan Burke at the Big Ten meetings, and we discussed their transition in basketball from Gene Keady to Matt Painter.

We talked about the benefits of Painter serving one year as an assistant under Keady — to learn the ropes — before taking over the program himself. That sold me on the process.

Over a period of time, I got together with Bret to talk, whether it was in my office, on the field, or during our noon-hour walks to Picnic Point. That gave me a feel for how he would handle certain things. I finally said, "You know what? I'm planning on stepping down as head coach. I like what you've done, and I want you to be the next head coach here."

I think he was thrilled and dumbfounded.

Bret later said, "When Barry first threw that out at me, we were alone and yet we weren't — we were still in a public environment with people around us, and I didn't know whether to high-five or hug him. There was so much emotion. It took me by surprise. I still can't remember exactly what happened. I was caught totally off-guard."

***

As a former head coach, I think I have an advantage over most athletic directors in dealing with coaches. Many universities have decided to go with a businessman as their AD, and I can understand the approach. It is a big business, bigger now than ever.

But you still have to remember that this is an athletic department, and it has to be accountable to the athletes and the coaches. I want to be hands-on with my coaches, and I think they feel comfortable coming to me with issues because there's nothing that's going to happen to them that hasn't already happened to me. Many will come in for advice or they will use me in recruiting.

In sitting down with head coaches, I'll tell them some of the same things I told my football assistants. "You've got some deficiencies, you've got some issues. Think about this, and come back with a plan for how it's going to be corrected and we'll discuss it."

I don't plan on changing how I handle things.

That seems to sit well with my coaches.

"I don't know how many times I've talked with Mike Eaves or Bo Ryan or Lisa Stone," Bret said, "and they've referenced how great it is to have an AD who knows and understands the difficulties we go through and the tightrope we need to walk.

"You can't put a price tag on something like this because no one else has such an avenue. There's no other Division I coach in America who has an AD — for whom they've worked — who can understand where this program is academically, socially, and athletically. We've been together two years and I understand his philosophies and thinking.

"I always say, 'He's 100 yards away' because I know I can walk down to his office at the other end of Camp Randall or pick up the phone and give him a buzz. He has seen every level of success as an assistant, a coordinator, and head coach, and so when different things are coming at me, at a million miles an hour, he can give me reference points.

"He has never told me, 'This is how you need to do it.' He just throws out an idea. 'I can see where you're coming from. Have you ever thought about this?' I appreciate that."

I don't ever want Bret looking over his shoulder. This is his show.

"Go with your heart, go with what you believe," I told him, "and have a little vision and confidence in what you see. Don't be overwhelmed. Don't make it bigger than what it is. This job is about solving problems and breaking them down to their simplest form."

Seems to me another young coach — who was taking over a college program for the first time — got the same advice from Lou Holtz.

It seemed to work out.

***

I didn't want the news to leak out that I would be stepping down as the head coach and Bret Bielema would be replacing me — at least not until we could hold a formal press conference. Cindy and I put a lot of time and thought into how to announce it.

I didn't tell anybody, not even Father Mike, until just before it happened. Cindy called some of our friends and said, "Barry is making an announcement. He'd like you to be there." They thought I was presenting an award to somebody or endowing a scholarship.

That day, I started getting phone calls from Lou Holtz and Brad Nessler and Tom Crean. There were rumors flying around that I had some type of illness. No one knew what I was planning on doing, which is really hard to pull off. But I did it.

And I thought the timing of the announcement — well in advance of the 2005 season and the start of training camp — worked out about as well as it could have worked out.

I'll tell you what some guys would do. If they weren't staying on as the athletic director and didn't care about the school, they would have coached the season and when it was over, they would have said, "Hey, that's it. Thanks for the memories."

But I was staying, and I just thought this was the best possible transition, especially for Bret and recruiting, since we already had a handful of verbal commitments that we were able to keep. To do it any other way would have been deceiving the kids.

There's no way we would have had a good recruiting class if I had waited and stepped down at the end of the season. That would have been unfair to many people, and there's no way we would have kept all the Wisconsin kids.

What was hard was sitting down with my assistants and telling them that I was retiring. I had coaches who had been with me for a long time. After I told the staff, I felt relieved.

Did I have any second thoughts about leaving coaching too soon? About a week after the press conference, according to Cindy, I sat up in the middle of the night and blurted out, "Did I make the right decision?" Without hesitating, I said "I did" and went back to sleep.

***

Even though it was my last go-around as a head coach, I didn't allow myself to get sentimental during the 2005 season, but that didn't stop others from bringing it up.

Whenever I walked out to midfield and chatted with an opposing head coach during the pregame warm-ups, they all wanted to talk about my retirement. What are you going to miss? What were you thinking? Why did you do it now?

They wanted to know these things because they're in the same racket, and they go through the same things on a daily basis. And unless you've been in these shoes and sat at this desk, you don't know all the issues that a head coach has to deal with.

Even Joe Paterno came up to me and said, "We've got to get together at the end of the season because some day I've got to start thinking about this."

When we're at midfield, I always try to read coaches. Some guys are nervous wrecks. Some guys are really confident. If you're friends, you just shoot the breeze.

Kirk Ferentz and I will talk about family or former coaches and that type of thing. We'll talk about the same things before a kickoff between our teams that we would talk about if we were sitting in Chicago at the Big Ten luncheon in early August.

What you say during those brief pregame meetings depends on the coach. If you don't respect the other guy, or have much in common with him, you try to be courteous. I can remember there were a few times when I didn't go out to the middle of the field and talk with the other coach before a game. That happened twice with Illinois.

I had nothing good to say, and I didn't want to be a phony.

I'm sure there were times when the other coach was ticked off at me, particularly during the early years when we were building our program. If they didn't want to see me, that was fine. It doesn't take long to find out who your true friends are in this profession.

Whether our teams were playing or not, I talked with Michigan's Lloyd Carr every week. Our friendship stems from our background. We recruited against each other as assistants. We're about the same age, and we both coached on defense.

Over the phone, we may share some ideas or just talk about what has been going on in the league. Who's hot, who's not. General things. We didn't get much into game-planning.

One of my favorites was George Perles, the former Michigan State coach. He was hilarious and as honest as the day is long. I loved George's wit.

One time before the kickoff, he was telling me, "You know, Barry, this is just a great job, just a wonderful job, just a terrific job." George went on and on and on about the job benefits and the time off and the compensation and how great this and that was.

Finally he says, "The only bad thing about this job is the games."

***

We played some memorable games in 2005. We've had other teams that were more talented than this squad. But to win close games, and to win them the way we did, and to win big games — to get a team to really stay focused — that's what coaching is all about.

That's when you get the most gratification, when all the pieces come together. The record was a testament to our program and what we had in place and how we trained our kids. They were not going to be distracted, though the opportunities certainly were there.

On the Sunday night following the Temple game I got the call telling me that my dad had passed away. He was 86. I flew to western Pennsylvania for his funeral on Wednesday. Bret ran the practice that day and I rejoined my team in Madison on Thursday.

That Saturday night, we played in a tough, hostile environment at North Carolina that included a 20-minute weather delay before the opening kickoff. There were plenty of distractions, but we stayed together as a team and pulled out the win.

Our starting left offensive tackle, Joe Thomas, said afterward that the players hadn't used my dad's death as a rallying cry or anything like that. But winning the game, Joe said, was just something everybody knew inside that they wanted to do for me.

That win was a gift, and you don't know how good that made me feel.

You also don't know how emotionally drained I was. I almost fell asleep on the bus ride to the stadium. To bury my dad on a Wednesday and to play an intense game like that on a Saturday completely wiped me out. I was on empty. I know when we played Central Florida in 2004, their head coach, George O'Leary, skipped the game to be at his mother's funeral.

That never entered into my thinking — not being with my team. Knowing what I had been through, Pat Richter looked at me and said, "You made the right decision."

I know this much — I was thankful that all my children and grandkids got their pictures taken with my dad that summer when our family spent some time in the Burgettstown-Langeloth area.

His quality of life was deteriorating, but he was able to recognize everyone. That meant a lot to him and me, and I'm sure some day it will mean even more to the kids.

***

Looking back on my final season, I know I took everything in and really did enjoy it. Much of that was because of how the players handled it. They were fun to be around and coach. They bought into what we were doing and how we were doing it. And when they're having fun, you're having fun. As a coach, you like some teams better than others. I liked this team, and I really liked the way our kids capped the season with a win over Auburn in the bowl.

I'll never forget that game. Nor the Minnesota game.

You don't win many like that — by recovering a blocked punt in the end zone. That was a game where we were outplayed and it looked like we were finished, but the players kept battling and we came back and found a way to win. That was unforgettable.

So was the Iowa game. That was a hard one to lose. Needless to say, that wasn't how I pictured my final home game in Camp Randall. We had all the momentum in the world, but we let it get away from us in the second half. That's why it was such a disappointing loss.

What was really hard was getting up on that stage for that post game celebration. But I'll never forget the video tribute or the words that were spoken. I cried when Joe Panos talked, and I know it was pretty tough on him, too.

"That video was pulling my guts out, it was awesome," Joe said. "And it was one of the most emotional things I've ever done — to be the guy to represent all the former players and captains. I was a wreck. I didn't want to mess up.

"All I wanted to hear from all the other players was, 'Joe, I thought that was a great speech because I would have said the same things. Boy, you really hit the right notes.'

"Basically, my speech was a thank-you. I was thanking coach for not only preparing us every week to play football, but for teaching us so many life lessons that we use every single day. He taught us to be better teammates which, in turn, made us better men.

"He had a plan, he had a vision, and he always had us prepared. There were even contingency plans for every possible scenario. He made us do the little things — to get better — that the others guys wouldn't do. And he really knew how to get us motivated.

"He was really good at pitting 'us' against 'them.' Some of his best teams were his hungriest teams — the teams that didn't get respect. I just think he loved being backed into a corner. He played that card so well, but it wasn't a gimmick.

"So I was very honored to be standing up there representing hundreds and hundreds of former players. And I was proud to be called his best captain because I learned from the best.

"I like Bret Bielema and I know he's going to be a great coach. But this is the end of an era. I'll still see Barry and we'll talk every week. He may even have more time for me now. But Wisconsin will not see another coach like him again."

***

My only expectation for Bret is to see the team managed properly. I want to see things run smoothly, and I have no reason to believe that won't happen. I want to see him implement his plan — to put his own stamp on it — and I want to see the kids execute it.

Not being on the sidelines will leave a void for me.

I won't be calling plays, but I will still be a part of what's going on. And it will still be important for us to be successful. In that respect, I'll be emotionally involved.

As far as coaching again, I'm really not planning on it. This season will give me an idea of how much I miss it, and if I miss coaching that much, then I'd have to reconsider.

What excites me about the future is that I have some options in what I can do, and they are things that I want to do — starting with the continued growth of the athletic department.

We're solid, and we've made a lot of improvement. But there's much more we can accomplish. We can continue to improve facilities, and I want to be able to allow all of our coaches to compete at the highest level.

You feel good about things because the football stadium is full, the basketball arena is full, and hockey is filling almost all the seats, too. We've done well with our Badger Fund and donations are up. We should get a windfall from the Big Ten's new TV contract.

But how do you protect yourself for the future?

Costs keep rising, so you have to be creative in how you raise funds and you have to stay ahead of the game and anticipate what is going to happen.

I know this: when I first came here, it was very easy to take cheap shots at the athletic department. Our competitors said, "They want to be big time, but they're bush league."

We were. But we're not bush league anymore, and I don't want to go back to that era. Pat Richter brought back pride to the department, and

I felt like I brought it back to football.

I know I will never take our fan support for granted because I know how hard it was to get them back. Look, they weren't given a very good product for a long period of time.

From my Iowa coaching days, though, I remembered how Camp Randall rocked. I thought the fans were unbelievable, even a little nasty to the visiting coaches who had to wind their way through the seating areas to get from the field to the press box.

Back then, I didn't know the ins and outs of Wisconsin's athletic department. But I saw good players and intense fans, and I just could never see why they couldn't win at Wisconsin.

Our people love football. They don't want to be embarrassed. They want to be competitive and win their share. Truth is, they were probably suspect of me when I took over. Here was a bold, young coach spouting off, and he doesn't back it up that first year. I kept saying, "Be patient, we're building a foundation and we're not taking short cuts."

That's how we did it, and as we gradually started filling Camp Randall, I appreciated the support. And I appreciate how that support has extended to our booster club, the Mendota Gridiron Club.

Wayne Esser, the executive director, has been through the good and the bad. I can't imagine what he went through during the early years when we weren't winning because he has been the sounding board for complaints. I think he has learned that you can't please everybody, no matter how much you win. He has been a valuable piece to the puzzle.

So were John Chadima and Steve Malchow. Our friendship dates back to when I was an assistant at Iowa and they were going to school there. They're family. I've always looked at them like two of my kids, and I've been really proud to watch them develop.

When I first hired John as my administrative assistant, I told him, "I don't like surprises. I just want to coach. Keep me informed, but you handle all the outside stuff."

And he has been meticulous in everything that he has done. I have so much confidence in John that I can concentrate on my job and know the rest is being taken care of.

As a player, you also want to have somebody on the front end running lead, someone who can stay on top of things. That was Steve Malchow's role in Sports Information.

He handled all the publicity for Ron Dayne and really managed it well.

He knew we weren't going to pad statistics, that we wanted Ron to break the record and win the Heisman within the context of the game, and Steve brought that out.

From my first day, Lisa Powell has been my secretary. Besides handling all the football-related business, Lisa has handled all of my speaking engagements and scheduling. She gets me to where I need to be, which isn't easy because the schedule is always changing.

In putting together this puzzle — athletically and administratively — one of the more indispensable pieces has been Father Mike Burke. I know that I can go to him and open up about staff issues, player issues, family issues, whatever it may be.

Cindy would agree our circle of friends has changed over the years. That's a natural progression as you get older. The fact is we both enjoy our kids and their spouses as much as we enjoy our friends. We'll do things with them socially and have as much fun as we do spending time with friends our own age. I look forward to going to Little League games and watching the grandkids grow.

For a lot of reasons, then, the future is really exciting. As I would tell my players or my own children, you need to do something that you really enjoy and you need to do it well enough that somebody will pay you for it. I've been able to do that my whole life.

***

At speaking engagements, I like to tell the story of how I pulled into the parking lot at Maple Bluff Country Club and some guy took one look at the car I was driving — a Cadillac, the Barry Alvarez edition — and he said, "Maybe I should become a college football coach so I can drive a big, fancy car like that."

I said, "Listen, pal, in this business, you don't start off driving Cadillacs."

People may not believe this, but I have a long history with junkers. My first car was a 1950 Ford. I was a freshman at Nebraska, and four or five of us chipped in 25 bucks each to purchase the car. To jazz it up, we got tape from the trainer's room and put racing stripes on it.

That winter, the starter went out, and we didn't have the money to replace it.

So we would have to push the car up on the sidewalk — right in front of our dorm — and a bunch of us would run behind it and push until we could jump-start the engine and take off. It wasn't easy getting it up to speed because there were no hills in Lincoln.

On a beautiful spring day, we created the first sun roof. We got out a chisel and a metal cutter and cut a big hole in the roof of the car. There were some obvious drawbacks, though, and it wasn't long before we drove the car to the junk yard and sold it for salvage.

During my senior year, we would often play the card game Pitch for money. I was pretty good at it, and one guy owed me so much money, I said, "Instead of cash, I'll just take your car." That's how I wound up with a 1957 Olds.

When I got my first head coaching job at Lexington High School, we needed a second car because Cindy was teaching and I needed a way to get to work. We didn't have any money, so I looked through the newspaper for the best deal.

I found a car with an option to buy. The option? I could buy the car, as is, for 35 bucks or the owner would fix the windshield wipers and sell it to me for 50 bucks.

I said, "Here's 35 bucks. I won't drive in the rain."

Cindy didn't need me to call and tell her when I was coming home for dinner. That car didn't have a muffler, so she could hear me from a block away.

When I got my next head coaching job at Mason City High School, I bought a second car there, too. This one wasn't too bad, just a little rusty.

We were in the process of trying to raise money for a new weight room, which meant that we needed to meet as many wealthy people in the city as we could.

I remember joining the local country club and taking one of my assistants out. He was embarrassed to be seen with me, I think. The parking lot was full of new cars and we were pulling up in a car with rusted out fenders. Didn't bother me a bit.

So don't talk to me about the car I may be driving today.

I paid my dues.

***

There's big money in the coaching profession. But the guys who are making it have worked their way up the ladder. They have proven they can win.

Most people can see what the value of a sold-out stadium is to an athletic department and a school and a community. So when someone can do that — win at a high level and fill the seats — the school is getting its money's worth from that coach.

It's not just about showing up on Saturdays and winning. It's about keeping everyone on the same page and holding things together and running the entire program.

You need to be a strong person because it's a hard job.

When I was hired, somebody questioned Chancellor Shalala about my contract. She agreed "that's a lot of money" but quickly added, "it's a very tenuous job."

Coaches aren't tenured like professors. And in coaching, you're not just criticized on Saturdays. It seems like you're criticized for something every damn day.

Someone is always keeping score.

Every time you open your mouth, you've got to be politically correct. Any time you go out in public, you have to be aware that people are watching.

Over the years, I've learned to be more guarded and more aware of where I'm at and who I'm with and who is around me. I don't go out less, I'm just more cautious.

There's a simple rule to follow — if you walk in somewhere and you don't feel comfortable, you need to do one thing: exit. It took me a while to learn that.

When we first got to Wisconsin, Cindy had no clue about the size of the fishbowl that we were stepping into. Or the lack of privacy that comes with the territory.

"There was a point," she said, "where I realized Barry was a celebrity and what we said and how we acted was going to be cause for discussion. When that first hits you, it's kind of a good feeling because you realize that you've made it. And that's what you're trying to do — be a success in your chosen field. But you also realize the responsibility you have."

I always felt Hayden Fry and Lou Holtz were loners. They were very guarded in their own way. They didn't go out very much. They were seldom seen in public.

When Hayden did go out, there was always a buzz. Wherever he went in Iowa, the reaction he created was ridiculous. Even when we were on the road, people would recognize him. With Lou, you couldn't get through an airport without someone stopping him. Paterno is the same way.

I enjoy people. I like being around people. I like going to restaurants.

From the first day I took this job, I was never afraid to go out. Whether it was going out and having dinner or a drink with John Jardine or an assistant coach, or just me and Cindy going out.

I wanted to be visible enough when I was out in public that it wasn't that big of a deal — so it was not strange for people to see me. I got that for the most part. But you find out that you're vulnerable. If you're in a room, everybody in the room is with you.

You can be as innocent as all get-out, but the next thing you know someone spots you in the crowd and they're saying to somebody else, "I was with Barry at so-and-so and he said blah-blah-blah" and they really weren't with you at all.

That's how rumors get started.

They were rampant in 1996. That was tough on everybody, especially Cindy, because people were making accusations about me and who I was with or seeing. The rumors were flying and kept snowballing, and I didn't know where they were coming from or who had started them.

To this day, when I'm out alone with my daughter Dawn, she'll scream out "dad" loud enough so everyone knows she's my daughter.

I hired a private investigator to track down where some of those rumors were coming from and things started to quiet down pretty quickly. I talked with Texas coach Mack Brown, who said he went through the exact same thing his seventh season at North Carolina.

Even the FBI got involved.

Every year, an agent will come in during training camp and make a presentation to our team about gambling. They will focus on what the players need to know, recognize, and stay away from, and they will alert them to the inherent dangers, even for innocent bystanders.

One year, the agent made the statement, "If you don't think this can happen, look at what happened to your coach a few years ago after the Badgers lost a tough game."

Afterward, I talked to the agent and he told me how the FBI was called in to investigate after Ron Dayne lost a fumble in the closing seconds. We were trying to protect the lead against Northwestern and, because of the turnover, we wound up losing the game.

The agent said, "We had to investigate because people lost a lot of money. But we were aware of the type of program you run — you run such a tight ship — nobody could infiltrate your team. We tracked down the rumors to an unhappy group of gamblers."

***

I never tried to shield my family from the scrutiny that comes with celebrity, with being a head coach, with being a public figure. The kids were always aware of it.

But I'll hear things now that will register more than they did early on when I was so engrossed with my coaching. I can't believe how ugly some of the professors were to my daughter Stacy, who was a freshman at the UW during my first season as head coach.

She never said a word to me that she had issues. But she later told Cindy about some of the things that happened in class. She's the tough one. She won't take guff from anybody, and she has been known to dress down people with declarations such as, "Like the play-calling is my damn fault?"

All my kids have been very successful in their own fields, and they don't want to be judged on who their father is. They want to be judged on what they've accomplished.

I know Dawn won't mention her last name sometimes because of the public reaction. And I know she doesn't want to be perceived as looking for favors because of who I am.

"As we've become more successful and more well-known," Cindy has said, "people will say things to me and the children that they wouldn't say to Barry."

Dawn's oldest son, Joe, won an award at Bo Ryan's basketball camp.

"Did you tell Bo who you were?" Dawn asked.

"No, I didn't want him to know," Joe said.

Meanwhile, their youngest son, Jake, who's 7, will go up to anybody on the street and say, "Do you know who my grandpa is?"

There have been negatives to having a high profile. But weighing everything, there have been far more benefits, far more positives, and it runs about 10 to 1.

You just have to take the good with the bad.

"What's the one thing you say to your children over and over?" Cindy asked rhetorically. "Please don't do anything to hurt yourself or somebody else. I never lost track of the fact that what Chad did was wrong, terribly wrong. But the reaction was amazing to me."

We both fully understood what Chad did was wrong when he killed a parrot in the microwave. He had been feuding with a fraternity brother for a long time and even though the hostilities towards each other escalated, it was still no excuse for his actions. He messed up big-time and that will be with him for the rest of his life.

But he paid his dues, and he has admitted what he did was wrong. Still, people want to bring it up and attack him and take pot-shots because he's my son.

During the trial, Cindy was like a mother bear protecting her cub. She wanted to fight everybody. She felt like some of the things that were being said were a direct attack on us.

She flinched. But so did the judge. He flinched big-time on the sentencing and some of the things that he brought up. He said to Chad, "We're not going to treat you special. We're not going to do anything different in this courtroom because you're a celebrity."

Chad's attorney interrupted and said, "Excuse me, he's not a celebrity. He's a college student. His father is a celebrity. You've got it confused."

Maybe because of the shadow I cast over my children, it hasn't always been easy to be Chad Alvarez. Even when he was playing high school football, it was a big deal for the other team to put a bulls-eye on his back. He enjoyed the sport, but there was always the scrutiny.

Cindy and I love our children: Dawn, Stacy and Chad. There's not enough time or space to talk about them. We could easily devote a chapter to each.

Chad, in particular, has shown all of us how to turn a negative into a positive. Cindy and I are so proud of what Chad has achieved as a student, who graduated from college with honors; and as a business professional.

A couple of years ago, we lost a tough game to an opponent we were supposed to beat, and I was concerned for my grandson, Joe, and what might be said to him at school.

I told Cindy, "You'd better talk to Dawn and make sure Joe is aware that some of the older kids might get after him about his grandpa's team. Just prepare him for the worst."

I don't think anything happened. But it still concerned me. It's the price you pay. Not that I'm complaining. What if one of my grandsons

— Joe, Jake or Jack — came up to me someday and said, "Grandpa, I want to be a coach."

I'd say, "Great. How can I help?"

Then I'd give him this advice:

Be committed.

Surround yourself with good people.

Learn the sport.

Be a good coach.

And never look back.

I haven't, and I've had a helluva run as a football coach.

I've lived my dream.

EPILOGUE

The Home Stretch
By Mike Lucas

Six months removed from one of his most satisfying career triumphs — the Capital One Bowl victory over heavily-favored Auburn — Barry Alvarez was making his way through the terminal in Milwaukee's General Mitchell Airport when he was recognized and intercepted by a middle-aged man traveling with his son.

The stranger greeted Alvarez like a long-lost friend. Extending his right hand to the former University of Wisconsin football coach, he said, "Barry, I just wanted to say thanks for making us care again. I was here for the bad years, and I don't ever want to go back."

Alvarez smiled and thanked the fan for his loyalty and support. As he walked away, Alvarez said, "People ask me all the time, 'What are you most proud of? What do you want your legacy to be?' That's it — that our program brought pride back to the state."

Once expectations were raised, Alvarez would later acknowledge, there was no going back, there was no lowering the bar. So much more was expected and demanded of Wisconsin football after the team won a share of the 1993 Big Ten championship and its first Rose Bowl.

Therein was the challenge — to maintain the level of play at a school that was so unaccustomed to "swinging for the fences" prior to the arrival of Chancellor Donna Shalala, athletic director Pat Richter, and Alvarez, in that order.

"We never, ever discussed having to hit certain milestones, like, 'We need to win this by this date or we need to go to a bowl by this date,'" Richter recounted of his first contract negotiations with Alvarez, who was then a highly-touted Notre Dame defensive coordinator. "I never even thought about bowl games. That was the furthest thing from my mind.

"Basically, I just wanted to find someone who was going to bring back respectability and pride. That was the essence of what we sat down and talked about — let's just be competitive, let's stop embarrassing ourselves, let's get some respect. I told Barry, 'If you win six games and go to a bowl, people will think that you hung the moon here.' That is as much as we ever discussed about a particular objective or timetable."

As he approached his departure gate, Alvarez said, "Anytime I travel, I will inevitably run into people from Wisconsin who will tell me their personal Rose Bowl story, or they will tell me about how many games they DIDN'T win when they were in school here. Now they know they have a chance to compete. Now they have pride in the program."

Upon boarding the flight to Pittsburgh — where he was to reconnect with family, friends, and fellow coaches in western Pennsylvania for the next two days — Alvarez said, "Sometimes you don't realize the impact that you've had until you leave Madison. But I've gotten the sense that a lot of people liked our hard-nosed brand of football."

***

From the front stoop of Bimbo's Ice Cream Shop — along Route 18 in Burgettstown — you can clearly see the area's most distinctive landmark. Rising above the hilly landscape is a tall smokestack from the Langeloth Metallurgical Company, which produces molybdenum products, metallic elements used to toughen alloy steels.

The American Zinc and Chemical Company had occupied the site until the mid-'40s, when the zinc smelting operation closed and the Langeloth mine was sold.

Bimbo, himself, is our historian.

Bimbo is David Vallina — Alvarez's cousin and business partner in the strip mall. They purchased the property in the mid-'80s when Alvarez was an assistant at the University of Iowa.

Besides the ice cream shop, the mall occupants include a physical therapy center, a justice of the peace, a liquor store, a medical clinic and a Kwik Stop/Deli, the busy hub for everything that happens locally and Badger Central during the Alvarez years.

"In the fall, from Thursday on, they all come in here to talk football; it's an agitating session for an hour every morning," Vallina said. "We get Penn State fans, Pitt fans, West Virginia fans." And for the last 16 years, Wisconsin and Barry Alvarez fans.

Vallina, like nearly everyone else, got his nickname from Alvarez. That was the Alvarez seal of approval. "A fast-pitch softball pitcher came through here named Bimbo," Vallina said. "When I was 10 or 11, I'd go to the games and pitch underhand on the sidelines, and Barry started calling me Bimbo. He damn near nicknamed everyone in town."

That included Alvarez's younger brother, Tony, who morphed into Woody. "There was this old, bald guy, Woody Houghton, who lived on Miner's Hill. Barry and I came home one day from playing ball and I didn't want to take a bath in the tub, so Barry said, 'You're a dirtball like that Woody Houghton.' He started calling me Woody and it stuck."

The tub — a big, steel tub — was in the cellar of the Alvarez home. "They finally put a shower in down there," Woody said. "That was later on, when we moved up in status."

Not far from the "Welcome to Langeloth, Home of Barry Alvarez" sign was the Alvarez home on 4th Avenue, a nondescript 30-by-30 cement structure with a living room, two bedrooms, and a kitchen. It meshed with the other homes: well-kept, but low-income.

"My mom and dad had one bedroom," Woody said, "and when Barry and I were younger, we both slept in the same bedroom with our grandmother. I slept in a crib until the second grade because we didn't have space."

An addition was eventually built on to the back of the house, and the two boys got their own room, which they shared with an uncle, a recent immigrant from Spain.

"The three of us were in bunkbeds — it was small, but it was home," said Woody. "A lot of people still had outhouses. Hell, we had an inside toilet."

Langeloth was an old mining town of maybe 200 homes, total. It was a town where everyone knew everyone; people were neighborly and bent on survival.

Woody Alvarez can still visualize his dad shoveling coal into the furnace, and he can still see his grandmother, Wella, feeding the ducks in the backyard.

"We had a garage with a pen and she would get duck eggs every morning," he said, adding the kicker to the story. "She'd make homemade Spanish sausage every month, and my Uncle John would smoke the sausage and sell it at his store. One day, though, the smokehouse caught fire and the garage burned down and killed all the ducks."

Uncle John was Bimbo's dad.

"He was a hard-ass, too — about 5-9 and 240 pounds," David Vallina fondly remembered. "He took Barry everywhere. He would play soccer on Sunday morning on the other side of Washington County and then he would play a softball doubleheader on Sunday afternoon, and Barry would never leave his side."

With the imposing smokestack in Langeloth framing his line of sight, Bimbo said, "Barry was definitely a product of this environment, the hardcore background. He has the same work ethic as the common folk here: work hard and good things will happen.

"If people would see how he grew up...I know some have come out here from Wisconsin and we'll take them up and show them where he lived, and they just shake their heads. They figure he came from some uppity school district and some high-class neighborhood, but he didn't. He came from sticks and stones, man."

Bimbo's brother, Jon Lynn Vallina — the longtime athletic director at Burgettstown High School — pointed out that Barry Alvarez was "your typical blue-collar coach," which was consistent with his upbringing and the personality of western Pennsylvania.

The high school field in Burgettstown — the one Alvarez starred on — was built on an old strip mine, and the players' locker room had been the miners' locker room.

"Steel mills and coal mines," Jon Lynn reiterated. "That was the way he was raised. He never had much. But no one around here had much. You had to work and you knew that you had to study and play hard to get out of this area and make something out of yourself.

"Today, they're spoiled, they're softer. We don't have the tough kids anymore in western P-A."

Back in the day — when there were no restrictions on what was pumped out of that Langeloth smokestack — you had to be tough just to breathe the air.

"They'd be releasing these acid by-products at the plant," Woody Alvarez said. "Some days the soot would lie over the ball field like a fog, and we'd have to go home for a couple of hours until it cleared out because we couldn't breathe. It was bad stuff."

"You could smell the sulfur, you could taste it," Barry Alvarez vividly remembered. "And you'd get blue splotches on your porch and cars — most of the cars were rusted out."

Without missing a beat, the follicle-challenged Woody chimed in, "You'd also get that blue stuff on your head. That's why everyone is bald here." He cracked himself up.

Since they had mined coal for over 100 years in this region, it was no great revelation that Raccoon Creek and its tributaries were polluted by the acid mine drainage.

"They also had two slaughter houses — packing houses — within a half mile of each other," Barry Alvarez said. "They'd butcher the cattle and let the blood run into the creek. I remember it would get a real bright orange when it mixed with everything else. Sometimes we'd be walking home and we'd see a bladder stuck on a twig or floating down the creek."

Things have changed over the years.

But there are still many constants in Burgettstown.

Barry Alvarez, for one.

"You see that bar, Tia's, right down the road," Bimbo Vallina said, gesturing to a cluster of taverns. "Barry could walk in there today and 50 people would know him, and he'd sit there and talk to them just like he talked to them 20 years ago."

***

Barry Alvarez pulled the rental car into the parking lot of Burgettstown High School and turned off the engine. He motioned to his right.

"That's where the old school was — it burned down when I was a junior," he said. "It was early in the spring, and we were practicing baseball in the gym, when the custodian came running down the steps yelling, 'The school is on fire. You've got to get out.'

"Our baseball coach, Pat McGraw, who was also my football coach, instructed us to put our gloves away and get outside. I thought, 'The hell with that.' I just got a new coat and glove, so I ran up to my second-floor locker and got my coat and stood out on the balcony.

"The curtains were going up in flames, like something out of *Phantom of the Opera*. I finally ran outside, stood across the street, and watched the school burn down to the ground. But I had my stuff — my coat and glove. I wasn't going to lose them."

They were much too valuable, especially the glove, to sacrifice, he stressed.

The high school setting brought back some memories for Alvarez, who had a flashback to his first head coaching job at Lexington High School in Lexington, Nebraska.

"I went to a state track meet to see this big, strapping kid — Mike Scully, who was 6-4, 230 pounds and only a sophomore," he said. "Scully's family is living in Cozad, which was a neighboring rival. I went up to him and said, 'Maybe you ought to consider moving to Lexington.'

"Now, there's no way I should be mentioning that. But the kid is fired up and the next thing I know his dad is buying a house on the lake in Lexington. Before they moved in, he has no place to stay, so I say, 'Hell, you can stay with us. You can sleep in the baby's room.'"

Alvarez broke out in laughter at the memory of Cindy's reaction. "She would have nothing to do with it," he said. "It was one of those 'enough is enough' discussions."

Soon he had another flashback, this time to his second head coaching job at Mason City High School in Mason City, Iowa.

Alvarez recalled confronting a young player who had skipped an out-of-season weight lifting workout. "The excuse he gave me for not being there was that he didn't have a ride to school. I said, 'OK, I'll pick you up at 7:15 every morning.'"

That became a part of the routine, and the player stuck it out.

"That year we won the state championship," Alvarez said. "He didn't play, he wasn't a contributor. But he was part of it, he experienced it. This past year I got a note from him thanking me for making him believe in something. He made a commitment.

"My whole thing was, 'If I make a sacrifice to pick you up and you make a sacrifice to get up every morning and lift, we'll all get better as a team.'"

Throughout his Wisconsin tenure, Alvarez has received phone calls from high school administrators and athletic directors seeking his advice on hiring a coach.

"I tell them, 'Go out and find a young lion — someone who's full of enthusiasm, someone who's going to throw his arm around the kids in the hallway and sell them five days a week,'" he said. "When you show commitment and excitement about your job, it's contagious through the school and the community.

"If I'm the head coach, and I'm making sacrifices, those kids know I care about them and I'm working just as hard as they are, and everybody jumps on the band wagon."

Alvarez started the engine and quickly put Burgettstown High School in his rearview mirror. A few hours later, he was in a Pittsburgh suburb kibitzing with Phil Mavrich, a lifelong friend, who competed alongside Alvarez in Little League baseball and prep sports.

"Barry had the home run trot perfected in baseball when he was 9 years old," chuckled Mavrich. "He was one of the few kids who could knock the ball over the fence. I wouldn't say he did it routinely. But he did it quite often."

The Alvarez confidence or swagger was the result of knowing he could do something well, or better than others, according to Mavrich. That extended to his coaching.

"Barry Alvarez, the high school football player," Mavrich said, "was a lot like Barry Alvarez, the head coach. He was a leader and motivator. When he played, he played 60 minutes, and when he wasn't pounding an opponent, he was smacking a teammate in the butt trying to motivate him to play harder. He mentored people and tried to make them better."

That night, Mavrich accompanied Alvarez and Pat Gallagher — another successful local businessman in the Alvarez inner circle — to an Italian fest thrown by Armand Dellovade, a generous University of Pittsburgh booster.

The annual event at Dellovade's home attracts a Who's Who of high school and college coaches from western Pennsylvania, ranging from Johnny Majors to Foge Fazio to Dave Wannstedt. Also in attendance this year was agent Ralph Cindrich, Pittsburgh Steelers offensive line coach Russ Grimm, and Iowa's Kirk Ferentz.

Although Pitt is his passion, Dellovade has also been a loyal supporter of Alvarez and Ferentz, who said, "To me, Armand is the kind of person who typifies the great people in western P-A — self-made, hard-working, unpretentious."

Ferentz was raised in Pittsburgh. His mom and brother still live there. "The town has changed dramatically since the '80s," Ferentz said. "But high school football, historically, was always a very strong part of the culture and fabric in this part of the state. Still is."

Jogging his memory to 1981, Ferentz, then a Pitt graduate assistant, interviewed for a full-time position on Hayden Fry's staff at Iowa. Alvarez picked him up at the airport.

"Barry had a swagger the first time I met him," Ferentz said. "I know he had the swagger in Mason City and Lexington and everywhere he has been. That's just his personality. I can never imagine him lacking confidence; if he has, he hasn't shown it.

"I don't know if it was because I was from western P-A, but he really made himself available to me right off the bat. Before my wife got to Iowa City, I spent a lot of nights over at the house, just sitting on the porch. Cindy would feed me, and Barry and I would talk football."

Ferentz spent nine seasons as an assistant to Fry before leaving for the NFL. "When I left Iowa City in 1989," Ferentz said, "Wisconsin had the worst program in the conference. If we could play the Badgers 10 times a season that would have been great for us."

Ferentz returned to replace Fry as the head coach in 1999. "In the nine years that I was gone, for my money, nobody did a better job in the Big Ten than Barry and his staff at Wisconsin," Ferentz said. "Believe me, I fully studied what was going on [in Madison]. And I definitely kept that model in my mind when I went 1-10 my first season.

"I respect the way he built the program with a solid foundation instead of going for the quick hit. We're very different personalities. But the things he believes in — things that he believes are paramount to having success — we would both embrace. I think there's a mutual respect and very similar values there. We're probably a byproduct of our background."

***

On the return flight to Madison, Alvarez was excited about the prospect of doing some television work for Fox Sports. As a coach, he was understandably curious about the way college football TV analysts went about their business. He often wondered how much homework or preparation went into the production and how much thought into the analysis.

To this end, Alvarez will get an opportunity to learn the nuances behind the craft when he steps into the Fox Sports booth for two BCS bowl games, including the 2007 national championship game from the new Cardinals Stadium in Glendale, Arizona. Alvarez will work as one of the two analysts alongside play-by-play voice Thom Brennaman.

Before auditioning for the job, Alvarez received clearance from UW Chancellor John Wiley. From there, he contacted ESPN's football analyst Bob Davie, the former Notre Dame head coach, and ESPN's basketball analyst Rick Majerus, the former Marquette and Utah coach. Alvarez has tried to go to school on their development as broadcasters.

"You want to give insight, but you should be fair," said Alvarez in response to the type of analyst he will try to be. "From being on the sidelines for so many years, I think I can offer something that maybe somebody else — who hasn't been down there — wouldn't see, feel, or understand. I think I can bring something to the table with my views."

The thought of joining the "media" probably amused Alvarez.

Asked how he felt he handled the press as a head coach, he said, "Better at the end, because I didn't have anything to prove and I could be very honest and straightforward. I wasn't trying to accomplish anything. I had accomplished it already."

That was not the backdrop during the early years.

"Early on, I felt like I had to battle with the media," he confided. "We weren't very good as a team, and we were trying to build a program. And when people attacked us, I fought for my team and my program. I wasn't going to back down from anyone.

"I tried to hold the media accountable. If you're going to write something or you're going to make an accusation about our program, it should be accurate and true. I just wanted to hold people to the same high standards that they were holding us to.

"If you want me to work hard and be productive and make all the right moves, then I feel like I have the right to expect the same from the media — that people would be thorough in their interviews and reporting and they wouldn't take quotes out of context.

"What really bothered me was when writers seemed to have their stories written before I even answered any of their questions. I never could understand how that worked."

As an Iowa assistant, Alvarez used to listen to how Chicago Bears coach Mike Ditka dealt with people on his radio call-in show. "Ditka challenged guys to fight, it was crazy," Alvarez said. "But I kind of liked that. He wasn't going to take crap from anyone. I could never be that rough. But if someone wasn't fair to me, I could make it tough on them."

As a high school senior, Alvarez took a journalism course.

Did he remember anything from the class?

"Hell, no," he said gruffly. "Other than it was very easy."

***

Alvarez has been called "arrogant" in print more than once.

What does he think?

"I've been confident, I've never NOT been confident," he said. "Some people may read that as arrogant, I don't know. Cindy, you ever feel like I've been arrogant?"

Cindy Alvarez, busy in the kitchen, doesn't hear the question.

"I'm going to tell you something," he went on. "In this job, if you're not confident, if you don't carry yourself and stand up for your program and have a presence, you don't last long. It's very easy to step on somebody, easy to take shots at somebody.

"I talk to everybody. I've always had time for people, I've had time for kids. But sometimes people can be very rude. I try to deal with them…."

Cindy entered the room and sat down.

Do you think Barry is arrogant?

"Yes, he is," she said.

Her husband cackled.

"But I think his arrogance is one of his strengths," Cindy went on, "because he believes in himself and he believes that he can get the job done."

"I see it as confidence, not arrogance," Barry pleaded. "What is arrogance? To me, someone who's arrogant looks down his nose at people."

"I can tell you where Barry may be a little arrogant," Cindy volunteered. "Barry feels that he doesn't have to wait in line like everybody else. Barry feels like he doesn't have to follow the rules like everybody else. This is arrogance."

"That's true," he said softly from his chair.

Cindy then cited an example. Shortly after beating UCLA in the 1994 Rose Bowl, the coaching staff was vacationing together in Hawaii.

"There were six or eight coaches and wives, and we were starving," said Cindy, picking up the play-by-play. "We go into this restaurant and the hostess said it was going to be a two-hour wait. Barry looks at me and says, 'Doesn't she know I'm Barry Alvarez?'"

There was a caveat. The group may have been over-served on Mai Tai's.

At an earlier stop, Barry was going to pick up the tab, so he held up a $100 dollar bill at the table and a girl walked by and plucked it out of his hand.

As they were leaving, the manager chased them down and demanded payment. Seems the girl who had pocketed the cash — the one Barry assumed was a waitress — didn't work at the restaurant. She didn't know who Barry Alvarez was, either. But a C-note is a C-note.

"Let me finish up on this," said Cindy, returning to the topic. "I think his arrogance is in combination with his confidence. But he's not snobbish. He loves people, and he will share himself with people.

"Many arrogant coaches won't do that. He doesn't think he's better than anyone. He just thinks he's entitled to certain things. The arrogance and the confidence are probably what make up his demeanor as a football coach. But he's definitely approachable."

Asked if Barry will coach again, Cindy said, "What will drive him back is his ego and love of the game. Someone will say, 'We know you're the right person for this job, the only person for this job, and we need you.' That will energize him and make him go back."

"I don't know," Barry said softly again.

No matter what transpires, Barry and Cindy Alvarez have found a peace of mind in Madison.

"Coaches tell us we're so lucky, we've achieved almost the impossible," Cindy said. "We have a sense of community, we have a sense of pride in what we've done here, our family is here, and we're going to retire here. This is home, and that's neat."

***

So has Barry Alvarez ever flinched?

"No, he hasn't," Cindy said. "We've had instances where he could have flinched, but Barry always looked for a solution. No, he hasn't."

Notre Dame was the genesis of the phrase, according to Barry, who recalled, "Lou Holtz asked me about a kid, 'Why don't you like him?' and I said, 'He's a flincher.'

"I learned in baseball, if you were a catcher, you had to keep your eyes open and not flinch when the batter swung the bat. You're trained to keep your eyes open, but some flinch.

"Or you go toe-to-toe — you bang people — and all of a sudden, there is a point where the person gives up. That's when he flinches.

"In football, you can be a flincher and not be a physical player; you can be a guy who backs off and doesn't take contact. Or, when the momentum swings away from you, there is a loss of confidence, and that's flinching as a team.

"That's why we always say, 'You can't flinch. You can never let losing enter your mind. You play the next play and you have the confidence that someone is going to make a play, and you'd better hope it's coming your way so you can swing the momentum back."

Barry Alvarez never met his paternal grandfather. But he has heard numerous stories about him. "He was a big guy, built kind of like me, and real proud," he said.

As the story goes, his grandfather was dressed up for a Saint's Day celebration in Spain when he began to have issues with a young police-man. Alvarez picks it up from here.

"The cop is telling him to take his hat off, and when my grandfather didn't hear him, the cop whacked him in the shins with his billy club.

"My grandfather is about 80 years old, but he gets up and beats the hell out of the cop and they throw him in jail.

"He's screaming all the way to his cell, 'This guy abused me, he had no business hitting an old man, he started this.'

"He wouldn't flinch."

Barry Alvarez smiled contently. "All of his buddies went down to the jail and played cards with him through the bars," he added.

Lou Holtz incorporated those two words into his Plan to Win.

So did Barry Alvarez.

Don't flinch.

The All-Alvarez Team

Position-by-position, here is the All-Alvarez team as chosen by Coach Barry Alvarez.

OFFENSE

WR: No. 3, Lee Evans (Bedford, Ohio) - Highly recruited. What helped us was Lee's relationship with Henry Mason and the fact that he's from the same school as Chris Chambers, who was already here when we were recruiting Lee. I thought he could be an excellent player. I don't know that I expected him to be as great of a player as he ended up being. I didn't know he was as fast as he was. Had the strongest hands of any receiver we've ever had. When Lee catches the ball, it's always with his fingers and hands, and he catches and runs with it better than most because he catches with his hands and his feet never leave him. He was an inspiration for all of us just by the way he handled his knee injury. I don't know that an injury affected me more than Lee getting hurt during the spring. After the surgery, I went to his apartment and I'm in the tank, but he's sitting there watching TV with a big smile on his face, ready to take on the challenge of rehabbing. Special kid.

WR: No. 88, Chris Chambers (Bedford, Ohio) - Henry Mason did another great job during the recruiting process. Michigan and Ohio State were also recruiting Chris, but he wanted to play basketball and football. We gave him that chance, and I think that was the main reason we got him. The whole package. Soft hands and could run and jump. Some NFL teams wouldn't take him in the first round because he was 5-11, not 6-foot. Most foolish thing I've ever heard. He plays like he's 6-4 because he's cut so high and his arms are so long. He can vertically jump 45 inches. It just shows you how inaccurate some pro scouts are. They're looking at the numbers instead of taking a look at the kid and what he can really do.

WR: No. 2, Lee DeRamus (Sicklerville, New Jersey) - Legitimate big-time receiver from New Jersey. Would have been a first round draft pick if he hadn't gotten injured. Green Bay wanted a big receiver, and DeRamus was their guy before he broke his leg. Had track speed. Big hands, soft hands. Bigger than most DBs. A fierce competitor. One of our most physical receivers. Match him against an All-American and he was going to crank it up and bring his game to a different level. He wanted to be challenged and he wanted to be good.

TE: No. 81, Mike Roan (Iowa City, Iowa.) - I knew him as a young kid in Iowa City. The Hawkeyes weren't sure whether to pull the trigger on him. We made the decision right away to take him. He could do it all. He was physical, he was very smart, he was a leader, and he could catch. Well-rounded athlete. If he split a two-deep, he's going to get hit as soon as he catches, but he was strong enough to catch, take the hit, and hold on to the ball. To run the zone and do the things we need in the running game, you have to block the edge. That's a hard combination to find at that position: a receiver/blocker. That's one of your best athletes.

FB: No. 37, Cecil Martin (Evanston, Illinois) - It came down to us and Iowa. We've had better blockers, we've probably had better runners, but as far as a team player, a captain, someone you wanted representing you, that was Cecil. The kids called him the Mayor. Everybody in town knew him. He was one of the best people I've ever coached.

TB: No. 33, Ron Dayne (Berlin, New Jersey) - Even though we had been to a Rose Bowl before he got here, when people think of Wisconsin right now, they think of Dayne. To many people, we were Ohio State and Woody Hayes and the three yards and the cloud of dust offense. That's how our offense was perceived. Woody handed it off to a fullback, we handed it off to a 270-pound tailback. The one run that really identified Dayne was late in the Purdue game his senior year. We were trying to run the clock out, and he was just bulling through tacklers, tossing them aside. One of the most violent runs I have ever seen.

TB: No. 33, Brent Moss (Racine) - I know I've got two tailbacks on my first team, but I've got to find a spot for Moss, especially since he was the MVP of the Big Ten and the Rose Bowl. Unlike Ronnie, he didn't hit any home runs. Brent would get you five yards all day, sometimes six yards, maybe 10. He finished every run. He was a piece of gristle. Quick, shifty in the hole, and a good blocker. Similar in some ways to Auburn tailback Kenny Irons.

QB: No. 5, Brooks Bollinger (Grand Forks, North Dakota) - A coach on the field. My kind of quarterback, a combination quarterback. I like someone who can beat you with his feet and his arm. One of our all-time best competitors. Loved playing. Gym rat. When he showed up at our summer camp, when he wasn't throwing, he jumped into the receiving line and ran routes. Brooks had just come from the Iowa camp, and they didn't offer him. We had a couple of coaches who didn't want to recruit him, either. I liked him, and so did his teammates, which is important, particularly for a quarterback who has to gain their trust.

LT: No. 75, Chris McIntosh (Pewaukee) - As a freshman redshirt, he was matched against our All-American defensive end Tarek Saleh in an inside drill. Saleh gets into it with Mac, who just flipped Tarek on his back. Wasn't intimidated by anybody. Real serious kid. Took the time to visit with Joe Panos to learn how to be a successful captain. We knew he was going to be a good player. Played through injuries. You couldn't get him off the field.

LT: No. 72, Joe Thomas (Brookfield) - Most gifted offensive lineman we've ever had. Runs around like a linebacker. Very athletic. Strong. Smart off the field. Studies the game. No doubt in my mind he will bounce back from knee injury. After breaking down film, one NFL general manager told me they had Joe graded higher than Virginia's D'Brickashaw Ferguson, who went in the first round to the Jets.

LG: No. 67, Dan Buenning (Bay Port) - Most of the pro teams that came to Madison and evaluated Dan felt like he was the best pulling guard in the draft. Tough, hard-nosed player. Everyone in the league has characterized him the same way: typical Wisconsin lineman. I really liked Joe Rudolph and his toughness, but Dan was a better player.

C: No. 52, Cory Raymer (Fond du Lac) - One of the real characters. He was fun. I lied to him during recruiting and assured him that he would play on the defensive line. He brought personality to the field, and he was really athletic. He could run. He gave you the flexibility to do a lot of things because he could pull, lead, and get around the corner.

RG: No. 58, Joe Panos (Brookfield) - Joe played center, guard, and tackle, and he had as much to do with our turnaround as anyone. Kids all respected him. He took being captain to heart. You knew what Joe stood for. He was a street fighter. He started the tradition of the linemen being real close: eating together, studying film together, looking out for each other.

RT: No. 79, Aaron Gibson (Indianapolis, Indiana) - Mom and dad worked as professional clowns. They did birthday parties. Lining up opposite Gibby was no laughing matter, though. He was the most dominant lineman I've ever been around. He threw defensive linemen around like dish rags. Not only a giant, but he could move.

DEFENSE

DE: No. 42, Tarek Saleh (Woodbridge, Connecticut.) - One of my favorites. Tenacious, 100 percent player. Really sound in his fundamentals and techniques. Didn't make any difference how big the tackle was. Used hands to get leverage. Showed his toughness and versatility when he went to the NFL and was converted into a fullback. Blew up Chris Spielman.

RUSH END: No. 90, Erasmus James (Pembroke Pines, Florida) - Probably the most gifted of our D-linemen. High cut, high waisted, could run, could bend, athletic. John Palermo did a good job teaching Ras techniques. As a senior, he was unblockable before injury.

RUSH END: No. 74, Tom Burke (Poplar) - Had the ability to totally disrupt an offense with speed and strength. Playmaker. Unbelievable motor. Much like Iowa's Matt Roth and Georgia's David Pollack. Off the field, he was a Strange Ranger.

DT: No. 66, Mike Thompson (Portage) - Might have been our first commitment. Was originally headed to Iowa State and jumped ship. Had great toughness. Not a great technician. Relied more on effort and hustle. He'd get to the quarterback. Was productive.

DT: No. 91, Don Davey (Manitowoc) - It's a shame we didn't have better people around him. Smart athlete who loved to play and played hard all the time. Could have started for any program in the country. Played faster than anybody else on our defense.

DT: No. 77, Wendell Bryant (St. Louis, Missouri) - Great ability. We would do different things with him to take advantage of his skills. Instead of having him just play as a one-gapper, we'd line him up inside where he could whip the guard and get to the quarterback.

LB: No. 44, Donnel Thompson (Madison West) - Had the linebacker mentality and attitude. As a freshman walk-on, he was hitting everybody in practice and nobody had pads on. Whacked people, because that's how he played. Really smart. Didn't get knocked off his feet.

LB: No. 48, Pete Monty (Fort Collins, Colorado) - Our most productive linebacker. Big, could run. Student of the game. Everybody liked him. Natural captain, natural leader. Played as true freshman in our first Rose Bowl. Tackled UCLA's Wayne Cook on final play.

CB: No. 22, Troy Vincent (Trenton, New Jersey) - Had it all. Big, fast. When you had Troy, you could play 10-on-10 because you would just put him on the best receiver and he's erased. Should have used him on offense as a receiver. Should have streaked him down the field or thrown him some hitch screens because he was a threat on kickoffs and punt returns.

CB: No. 2, Jamar Fletcher (St. Louis, Missouri) - Tremendous confidence. Not near the ability of a Vincent, but more productive as far as interceptions. Great anticipation on the ball. Our first trash talker, but he backed it up. I told Fletch, "Don't let your mouth write a check that your ass can't cash." But he cashed it on Michigan State's Plaxico Burress.

SAFETY: No. 8, Jason Doering (Rhinelander) - Walk-on. Big hitter. Watched him stone people in practice every day, so I just threw him into the Michigan game and he made a bunch of tackles. He wasn't intimidated. Receivers coming over the middle were.

SAFETY: No. 18, Jim Leonhard (Tony) - Another walk-on. More athletic than most would give him credit for. Faster, too. Great punt returner. Helluva player. Unassuming. People are amazed the first time they meet Jimmy because of his size. Played big.

PUNTER: No. 14, Kevin Stemke (Green Bay) - Consistent. Gave us hidden yardage. Good athlete. Helped us off the field with his leadership and maturity. One of the kickers everyone liked. You can't always say that about kickers. At least I couldn't.

PLACEKICKER: No. 28, Matt Davenport (Mission Viejo, California) - When he got here, he could barely get the ball over the crossbar on extra points. I'm looking at Kevin Cosgrove and saying, "Cos, where the hell is the 50-yard field goal kicker you promised me?" Really developed. Won back-to-back games with kicks. Really clutch. Money.

BARRY ALVAREZ BIOGRAPHY (as of June 2006)

What is the common denominator between Steve Spurrier, Ron McBride, Randy Walker, Nick Saban, Bill Curry, Paul Hackett, Gary Moeller, Doug Graber, George Allen, Gene Stallings, Jim Hess, George Chaump, Jim Strong, Tom Lichtenberg, John Jenkins, Ken Hatfield, Barry Wilson, Jack Crowe, and Barry Alvarez?

Before the start of the 1990 season, these 19 diverse individuals were all named head coaches of Division I-A college football programs. The survival rate wasn't very high, and, in the end, Alvarez was the only one still coaching at the same school he began at — UW. He outlasted them all, despite inheriting arguably, the worst job of them all.

Today Barry Alvarez is in his third year as Director of Athletics at Wisconsin, but his first without the additional title of head football coach. Alvarez guided the fortunes of the Badger football program from 1990-2005, including the last two seasons in a dual role as AD and head football coach.

He retired from coaching at the conclusion of the 2005 season in order to concentrate on running the Division of Intercollegiate Athletics. Alvarez has made a lasting impression on the Wisconsin sports scene.

His well-documented turnaround of the once-moribund Badger football program has helped the school's entire athletic department to blossom into one of the nation's finest and most respected organizations in college sports.

When Alvarez arrived in Madison in 1990, Wisconsin had compiled a 9-36 record during the previous four seasons, and attendance at Camp Randall Stadium had dipped to an average of 41,734 per game (54 percent of capacity).

The program sorely needed a boost and got it when new Director of Athletics Pat Richter hired Alvarez from Notre Dame, where he had been an assistant coach under Lou Holtz.

Over the next 16 seasons, Alvarez transformed the football program and, subsequently, the culture of athletics at the UW. The success of the football program ignited and heightened interest in Badger sports. Alvarez's list of accomplishments at Wisconsin is remarkable.

Consider just a few of the most notable:

•winningest coach in school history (record of 118-73-4, .615)

•highest bowl winning percentage of all-time (8-3, .727)

•coached team to three Big Ten and Rose Bowl championships

•only Big Ten coach ever to win the Rose Bowl in consecutive seasons

•just the 10th coach in Big Ten history with 100 victories at one conference institution

•coached five national award winners, including Ron Dayne (Heisman, Doak Walker, Maxwell); Jamar Fletcher (Jim Thorpe); and Kevin Stemke (Ray Guy)

•guided UW to back-to-back Big Ten titles in 1998 and 1999 (hadn't happened at Wisconsin since 1896-97)

•coached the four winningest teams in school history

In 2004, Barry Alvarez became just the 10th coach in Big Ten history to win at least 100 games at one conference school.

The list:

205 wins-Woody Hayes, Ohio State

199-Amos Alonzo Stagg, Chicago

194-Bo Schembechler, Michigan

165-Fielding Yost, Michigan

143-Hayden Fry, Iowa

136-Henry Williams, Minnesota

131-Robert Zuppke, Illinois

118-BARRY ALVAREZ

111-John Cooper, Ohio State

109-Duffy Daugherty, Michigan State

THE ALVAREZ ERA, YEAR-BY-YEAR

2005 (10-3): Wisconsin capped the Alvarez era with a stunning 24-10 upset win over seventh-ranked Auburn in the Capital One Bowl. UW won 10 games for just the fourth time in school history. The Badgers set school records for scoring and passing yardage and were led by running back Brian Calhoun, who became just the second player in NCAA Division I history to accumulate 1,500 rushing and 500 receiving yards. Wisconsin finished ranked No. 15 in the media and coaches polls. Calhoun, OT Joe Thomas, WR Brandon Williams, and P Ken DeBauche earned All-America honors.

2004 (9-3): The Badgers won their first nine games en route to a No. 4 national ranking in both polls. In that winning streak, UW beat both No. 18/17 Ohio State and No. 5/5 Purdue on the road and led the nation in scoring defense with 9.1 ppg. Wisconsin finished third in the Big Ten and earned a bid to play Georgia in the Outback Bowl. Five Badgers were named All-Big Ten, including DE Erasmus James, a consensus All-American. Seven Badgers were NFL draft choices, including all four starters on the defensive line.

2003 (7-6): Wisconsin won six of its first seven games, including a 17-10 upset victory that ended No. 3-ranked Ohio State's 19-game winning streak. Four Badgers earned first-team All-Big Ten mention, including WR Lee Evans, who finished his career ranked No. 2 on the all-time Big Ten receiving yardage list. UW qualified for its ninth bowl game in 11 years. UW lost to Minnesota on a FG as time ran out; to Purdue on a FG with 0:03 left; and to Iowa when the Badgers were unable to score on a last-minute drive.

2002 (8-6): A season-opening five-game winning streak and league wins over Michigan State and Minnesota qualified the Badgers for their eighth Alvarez-era bowl game, a 31-28 OT win over 14th-ranked Colorado in the Alamo Bowl. First-team All-American Jim Leonhard led the nation with a Big Ten record-tying 11 interceptions. Anthony Davis (1,555 yards) gave UW a 1,000-yard rusher for a Big Ten-record 10th straight year.

2001 (5-7): Several individual achievements highlighted a season in which the Badgers never won or lost more than two straight games.

WR Lee Evans set the Big Ten record for receiving yards in a season with 1,545, and RB Anthony Davis led the conference in rushing. Evans and Davis were All-Americans and six Badgers earned first-team All-Big Ten acclaim, including DL Wendell Bryant who became a first-round NFL draft choice. The Badgers lost by a field goal to both Oregon and Michigan.

2000 (9-4): A five-game winning streak to end the season highlighted the Sun Bowl champions' 9-4 season. Fighting injuries and suspensions, the Badgers had a difficult time getting consistency in the early part of the league season. Jamar Fletcher (Jim Thorpe Award) and Kevin Stemke (inaugural Ray Guy Award) allowed UW to be the only school in the nation with two different players winning major awards.

1999 (10-2): A 17-9 win over Stanford in the Rose Bowl allowed Wisconsin to become the first Big Ten school in history to win the "Granddaddy of Them All" in back-to-back campaigns. The 10-2 Badgers finished fourth in both the media and coaches final polls. Wisconsin defeated five nationally-rated foes for the first time in school history and concluded the year with eight consecutive victories. The Badgers led the Big Ten in both scoring offense and scoring defense. Ron Dayne became the NCAA's all-time leading rusher and then walked away with the Heisman Trophy, Maxwell Award and Doak Walker Award. Chris McIntosh (Outland Trophy) and Vitaly Pisetsky (Mosi Tatupu and Lou Groza Awards) were major award finalists. Alvarez was forced to coach from the press box or hospital in eight games after mid-season knee surgery.

1998 (11-1): The winningest season in school history ended in dramatic fashion with a thrilling 38-31 upset of sixth-ranked UCLA at the Rose Bowl. Game MVP Ron Dayne keyed the win with 246 yards rushing. Wisconsin led the nation in scoring defense and turnover margin. The Badgers' nine-game win streak to open the season tied a school record. Tom Burke (NCAA sack leader) and Aaron Gibson (a finalist for the Lombardi Award and the Outland Trophy) were consensus All-Americans. Alvarez was Big Ten Coach of the Year.

1997 (8-5): A six-game winning streak catapulted the Badgers to a second consecutive eight-win season and berth in the Outback Bowl vs. Georgia. The Badgers joined the '37 Michigan team as the only squads in league history to win three one-point decisions. Ron Dayne earned first-team All-America honors and Matt Davenport won two games with last-second field goals.

1996 (8-5): The Badgers opened quickly with a 3-0 non-league slate before losing four games (three by a combined total of 10 points) to highly ranked foes. The UW closed 4-1 and posted a 38-10 win over Utah in the Copper Bowl. Ron Dayne set an NCAA freshman rushing record and had 2,109 yards, including the bowl win.

1995 (4-5-2): With the most inexperienced squad in the Big Ten and facing the nation's most difficult schedule (according to the Seattle Times), the Badgers posted a 4-5-2 mark. Darrell Bevell broke several passing records at the UW. The 17-9 upset at Penn State broke the NCAA's longest win streak (20 games).

1994 (8-3-1): Wisconsin won its second straight January bowl game by defeating Duke in the Hall of Fame Bowl. The regular season featured a win at Michigan for the first time since 1962. Center Cory Raymer was a consensus All-American. Seven players were drafted by the NFL.

1993 (10-1-1): The Badgers were Big Ten co-champions, beat UCLA in the Rose Bowl and were ranked as high as fifth (coaches) in the final polls. The UW had the NCAA's largest attendance increase, and its .875 winning percentage was the best by a Big Ten team since '79. A school-record eight players were named first-team All-Big Ten. Brent Moss was the Badgers' first Big Ten MVP since 1962.

1992 (5-6): UW was 5-6 and climbed in the Big Ten standings for the third season in a row. The Badgers upset 12th-ranked Ohio State, their first win over a nationally-rated foe in eight years. Wisconsin received votes in the national polls for the first time in Alvarez's career and ended the year one victory short of a bowl bid. Three of the losses were by a total of four points.

1991 (5-6): Wisconsin improved its win total by four games, the fourth-largest improvement in the NCAA. Troy Vincent was an All-American, runner-up for the Jim Thorpe Award, and the No. 7 pick in the NFL draft. A victory at Minnesota broke a 23-game road losing streak.

1990 (1-10): Wisconsin was within striking distance entering the fourth quarter in 10 games, although its only victory was over Ball State. UW had the third-best attendance gain nationally.

Alvarez's coaching career began at the high school level. He served as an assistant at Lincoln (Nebraska) Northeast High from 1971-73 before taking over as head coach at Lexington (Nebraska) High from 1974-75. His last prep coaching stop was at Mason City (Iowa) High where he was head coach from 1976-78 and where his team won a 4-A state title in his final year.

Iowa's Hayden Fry hired Alvarez as an assistant coach in 1979. The Hawkeyes played in six bowl games (two Rose Bowls) during Alvarez's eight years in Iowa City, compiling a 61-33-1 mark in the process. Alvarez's standout player with the Hawkeyes was LB Larry Station, a two-time All-American and two-time Academic All-American.

Alvarez left Iowa after the 1986 season to become linebackers coach at Notre Dame. He was promoted (linebackers to defensive coordinator to assistant head coach) by head coach Lou Holtz each of his three seasons, as the Fighting Irish went 32-5 and won the 1988 national title. While in South Bend, Alvarez coached All-American linebackers Michael Stonebreaker, Ned Bolcar, Cedric Figaro, and Wes Pritchett.

ALVAREZ'S YEAR-BY-YEAR COACHING RECORD

Year	School	Wins	Losses	Ties	Big Ten	Bowl	Results
1990	Wisconsin	1	10	0	10th		
1991	Wisconsin	5	6	0	8th (tie)		
1992	Wisconsin	5	6	0	6th (tie)		
1993	Wisconsin	10	1	1	1st (tie)	Rose Bowl	Defeated UCLA 21-16
1994	Wisconsin	8	3	1	3rd	Hall of Fame Bowl	Defeated Duke 34-20
1995	Wisconsin	4	5	2	7th (tie)		
1996	Wisconsin	8	5	0	7th	Copper Bowl	Defeated Utah 38-10
1997	Wisconsin	8	5	0	5th	Outback Bowl	Lost to Georgia 33-6
1998	Wisconsin	11	1	0	1st (tie)	Rose Bowl	Defeated UCLA 38-31
1999	Wisconsin	10	2	0	1st	Rose Bowl	Defeated Stanford 17-9
2000	Wisconsin	9	4	0	5th	Sun Bowl	Defeated UCLA 21-20
2001	Wisconsin	5	7	0	8th (tie)		
2002	Wisconsin	8	6	0	8th (tie)	Alamo Bowl	Defeated Colorado 31-28
2003	Wisconsin	7	6	0	7th (tie)	Music City Bowl	Lost to Auburn 28-14
2004	Wisconsin	9	3	0	3rd	Outback Bowl	Lost to Georgia 24-21
2005	Wisconsin	10	3	0	3rd (tie)	Capital One Bowl	Defeated Auburn 24-10

16-YEAR TOTAL: 118 wins   73 losses   4 ties

BOWL RECORD: 8-3

ALVAREZ TALKING POINTS

Can Wisconsin win a national championship in football?
Yes. I never said no. I never set it as a goal. But you can win one here. We were close. If you win this league, you're right there, you're a Top Five team.

Do you favor an NCAA play-off?
No. I think the bowl system is good. Bowls reward kids. People say, "There are too many bowls and no one cares." Yeah, they do care. The guys who play in the bowls care. Besides, it's more complicated than just saying, "Let's have a play-off. For one thing, if there are multiple play-off games at multiple sites, what are the logistics for your fan base? How are the fans going to follow their teams?

Will the Big Ten ever expand to 12 teams?
Considering today's landscape, with teams jumping leagues, I see it happening someday. I don't know who that team would be. It makes sense. And we were very close a couple of times.

Would Notre Dame ever be the 12th team?
I don't think their alums will let that happen. They like being an independent in football, they like being on a pedestal and having their own TV contract. It got close once, and they were the ones asking the questions of the Big Ten. But when they took their straw vote, they didn't want to do it.

Were you ever considered for the head coaching job at Notre Dame?
I was never contacted. But Lou Holtz called me two days before he retired and said that he was going to recommend me for the job. He also said that would probably hurt me, not help me.

Do you think players should be paid?
We could do more for them. When I played, we got $15 dollars a month. If we could give them some type of a stipend, I think it would help. We're more lenient today than ever with some funding. But I'd like to be able to do more.

Have players changed over the years?
They're different today because they're more aware. They have more choices than we had in the '60s. But they want the same things: they want to be coached, they want to get better, and they want direction.

How has the game of college football changed over the last 16 years?
Two of the biggest changes have been the spread offense and the

pressure defenses, the zone blitzing. The game has gone away from standard one-back sets. You spread the field, you're deceptive with your hand fakes, like the old Wing-T, and you stretch the defense.

Has the NCAA done a good job governing football?
Anytime there's an issue, there's a new rule. And many of the new rules are reactionary. Some are so trivial and convoluted and complex, there's no way anyone could know the manual.

Do you think the NCAA makes fair decisions?
No, the decisions are not always fair. But I think they're trying to err on the side of the athlete. That's what they claim. I haven't seen it.

How has the scholarship reduction impacted the game?
It has created more parity, so it has been good for the sport. Powers can't stock-pile players anymore.

Should athletes be held to a higher standard on campus?
Yes, because they're more visible and have more responsibility to the public.

How has the Internet changed coaching?
It has become an integral part of recruiting. There are a lot of rumors and false information available on the Internet now. People can attack coaches and players and programs without being accountable for what they're saying.

Is firing a coach ever easy for a head coach?
Never. That's the hardest thing I've ever had to do. After my first year here, I had to let two coaches go and I didn't sleep for a week, but I had to do something because I knew the problem wasn't going to correct itself. Lou Holtz always said, "Do it in a Christian way." But there's no easy way.

Is there any coach you've admired from afar?
I always got a kick out of Bo Schembechler. I respected him. I liked the way he coached. His teams were always well-coached and tough. He coached the game like I coached the game.

Anyone else?
Jimmy Johnson. He had great players, but you still have to manage them and he always did.

What one thing do you cherish the most about being a head coach?
I've always had special relationships with the players. When a player comes back on campus and says that I've affected his life and he's still leaning on principles I gave him to be successful in life, that's what coaching is all about to me.

"I didn't take this job to get another job. I didn't have someplace else where I wanted to end up. Some guys want to be NFL coaches. Some guys want to be coaches at Penn State and Southern Cal. Some guys want to coach in their home state, or at their alma mater. But I didn't take this job to leave. I said from Day One, I wanted to do at Wisconsin what Bob Devaney did at Nebraska. I wanted to take a program that was down, build it up and sustain it. And today it's really touching and gratifying for me to hear these words: "Thanks coach, job well done."

-Barry Alvarez